ORDER AND THE VIRTUAL

Crosscurrents

Exploring the development of European thought through engagements with the arts, humanities, social sciences and sciences

Series Editor
Christopher Watkin, Monash University

Editorial Advisory Board
Andrew Benjamin
Martin Crowley
Simon Critchley
Frederiek Depoortere
Oliver Feltham
Patrick ffrench
Christopher Fynsk
Kevin Hart
Emma Wilson

Titles available in the series
Difficult Atheism: Post-Theological Thinking in Alain Badiou, Jean-Luc Nancy and Quentin Meillassoux
Christopher Watkin
Politics of the Gift: Exchanges in Poststructuralism
Gerald Moore
Unfinished Worlds: Hermeneutics, Aesthetics and Gadamer
Nicholas Davey
The Figure of This World: Agamben and the Question of Political Ontology
Mathew Abbott
The Becoming of the Body: Contemporary Women's Writing in French
Amaleena Damlé
Philosophy, Animality and the Life Sciences
Wahida Khandker
The Event Universe: The Revisionary Metaphysics of Alfred North Whitehead
Leemon B. McHenry
Sublime Art: Towards an Aesthetics of the Future
Stephen Zepke
Mallarmé and the Politics of Literature: Sartre, Kristeva, Badiou, Rancière
Robert Boncardo
Animal Writing: Storytelling, Selfhood and the Limits of Empathy
Danielle Sands
Music, Philosophy and Gender in Nancy, Lacoue-Labarthe, Badiou
Sarah Hickmott
The Desert in Modern Literature and Philosophy: Wasteland Aesthetics
Aidan Tynan
Visual Art and Self-Construction
Katrina Mitcheson
Proust Between Deleuze and Derrida: The Remains of Literature
James Dutton
Saint Paul and Contemporary European Philosophy: The Outcast and the Spirit
Gert-Jan van der Heiden
Order and the Virtual: The Philosophy and Science of Deleuzian Cosmology
Bill Ross

Visit the Crosscurrents website at www.edinburghuniversitypress.com/series-crosscurrents.html

ORDER AND THE VIRTUAL

The Philosophy and Science of Deleuzian Cosmology

Bill Ross

EDINBURGH
University Press

Edinburgh University Press is one of the leading university presses in the UK. We publish academic books and journals in our selected subject areas across the humanities and social sciences, combining cutting-edge scholarship with high editorial and production values to produce academic works of lasting importance. For more information visit our website: edinburghuniversitypress.com

© Bill Ross, 2024, 2025

Edinburgh University Press Ltd
13 Infirmary Street
Edinburgh EH1 1LT

First published in hardback by Edinburgh University Press 2024

Typeset in 10.5/13 Sabon by
Cheshire Typesetting Ltd, Cuddington, Cheshire

A CIP record for this book is available from the British Library

ISBN 978 1 3995 2735 4 (hardback)
ISBN 978 1 3995 2736 1 (paperback)
ISBN 978 1 3995 2737 8 (webready PDF)
ISBN 978 1 3995 2738 5 (epub)

The right of Bill Ross to be identified as the author of this work has been asserted in accordance with the Copyright, Designs and Patents Act 1988, and the Copyright and Related Rights Regulations 2003 (SI No. 2498).

Contents

Series Editor's Preface	vii
Preface by Robin Durie and David Webb	ix
Abbreviations	xii

1. Chaos — 1
   - Chaos and Complexity Theory — 1
   - Nietzschean Chaos and the Superior Principle of Sufficient Reason — 5
   - The Eternal Return and the Disparity of Forces — 8
   - Ergodicity and Infinite Duration — 10
   - Post-Classical Physics and the Question of Entropy — 15

2. Entropy and the Complete Concept in Leibniz and Deleuze — 24
   - Dissymmetry, Energy Gradients and 'the Ultimate Origination of Things' — 29
   - On the Ultimate Origination of Things — 30
   - From Many Worlds to Chaosmos — 34
   - The Calculating God — 36
   - Mathematical Thought, the Problem and the Cosmos — 38
   - The Compete Concept and Disjunctive Synthesis in Sufficient Reason — 44
   - Physical Systems, Disparity and Disjunctive Synthesis — 50
   - Chaosmos as Cosmology — 56
   - Absolute Zero, Limits and the Infinite — 60
   - Simple Order — 68

3. Order — 71
   - Mechanism and Vitalism, Order and Complexity — 73
   - The Game Analogy #1: Leibniz and Kant — 81
   - The Game Analogy #2: Claude Shannon and Michel Serres — 85

Game #2.1: Claude Shannon's 'A Mathematical Theory of
      Communication'   86
   Game #2.2: Michel Serres' *The Birth of Physics*   94
   Game #3.0: Deleuze's Ideal Game   98

4. Order as Complexity   109
   Complexity as Principle   122
   Limits without Negation   127

5. Sufficient Reason as Dissymmetry and the Evolutionary
      Paradigm   131
   Limits and Non-Locality   135
   A Network Paradigm: Loop Quantum Gravity   150
   A Holographic Paradigm: David Bohm's Implicate Order   154
   Evolutionary Expansiveness   161

Conclusion   175
Notes   182
Bibliography   207
Index   217

Series Editor's Preface

Two or more currents flowing into or through each other create a turbulent crosscurrent, more powerful than its contributory flows and irreducible to them. Time and again, modern European thought creates and exploits crosscurrents in thinking, remaking itself as it flows through, across and against discourses as diverse as mathematics and film, sociology and biology, theology, literature and politics. The work of Gilles Deleuze, Jacques Derrida, Slavoj Žižek, Alain Badiou, Bernard Stiegler and Jean-Luc Nancy, among others, participates in this fundamental remaking. In each case disciplines and discursive formations are engaged, not with the aim of performing a predetermined mode of analysis yielding a 'philosophy of x', but through encounters in which thought itself can be transformed. Furthermore, these fundamental transformations do not merely seek to account for singular events in different sites of discursive or artistic production but rather to engage human existence and society as such, and as a whole. The cross-disciplinarity of this thought is therefore neither a fashion nor a prosthesis; it is simply part of what 'thought' means in this tradition.

Crosscurrents begins from the twin convictions that this re-making is integral to the legacy and potency of European thought, and that the future of thought in this tradition must defend and develop this legacy in the teeth of an academy that separates and controls the currents that flow within and through it. With this in view, the series provides an exceptional site for bold, original and opinion-changing monographs that actively engage European thought in this fundamentally cross-disciplinary manner, riding existing crosscurrents and creating new ones. Each book in the series explores the different ways in which European thought develops through its engagement with disciplines across the arts, humanities, social sciences and sciences, recognising that the community of scholars working with this thought is itself spread across diverse faculties. The object of the series is therefore nothing less than to examine and carry forward the unique legacy of European thought as an inherently and irreducibly cross-disciplinary enterprise.

Christopher Watkin
Cambridge
February 2011

Preface

Playing Cortázarian Hopscotch

Gilles Deleuze argued that the most significant characteristic of an encounter is that it forces us to think. *Order and the Virtual* dramatises multiple encounters between the philosophies of Deleuze, Michel Serres, Henri Bergson, Alfred North Whitehead, Leibniz and Lucretius, and the scientific theories of general relativity, quantum mechanics, information theory, thermodynamics, evolutionary theory, chaos theory and complexity theory. Each of these encounters forces the reader to think anew, to imagine new possibilities for both philosophical and scientific thought. Each encounter also reveals the depth with which Bill Ross himself had thought about these matters.

At the heart of *Order and the Virtual* is a sustained examination of the complexity of Life. But the book itself is an articulation of a life's work, of the work of a Life that was itself remarkable. Philosophy today is almost exclusively practised within the confines of academia, and those who would be philosophers follow a tightly circumscribed path from PhD work to professional employment. Bill Ross's life explored many different pathways, only some of which circled around the institutions of academia.

He graduated from Edinburgh University with a General MA, that distinctively Scots degree which the philosopher and historian George Davie has described as the bedrock of the Scottish Democratic Intellect. The General MA compels its graduates to develop expertise in multiple disciplines, cutting across traditional distinctions between arts and humanities, and natural and social sciences. Bill's affinity for synthesising learning from disparate disciplines was already manifest during conversations in University cafés that ranged over metaphysics, psychology, the paradoxes of quantum theory, amongst many other topics.

After university, Bill took on an array of jobs, from bar work in some of Edinburgh's most 'couthy' pubs, to working in bookshops, to teaching English to secondary school students. Then, in the late 1990s, he seized with unconcealed joy the opportunity to set up Clinamen Press with Ben Stebbings. Devoted primarily to publishing works in the philosophy of science (including Bergson's *Duration and Simultaneity* and Serres' *The Birth of Physics* – key texts that figure prominently in *Order and the Virtual*), alongside new editions of 'forgotten' texts from the Enlightenment, Clinamen Press embodied Bill's commitment to bringing philosophy and science into contact with one another. It was, of course, telling that he should have appropriated the word 'clinamen' to name the Press: a core notion for *The Birth of Physics*, and one which figures throughout *Order and the Virtual*, 'clinamen' is the word Lucretius used to name the infinitesimal swerve that brought atoms into contact in the void, generating the turbulence of complex order.

Latterly, Bill returned to academia, completing a PhD at Staffordshire University for which he had in reality been preparing half his life, and then teaching, supervising doctoral research, devising new courses, writing, translating and editing. He delighted in it all. He was set fair. The winds were good and the weather fine.

CLINAMEN – THE EVENT OF AN ENCOUNTER

In some of its most impressive pages, *Order and the Virtual* seeks for ways to respond to Deleuze's most fundamental problem: how we can think the principle of sufficient reason as difference. In *Difference and Repetition*, Deleuze talks of disparity, and of the dark precursor, as the differential means of communication bringing heterogeneous series, or systems, into differential relation with one another. We could also name this disparity, *clinamen*.

Clinamen, then. The inclination of an encounter, such as the possibility of a productive encounter between philosophy and science. But also, the encounter between friends. Everyone who was fortunate enough to come into contact with Bill Ross will recall his friendliness – his laughter, his generosity, his joy in language, his delight in life itself, the life of which he was so full. But they will also recall that every encounter, whatever the circumstances, was an occasion that prompted thinking. Even when he was laughing, Bill was thinking – and he always wanted to laugh with you, and think with you; to share his laughter with you, and to share his thinking with you.

Bill Ross completed the final revisions to *Order and the Virtual* only a few months before he died so unexpectedly. In the text he writes that life begets life, complexity begets complexity. In his life, encounters begot encounters; and each encounter begot friendship, and each friendship begot thinking. One encounter in particular begot friendship, thinking and also love – the encounter with his soul mate Kerry Gorrill, with whom he led a life of profound connection and happiness, and to whom this book would surely have been dedicated had Bill lived to see its publication.

The thinking of Bill Ross's Life is expressed here, in *Order and the Virtual*, for the first time. It is our tragedy that it will have also been the last time.

Robin Durie and David Webb

Abbreviations

ATP Gilles Deleuze and Félix Guattari, *A Thousand Plateaus*
B   Gilles Deleuze, *Bergsonism*
BP   Michel Serres, *The Birth of Physics*
CE   Henri Bergson, *Creative Evolution*
DR   Gilles Deleuze, *Difference and Repetition*
FLB Gilles Deleuze, *The Fold: Leibniz and the Baroque*
LS   Gilles Deleuze, *The Logic of Sense*
NP   Gilles Deleuze, *Nietzsche and Philosophy*
PR   Alfred North Whitehead, *Process and Reality*
WP   Gilles Deleuze and Félix Guattari, *What is Philosophy?*

1. *Chaos*

CHAOS AND COMPLEXITY THEORY

Commentators attending to relations between the philosophy of Gilles Deleuze and developments in contemporary science have for the most part focused on chaos and complexity theory. To be sure, there are a number of rich cross-pollinations to be gleaned from a consideration of the frameworks of chaos and complexity theory and Deleuze's work, as has been demonstrated by writers such as Manuel DeLanda, John Protevi and Brian Massumi, amongst others.[1] Indeed, these connections are not simply adduced 'after the fact'. Deleuze is cited as an influence in the first work to catalyse chaos theory as such, *Order Out of Chaos*, by Ilya Prigogine and Isabelle Stengers. Equally, Deleuze recognised the resonance of chaos theory with his own work. In a discussion of 'inexact yet completely rigorous notions'[2] which are capable of crossing disciplinary boundaries, he says: 'One of the many concepts created in [*Order Out of Chaos*] is that of a region of bifurcation. Prigogine draws it out from his own field, but it's a good example of a concept that's irreducibly philosophical, scientific and artistic too.'[3] We might note a further such transdisciplinary instance in Deleuze and Guattari's co-option of Mandelbrot fractals in elaborating the term 'smooth space' (ATP, 486–7).

It is a moot point, in short, how far we might go in aligning Deleuze's work with the fields of chaos and complexity, all the more so since the general spirit of his thought is far from precious over the co-habitation of the philosophical apparatus with promising concepts and modes of thought in the mathematical and natural sciences. I would argue, however, that there are points in the commentary on Deleuze which exceed productive cross-pollination with these particular fields in the direction of too close an identification. This is counter-productive for two essential reasons: firstly, it is reductive to identify Deleuze's work too neatly with any one branch of science; secondly, it runs the risk of closing down illuminating connections to other fields, most notably for our purposes, quantum physics and relativity.

The example of 'bifurcation', in which Deleuze expresses interest in the quotation above, is a quite important instance of this too-close conflation. In chaos theory, a system is said to bifurcate at that point when there are two equally possible developments of its activity, two possible reconfigurations of its state space, and one of these comes to pass but not the other. For as long as neither path is 'chosen', the system remains in the 'region of bifurcation' which Deleuze alludes to; a region of state space associated with far-from-equilibrium conditions.[4] What is the appeal of this concept for Deleuze? There is an undoubted affinity here with a key tenet for Deleuze: he holds that divergent series are prior to convergent series. For Deleuze, divergent series are primordial phenomena, convergent series secondary. 'Series' may be series of anything; a trajectory is a series of points, the relative density of given chemical components and products may be a series in a cyclical reaction. The priority given to divergent series may be read in a similar way to the central place of the *clinamen* in Lucretian cosmology: the initial strict parallel paths of atoms in a downward fall through the void is broken by a swerve, a divergence, a *clinamen*, on the part of a single atom, bringing it into contact with others, and, by chain reaction, a convergence into structure and form which ever and again undoes and remakes itself, diverging first then reconverging. For Deleuze, this sense of divergence belongs equally primordially to the question of genesis; if it were not for divergence from an initial stasis, nothing would happen at all. 'The only way to escape from chaos', he says, 'is to form a series'.[5]

Bifurcation, then, offers us a bridge between our metaphysics and the rolled-up sleeves of the scientific discipline. John Protevi considers the link significant enough to make a firm association between chaotic bifurcation and the Event, which is without doubt one of the key concepts in the Deleuzian vocabulary: 'Deleuze calls the triggering of a bifurcator an "Event", which unleashes an "emission of singularities", providing for a new set of attractors and bifurcators, or patterns and thresholds of the intensive processes that are "buried" under forms of actual behaviour.'[6] Indeed, beginning from the twin terms 'divergence' and 'bifurcation', both indispensable initial conditions of the respective frameworks, it is possible to elaborate a far-reaching set of correspondences, as Protevi does. Where Deleuze attributes to the Event a power of 'redistribution of singularities', chaos theory attributes to Bifurcation the generation of a 'new set of attractors and bifurcators', which are in turn themselves termed singularities. We might, for instance, discover a chaotic cycle to shift from a state space featuring one basin of attraction to another featuring two or more; it is not just that the system itself has evolved along a particular path through its attendant state space, but that the state space itself is recast as a result of the evolution of the system, perhaps acquiring more degrees of freedom. Its long-term tendencies, its attractors, are, so to speak, redistributed. Moreover, the singularities spoken of in each framework occupy an ontologically comparable role. Where for Deleuze singularities as such belong to the virtual domain, serving as conditions for actualisation which may never themselves fully actualise, so too for chaotic attractors, which are to be understood as ideal points in state space, which the system will tend to approach but on principle cannot occupy. This is an inherent feature of the formalisation of state space structure proposed first by Henri Poincaré, the 'knots' and 'saddles', etc., of chaos theory. There is in a quite straightforward sense a chaotic 'virtual'. It seems we can legitimately map (if not translate) the two systems of thought onto one another, as Protevi does:

> The actual behaviour of the system, its oscillation at frequency #1 or #2, would be a trait, while oscillation frequencies #1 and #2 would occur as the result of a (near-) actualisation of virtual attractors, a selection of divergent series that actualises a certain set of virtual singularities.[7]

This set of mappings, however, is conditional on the relegation of a particular feature of Deleuzian 'divergence' to the background. For Deleuze, divergence, the motor of the Event, is continuous, without interruption, just as is the Event itself. In the passage below we can detect the mark of a power attributed to divergent series which far transcends the relatively domestic shifting between phases portrayed above:

> The basic series are divergent: not relatively, in the sense that one could retrace one's path and find a point of convergence, but absolutely divergent in the sense that the point or horizon of convergence lies in a chaos or is constantly displaced within that chaos. This chaos is itself the most positive, just as the divergence is the object of affirmation. It is indistinguishable from the great work which contains all the complicated series, which affirms and complicates all the series at once. (DR, 123)

We are rather here presented with a chaos of another stamp entirely than that of the scientific field, belonging more squarely to the ancient cosmologies of the Greeks: a tract from which existence or becoming pours. A Chaosmos, as Deleuze has it. Singularities are indeed redistributed within the Event, but there is no punctuation, no tipping point or bifurcation; rather a 'constant displacement'. It could not be otherwise according to the syntheses of time which Deleuze propounds in *Difference and Repetition*. The past, with all its conditions for the present, returns at each moment, in its entirety, but reshuffled and recombined subject to the exigencies, accidents and evolutions of the present. What is added from the present is no mere addition, but serves to promote some of the series ramifying out of the past and mercilessly to demote others; the past is cast anew at each moment instantaneously and forever, like the instant reconfiguration of a magnetic field. The future is another covariant field whose potentialities reconfigure accordingly; what was likely, possible or hypothetically necessary no longer is so, but the adjacent possible shivers into view as if the sensors for a lighting system in some vast hangar were triggered.

There are numerous indications that Deleuze took the Event to be continuous in nature. Leonard Lawlor draws our attention to the number of times he insists on this: 'Despite its singularity and novelty, the event does not end; it is incessant (Deleuze negates the French verb, *cesser*, at crucial points in his discourse). The event has a potency that cannot be stopped ("*il ne cesse pas*").'[8] Lawlor cites some seven instances of this construction in *The Logic of Sense*. Deleuze leaves little doubt on this matter in a chapter entitled 'What is an Event?' in *The Fold*, when he adopts a particular exemplification offered by Whitehead. Whitehead includes the apparent permanence and fixity of a structure such as a pyramid under the category of Event:

> A permanence has to be born in flux, and must be grasped in prehension. The Great Pyramid signifies two things: a passage of Nature or a flux constantly gaining and losing molecules, but also an eternal object that remains the same over the succession of moments. (FLB, 79)

Finally, this sense of the Event is arguably inherent in Deleuze's terminology; he coins the phrase 'constant variation', which connotes a continuous divergence of series, of form in relation to environment.

Pace Protevi, there is no straightforward identification to be made between Deleuze's chaotic 'divergence' and the 'bifurcations' of chaos theory, nor can such an identification underwrite the Deleuzian Event *qua* Event; this is in effect akin to comparing the knots in a piece of wood to the sap which laid the grain. But it would only be pedantry, and of a distinctly un-Deleuzian stamp, to labour the point if it were merely to stand on the letter of the Deleuzian text. Rather, to insist on the incessant nature of the Event is to recoup and remobilise a certain momentum in the Deleuzian metaphysics which opens up connecting lines to fields rather less explored in the commentary. This is at the heart of the motivation for this book. It will entail foregrounding elements of the Deleuzian text which are less frequently treated. When Deleuze refers to *décalage* ('delay', or 'retardation') in the passage of nature, he is on that same shared territory which Bergson forged between philosophy and relativity theory; but then how are we to understand the continuous Event – the Event that elapses at each given moment – in a 'retardative' cosmos which admits of no absolute simultaneity, no simple 'given moment'? The answer I will put forward bears heavily on what concept of order we can attribute to the Event, and to nature, and suggests a schism between Bergson and Deleuze in terms other than Deleuze himself offers. Equally, the continuity attributed to the Event must ultimately be at the expense of any restriction of *location* for the Event as such. To subscribe to the Deleuzian Event is to be obliged to entertain those same questions of 'non-locality' which have occupied quantum theorists since the early twentieth century. Questions of 'the limit', the 'constant' and 'the law' underlie Deleuze's orientation to science, and must be placed in context of continuous variation, of divergence. These questions, and Deleuze's response to them, suggest correspondences to modern developments in physics which extend far beyond those offered by chaos theory. They entail attitudes to the values of symmetry and symmetry-breaking, a trope which is by no means confined to that field. They circle around questions of energy and entropy, ever-present throughout the discourse of natural sciences, and force us to address not merely whether the universe is 'open', but what it is that might constitute such 'openness'. Finally, these questions conjoin with the increasingly prevalent paradigm of evolutionary cosmology. These themes will form the basis of the discussion in the chapters to come, but there is (at least) one other aspect of chaos to address first.

NIETZSCHEAN CHAOS AND THE SUPERIOR PRINCIPLE OF SUFFICIENT REASON

The Chaos which Nietzsche describes in his work leaves a lasting imprint on Deleuze's own. Without Nietzschean Chaos, there would be no Deleuzian Difference; it is the only motor of recurrence in the eternal return, just as Difference is the only motor for Deleuze's Repetition. Deleuze makes this connection in his early monograph on Nietzsche, published some six years prior to *Difference and Repetition*: 'This is why we can only understand the eternal return as a principle which serves as an explanation of diversity and its reproduction, of difference and its repetition' (NP, 45).

What, then, is Nietzschean Chaos, and more importantly, how does Deleuze understand and ultimately come to modify it? Tackling these questions will reveal a great deal about one of the stated motivations for writing *Difference and Repetition*: the search for a superior form of the principle of sufficient reason; and as we shall see Deleuze's stand on this point is decisive in triangulating his attitude to symmetry with those arguments from symmetry on which so much of science relies.

In a scientific register, Nietzschean Chaos represents a denial of any substantive state of equilibrium in nature. In Nietzsche's iconoclastic attacks on scientific principles, it is this denial which justifies the appeal to the eternal return. The point is encapsulated in the following two quotations: 'The total character of the world, however, is in all eternity chaos.'[9] 'If the universe were capable of permanence and fixity, and if there were in its entire course a single moment of being in the strict sense it could no longer have anything to do with becoming.'[10] The first quotation occurs in context of a number of injunctions to the reader regarding natural order. Nietzsche warns us not to view the apparent uniformities in the world as tokens of a universal order; even the regularities of our neighbouring stars: 'the astral order in which we live', he says, 'is misleading'. We should be wary of believing there to be laws in nature. In the commentary, this quotation has been taken as a precursor to the thought of eternal return; it is a marker of the role which chaos plays in that idea. Chaos is the primordial fact; it is due to chaos that Zarathustra's moonlit road stretches endlessly forward and backward to eternity; it is due to chaos that there are no laws in nature. The second quotation reveals why this should be so. The potential to achieve 'permanence' or 'fixity' cannot be any part of nature's 'total character', since, according to Zarathustra's observations, that state of fixity, of equilibrium, must already have been reached in a universe which has endured from all eternity. All permutations of the cosmic fabric must already have been visited, yet still nature advances. Given these premises – the world as eternal, the passage of nature as ergodic – it is a matter of deduction for Nietzsche that no state of equilibrium, no heat death, is achievable in nature. For it would mark a terminal impasse from which nature could not escape. And yet it moves. Hence Deleuze's claim that the eternal return is an answer to the 'problem of *passage*' (NP, 45), the passing of one moment into the other. Nietzsche intends to establish that time *cannot help* but pass in a world without stasis, and that for this reason eternity is its condition.

Nietzsche's chaos is a denial of equilibrium, then, but the other aspect is no less important: a lack of law. Babette Babich expresses this neatly: 'The primordiality of the void, understood as raw possibility, that is, as becoming recurs in Nietzsche's notion of the world taken as chaos *to*, and thus in this wise: *from* all eternity.'[11] Raw possibility, radical chance, is the total character of the world. And this is so because there never has been and never will be, neither locally nor globally, any actual state of equilibrium. Babich's characterisation is in the context of a discussion of Nietzsche's debt to Greek cosmologies – chaos as the void – but Nietzsche's standpoint on the matter is not confined to metaphysical reflections on the eternal return or cosmological origin. It has as much to do with the nature of energy, which he understands fundamentally as a conflict between forces, superior versus inferior. A conflict which can never be resolved, since competing forces are in their nature incommensurable; there is no common measure by which any given force can be quantified against any other, and this inequality guarantees a remainder in every least phenomenon, every quantum of action. Disequilibrium is a precondition for any event of any kind whatsoever. One of the main threads of Nietzsche's critique of scientific reasoning (and of philosophy) concerns its tendency to impose common measure, equalities, on phenomena which are fundamentally unequal:

> In our science, where the concept of cause and effect is reduced to the relationship of equivalence, with the object of proving that the same quantum of force is present on both sides, the driving force is lacking: we observe only results, and we consider them equivalent in content and force.[12]

Pierre Klossowski emphatically underlines this aspect of Nietzsche's thinking in his monograph *Nietzsche and the Vicious Circle*: '*The will to power appears essentially as a principle of disequilibrium.*'[13] Deleuze marshals and foregrounds these often disparate elements of Nietzsche's thought in ways which will serve his philosophy of difference:

> What is the body? We do not define it by saying that it is a field of forces, a nutrient medium fought over by a plurality of forces, for in fact there is no 'medium', no field of forces or battle. There is no quantity of reality, all reality is already quantity of force in mutual 'relations of tension'.[14]

This differential nature of energetic forces, this resistance to the notion of equilibrium, is of crucial importance to Deleuze. It informs his thinking of Disparity with Simondon; it is the 'remainder' without which the Event is nothing; it is what forces the movement in the Ideal Game. It underpins Life. Disequilibrium, radical chance, is a positive, indispensable, internal motor of the Chaosmos:

> The eternal return is not the effect of the Identical upon a world become similar, it is not an external order imposed upon the chaos of the world; on the contrary, the eternal return is the internal identity of the world and of chaos, the Chaosmos. (DR, 299)

There are a number of problems this raises with respect to the concept of entropy, to which we will come presently, but first it will be useful to clarify the role of this positive disequilibrium in the 'superior principle of sufficient reason' which Deleuze requires for the philosophy of difference. He states on more than one occasion in the course of *Difference and Repetition* that the rationale is to investigate the possibility of formulating a *superior* form of Leibniz's principle of sufficient reason. He identifies the resources for such a formulation as belonging to the idea of the eternal return. This is striking not merely because Nietzsche is notoriously dismissive of the power of reason as such, and thus an unlikely substitute for the arch rationalist Leibniz, but more particularly in the very nature of the theatre played out in Nietzsche's presentation of the idea to us: the overdetermined allegory seems irremediably removed from any claims to this intellectual principle. What is at stake in the translation? Where is the point of departure from Leibniz's system? What is it about the eternal return such that it can provide a superior sufficient reason? It is a matter of a certain Nietzschean necessity which, we shall see, is ultimately played off against a certain Leibnizian necessity.

THE ETERNAL RETURN AND THE DISPARITY OF FORCES

At first glance – or, more accurately, on a reading of the first formulation of Nietzsche's notion of the eternal return – there is not much to support Deleuze's interpretation of this core notion. Moreover, there is much to contradict it; indeed, Deleuze's philosophy of time and the role of difference therein seems directly at odds with the dramatised cosmogony that Nietzsche offers in *The Gay Science*:

> This life as you now live it and have lived it, you will have to live once more and innumerable times more; and there will be nothing new in it, but every pain and every joy and every thought and sight and everything unutterably small or great in your life will have to return to you, all in the same succession and sequence.[15]

If this passage were not (as of course it was not) written explicitly to refute any prospective alignment of Deleuzian 'repetition' with Nietzschean 'recurrence', it is nevertheless difficult to imagine one that could do so more definitively. Nietzsche's claustrophobic 'nothing new' seems to clash definitively with Deleuze's central insistence on the world as creative, on the ineradicable newness of the lived present; Nietzsche's 'same succession and sequence' stands against Deleuze's extended philosophical project devoted to clarifying the mere epiphenomenal dependence of concepts such as 'the same' and 'identity' on the operations of difference.

This seems to derail the claim above that Deleuze's 'repetition' belongs with Nietzsche's 'return'. Is the scenario of the Eternal Return merely a conveniently allusive and suggestive figure of cyclical temporality, sparse and austere enough for Deleuze to colour in as he requires? On one level, yes; the extent to which Nietzsche omits to flesh out the thought of the eternal return (an omission which Deleuze notes in *Difference and Repetition*)[16] is matched by the readiness of subsequent philosophers to lend their own apparatus – ethical, metaphysical, deconstructionist – to its interpretation; alongside Deleuze we can readily place any number in this vein: Vattimo, Klossowski *et al*. Yet as we have already seen, there are deep resources in Nietzsche on which Deleuze draws, and many Nietzschean tributaries to the Deleuzian philosophy of difference.

A more amenable place to start is with one of the famous passages dealing with the eternal return in *Thus Spoke Zarathustra*: the dialogue between Zarathustra and the dwarf in the section entitled 'Of the Vision and the Riddle'.

> 'Behold this moment!' I went on, 'From this gateway Moment a long, eternal lane runs *back*: an eternity lies behind us.'
>
> 'Must not all things that *can* run have already run along this lane? Must not all things that *can* happen *have* already happened, been done, run past?'[17]

We encounter again the two principles on which the reasoning rests: that the world is eternal, and that nature as a whole proceeds ergodically through its possible repertoire. Yet it is the closely subsequent utterance which carries the real import and helps us to understand why for Deleuze the eternal return might offer an apt model for his difference and repetition, an image of becoming and creativity: 'And are not all things bound fast together in such a way that this moment draws after it all future things? *Therefore* – draws itself too?'[18] This is the point in Nietzsche's text where a certain necessity is attached to chance. The 'gateway Moment' sits at the intersection of all that comes before and after, a pivot on which the development of all series rests, both backwards and forwards, yet it is destined to suffer the same redistributions at the very next moment as all other elements of nature. It is not contingently true that no pivot, no crux, no law persists; it is necessary. There is simply nothing in nature that could serve this function. It is this necessity to which Deleuze refers when he writes of 'the necessity of chance' in Nietzsche's work.[19] It is this necessity which secures the superiority of Nietzsche's thought for sufficient reason.

ERGODICITY AND INFINITE DURATION

> Everything which happens and everything which appears is correlated with orders of differences: differences of level, temperature, pressure, tension, potential, difference of intensity. Carnot's principle says this in one way, Curie's principle in another.
> Gilles Deleuze (DR, 222)

In a positive sense, the resistance to equilibrium affirms the ultimate irreducibility of differences in energetic potential between phenomena; those very phenomena which natural science takes as its object: temperature, pressure, tension, etc. And the science of thermodynamics both classical and modern would agree without hesitation, would equally forcefully confirm, that 'everything that happens and everything which appears' is a consequence of gradients of energy. The presence of an energy gradient is what constitutes free (as opposed to bound) energy in thermodynamic terminology. Without free energy no system will evolve, nothing will happen. The point of contention arises over the *irreducibility* in principle of those gradients. For classical thermodynamics, energy gradients within any closed system will always equalise; any action by definition requires some expenditure of free energy, some cancellation of the difference in potential. And because this is true of each and every system without fail, it will ultimately be true of the universe as a whole. Our fate in the long term can only be the moribund state of maximum entropy, a final equilibrium. It is difficult to overstate how central a position the concept of entropy – the long-term tendency of all systems toward equilibrium – occupies in classical thermodynamics. Arthur Eddington, a pre-eminent contributor to the physics of relativity, is often quoted on this: 'If your theory is found to be against the Second Law of Thermodynamics, I can give you no hope; there is nothing for it but to collapse in deepest humiliation.'[20] The second law is the very one which states that the universe tends to maximum entropy. To this day, as if in deference to Eddington's warning, it is not uncommon to find lines of argument in physics debunked because they contain some (usually unintended) consequence which transgresses the second law. No less a contemporary figure than Roger Penrose presents his theory of Conformal Cyclic Cosmology explicitly as a rebuttal of those cyclical cosmologies positing the birth of new universes from old without heed to the second law; this amounts, for him, to the illegitimate assumption of energy from nothing.[21]

As a matter of the history of science, both the notions of the universe as ergodic and as eternal play their part in the classical formulations of entropy – for Boltzmann, Maxwell, Kelvin and Poincaré – but in all cases in ways too nuanced to yield to Nietzsche's metaphysical dismissal without supplement. In particular, the dead-stop of all becoming which Nietzsche attributes to thermodynamic cosmological theory is at least an insufficient reading. Nor does its denial alone furnish the necessity of chance which both Nietzsche and Deleuze champion.

The Ergodic Principle rests on what is called the principle of indifference, which states that all relevant microstates are equally accessible to a system in evolution. The corollary is that all microstates stand an equal chance of expression during that evolution. The Ergodic Principle is an assertion on this basis that all microstates will eventually be occupied in the lifetime of a system if it endures long enough. To subscribe to the Ergodic Principle on a cosmic scale – to an ergodic universe – places us ostensibly on that same ground as Nietzsche illuminates with the allegory of the eternal return. First, he takes it as given that the universe endures infinitely both backward and forward in time, which would indeed (of course) secure the elapse required for an ergodic universe to cycle through the same states many times. Infinitely many. 'Must not all things that *can* happen *have* already happened, been done, run past?' asks Zarathustra. Which we might translate as: 'Must the world not already have visited all its possible microstates?'

The reasoning appears the same. Nietzsche's argument seems no less to require that all states are equally accessible, regardless of unlikelihood, in an evolution lasting long enough. Over sufficient time, what is impossible remains impossible, but what seems unlikely becomes inevitable.

But the devil is in the detail. For Nietzsche, this line of argument dictates that no 'macrostate of the universe' could ever be in equilibrium, whereas by the principles of classical statistical mechanics, *most* possible states of the universe, taken as an average over the course of its entire elapse, would be in equilibrium. It is probability which dictates the heat death of the universe; there are far fewer possible microstates corresponding to far-from-equilibrium macrostates than there are for equilibrial. This is often expressed in the form 'there are far more ways to be disordered than ordered' (far more ways for broken eggs to remain broken than to reassemble).[22] Indeed, to the degree that both Nietzsche and classical thermodynamics subscribe to the principle of indifference, the guarantor of an ergodic universe, they are equally subject to an apparent paradox, a 'paradox of ergodicity'. This paradox both heightens the stakes for Nietzsche's position, and demands an account on the part of thermodynamic science. Briefly, if by far the most numerous microstates correspond to equilibrial macrostates, how does it come about that our observed universe is so far from equilibrium?

The principle of indifference should guarantee that our present state lacks (precisely) the degree of differentiation, the structuration and complexity, that we see, due to its overwhelming rarity. And if we are to acknowledge a universality to entropic processes which dictate a march to indifferentiation, how is it that a universe which has lasted for eternity is not already arrived at its heat death? Must its initial condition not have been a microstate so improbably ordered, so exquisitely rare, that cosmic history could suffer the encroachments of entropy to this day, yet still not have run aground on the infinitely more probable state of equilibrium? How, in short, could nature maintain itself so long in the margins of its manifest destiny? This paradox was not lost on the pioneers of thermodynamic theory – Maxwell, Gibbs and Boltzmann himself – and has never yet been resolved to general satisfaction.

Here then are the two factors separating Nietzsche's eternal return from the ergodic universe of statistical mechanics: the distinction between microstate and macrostate which serves the latter as the index for probability; and consequently the nature of the 'heat death' assumed in each case.[23] Whereas for Nietzsche, arrival at cosmic equilibrium can only entail the instantaneous dead-halt to the passage of nature, a definitive blackout in 'permanence and fixity', this is not so for statistical mechanics. On the level of macrostate, in a state of heat death, nature is unlikely to change or evolve, while nevertheless free to run through all and every available permutation of microstates conforming to that same macrostate, much like shuffling a deck of blank cards, or the cycling of a disengaged flywheel. Nevertheless, the ergodic hypothesis, based as it is on probability, is inherently constrained from asserting the finality of heat death.

> I do not know if it has been remarked that the English kinetic theories can extract themselves from this contradiction. The world, according to them, tends at first to a state where it remains for a long time without apparent change; and this is consistent with experience; but it does not remain that way forever, if the theorem cited above is not violated; it merely stays that way for an enormously long time, a time which is longer the more numerous are the molecules. This state will not be the final death of the universe, but a sort of slumber, from which it will awake after millions of millions of centuries. According to this theory, to see heat pass from a cold body to a warm one, it will not be necessary to have the acute vision, the intelligence and dexterity of Maxwell's Demon; it will suffice to have a little patience.[24]

This observation by Henri Poincaré serves to undermine the 'contradiction' of the paradox of ergodicity; the contradiction does not exist. His 'recurrence theorem' states that all self-enclosed systems (of which we might take the universe to be one) will over the course of long enough time return arbitrarily close to initial conditions. This is to assert ergodicity, but in a way that, rather than underpinning the *prima facie* implications of the second law of thermodynamics, must rather be at odds with them. Enclosed systems must surely increase in entropy, but they must also just as surely exit from it. The recurrence theorem does not so much serve to contradict statistical mechanics as to extend its application, and in doing so reverse the long-term diagnosis.

The classical thermodynamics which Nietzsche resists refuses in turn to provide any simple foil, serving both to confirm and frustrate his metaphysical logic. While on the one hand it points to a moribund heat death, this is not definitive, no dead-halt. It both is and is not what Nietzsche requires. But this is so, it *seems*, precisely *because* of the key Nietzschean tenet which Deleuze brings so much to the fore: the necessity of chance, in the form of an irreducibly probabilistic direction for the passage of nature (although as we shall see, Deleuze does much to supersede this conception of chance in nature, through his notion of the Ideal Game). According to Poincaré, a form of eternal recurrence is *implicit* in the principles of classical thermodynamics, yet on maddeningly long time-scales that are mostly desert. This being so, we are deprived of another important facet of the Nietzschean-Deleuzian framework, the *incessant* nature of becoming, predicated on the perpetually out-of-kilter tension between incommensurable forces.

Finally, in the context of meaningful dialogue between our metaphysics and contemporary cosmology, it is abundantly clear that the incommensurability of energetic phenomena, and the consequent necessity of chance, must be *asserted against*, not *derived* as an unacknowledged implication *from* (as Nietzsche has it) the overwhelming body of opinion. This is because Nietzsche's second premise, the prior eternity of the universe (a premise shared by the classical theorists including Newton), has been definitively abandoned. Its last serious defence was put forward by astronomer Fred Hoyle (among others) in the 1940s and '50s, in resistance to what he dubbed derogatorily the Big Bang. His 'Steady State' cosmology has been taken to be definitively refuted by the discovery of cosmic microwave background radiation in 1976 by Penzias and Wilson. This background radiation had been a specific prediction of the Big Bang hypothesis, serving to elevate it to an almost unanimously subscribed theory. Current estimates of the age of the universe place it at some 13.8 billion years.[25] Even in an outrightly ergodic universe, which may or may not be ours, this is a woefully inadequate timeframe in which to furnish the required demonstration of the eternal return. For Nietzsche, everything that can happen, must already have happened. If it has not, the permutations of the universe remain unexhausted, and among those permutations may lie the dead-stop of equilibrium which he wishes to refute. Only the circumstance of *having survived* a cycle (in truth, an infinite number of cycles) can guarantee the necessity of chaos and chance.

If Deleuze were relying on the dramaturgical metaphysical arguments Nietzsche adopts with respect to the eternal return to underpin the principle of chaos, we should cede him somewhat less than a deductive status for them. Somewhat less than a necessity to chance. Yet to consign the promise of the Deleuzian cosmology so quickly to the same dustbin as classical physics would be to ignore the great suppleness and resourcefulness of his body of work; it is perfectly possible to make the case for the open-ended novelty which must belong to any cosmos we might call Deleuzian without reliance on the critique he borrows from Nietzsche. In making such a case, I shall not restrict myself to consideration of the physics contemporary to Deleuze's own lifetime, much less to that science only about which he was demonstrably aware and made comment. Both physics and metaphysics are open-ended projects, and it would be remiss to pass over the wonderful and inspired variety of contemporary speculative theory; it would be to fail to recognise the same speculative spirit animating Deleuze's work. What makes a metaphysics robust is its ability to engage with and throw light on even the most current strands in physics and science more broadly. The concomitant danger is of course that we force an application of our favoured metaphysics into areas and frameworks which could not be foreseen at time of writing. Deleuze never heard, could not possibly have heard, of loop quantum gravity, for example. Yet few if any new paradigms in science start completely afresh, with a whole new toolkit. Loop quantum gravity, just like any new contemporary proposal, must fashion itself in such a way as not to contradict the successes of either relativity or quantum theory. Like any new theory, it must align itself with respect to questions (among many others) of the continuous or discontinuous character of space, to questions regarding symmetry and the role of symmetry-breaking in nature, of local action versus 'spooky action at a distance', to thermodynamic considerations. These questions are 'written into the script' for any modern physics, and the particularities of a given position will determine the fruitfulness or otherwise of any potential conversation with a given metaphysical schema. There are rich reflections on all these questions in Deleuze's work, which will be addressed in detail in the chapters to come. For that reason, there is no inherent anachronism to a carefully evaluated dialogue on these matters between the science and the metaphysics. Indeed, in my opinion, it is on the terrain of speculation that metaphysics and science meet most naturally; there is no question which metaphysics would put in play that science does not also want to resolve. The distinction for me is that metaphysics lives in that plane above where the concepts are not tied specifically to one field, but remain free to mobilise the salient questions as they play out among several fields. As such, the implicit definition of metaphysics I employ here is rather loose and somewhat pragmatic; but in the sense that it entails a 'continuity' of sorts with science, and ultimately in the very long run must risk susceptibility to discreditation through empirical enquiry, it is not dissimilar to that 'naturalised metaphysics' defended by Anjan Chakravarty.[26] On the matter of general framing, a word is also due about the notion of 'speculation' here, to disambiguate any perhaps assumed association with the recent, somewhat diverse, philosophical movement called 'speculative realism', which engages with scientific frameworks. No such association is intended; indeed I take issue in the conclusion with the work of Quentin Meillassoux, whose work falls under that umbrella term. Equally, the work of the speculative realist Graham Harman can, it seems to me, bear only a tangential relationship with the material treated here. His 'object orientated ontology', while a useful corrective to the 'disappearance' of the object from contemporary science and philosophy, nevertheless advocates a conception of the object (electron and positron included) in relative isolation, which is essentially at odds with what I see as most valuable in the work of Deleuze and Whitehead, and indeed is hard to square with the messages from quantum physics.[27] Rather, by 'speculation' I intend those areas of enquiry (metaphysics and physics alike) which are working to push the salient concepts to the limit; this is, if you like, a Deleuzian form of speculation.

It remains, then, to frame the post-classical question in relation to Deleuze: what are the prospects of bolstering Deleuze's resistance to the question of entropy from among the paradigms which we encounter in the post-classical age? Which fields of physics speak most directly to his metaphysics? The following section attempts merely such an initial framing, with no claim to completeness; a more developed response will be proposed in the final chapter with respect to the more speculative strands of contemporary physics.

POST-CLASSICAL PHYSICS AND THE QUESTION OF ENTROPY

There are implications of chaos theory which both marry well with a Deleuzian metaphysics and shine further light on the argument. As Isabelle Stengers points out, the presence in systems of sustained fluctuation, or resonances such as those which Poincaré identified, are inimical to the formalisation of entropy adopted by Boltzmann:

> We have to accept as only a partial truth the idea that chaos is inevitably subjected to the law of indifference and statistical compensation. Chaos can also, at what are called 'second order phase-transitions,' become actual illegality, a chaos of fluctuations that no longer fluctuate around an average, because none can any longer be defined, but rather reverberate throughout the whole system, confusing that which the distinctions between microscopic and macroscopic had differentiated.[28]

Whereas Boltzmann's formulation rests upon an ideal ergodicity, underpinned by the principle of indifference, the synchronic mobilisations of systems in turbulence (which chaos theory brought so squarely to the fore) serve to problematise that framework. Boltzmann posits each atom in a system as essentially autonomous, with an attendant indifferent probability of occupying this or that position within its milieu. The sum total of those positions for a given large number of atoms defines its microstate, along with the properties of its macrostate. Chaotic, resonating phenomena problematise the distinction between microstate and macrostate, in that the micro-elements act in concert, far from indifferent to each other. The question of whether the universe as a whole is ergodic becomes entirely more complex, no longer amenable to the mathematics of simple distribution, no longer a straight road leading backward and forward in the moonlight: all the straight roads are made crooked. Stated another way, Boltzmann's equation is misleading in that it may serve perfectly well as an *external index* of a system, but will tend to mask any *internal structuring principles* such as turbulence. In this sense, while chaos theory serves to loosen the foundations of the Nietzschean-Deleuzian metaphysics of eternal return, this focus on *internal* structuring principles can be read as an episode in the history of science belonging squarely to the spirit of Deleuzian natural philosophy. Again, the importance of this distinction between internal and external order for Deleuze's philosophy of difference will come to the fore as the argument progresses. At this point, however, we might note that the insights driving the revolution that was chaos theory conjoin with Deleuze's own. It is, strictly speaking, false in light of chaos theory to assume of atomic phenomena that they are susceptible to a neutral, indifferent range of possibilities; in those circumstances where fluctuations and resonances propagate, in those states far from equilibrium, the flat landscape of possible permutations are distinctly no longer so; systems act as populations, precluding indifferent distribution.[29] This is in no way different to Deleuze's assertion (after Bergson) that the possible is the 'sterile double' of the world:

[Every] possible is not realized, realization involves a limitation by which some possibles are supposed to be repulsed or thwarted, while others 'pass' into the real. The virtual, on the other hand, does not have to be realized, but rather actualized; and the rules of actualization are not those of resemblance or limitation, but those of difference or divergence and of creation. (B, 97)

Chaos theory's unwillingness to neglect apparently negligible phenomena speaks to that same unwillingness on Deleuze's part to trust to the indifferentiation of the possible. The patterns and capacities in nature are to be sought in the active fuse of process, not in the mere succession of states. And never indifferently, always internally; there is no such thing, Deleuze says, as 'any multiplicity whatever' (WP, 152). The truth is consequently that, paradoxically, the realm of the virtual is a much less capacious tract, understood as a range of possibilities, than the realm of the possible. But it is not to be so understood, and for precisely that reason it is vital and open.

As is well-known, chaos and complexity theory offer many resources which place in doubt, we might say supersede outright, the 'Newtonian Paradigm' on which classical dynamics and thermodynamics is based. In essence, the Newtonian Paradigm entails the calculability of a system's evolution given sufficient knowledge of that system in terms of salient variables. In the case of the trajectory of a projectile, this will include the angle of launch, speed, momentum, wind-resistance, relative strength of gravitational pull at the given location in the gravity well, etc. The body of chaos theory has resolutely problematised the very possibility of determining initial conditions in sufficient detail to guarantee calculability. Indeed, perhaps its most signal message is that science should be conscious of the potential for even the slightest variation in initial conditions to produce wildly varying evolutions of a given system. Exact calculability in effect would depend on an infinite knowledge of those conditions, and is therefore in principle ruled out; what remains is the possibility of defining the long-term tendencies of a system. Equally, chaos theory has upended the usefulness of extrapolating from the behaviour of closed systems to the behaviour of natural processes in general. The closed system had been taken as a paradigm for all systems, affording empirical scrutability and legitimating generalisations about the way systems as a whole could be expected to evolve. Now, it is held that open systems are vastly more prevalent in nature than closed, and are significantly different in kind to isolated systems, displaying a much greater elasticity of behaviour in contrast to the obedient tendency of closed systems to succumb to equilibrium in a predictable and timely manner. Indeed, another of the definitive lessons from chaos theory is that there is no such thing as a truly closed system;

even where all other forms of energy are shielded, no system can be insulated finally from the effects of gravity. All systems are potentially subject to fluctuations which may amplify, deferring the route march to equilibrium. All open systems have the potential to occupy states far from equilibrium more or less indefinitely.

We should be wary of assuming, however, that the Nietzschean-Deleuzian suspicion of classical thermodynamic principles is vindicated straightforwardly by the advent of the Post-Newtonian Paradigm. From the purview of chaos theory, it is not the *incommensurability* of energetic phenomena as such which underwrites deviations from equilibrium, but the fact of the *open nature of all systems*. The distinction is a critical one. It serves to clarify the capacity of given systems to maintain order against chaos, indeed, to adopt increasingly complex levels of structuration, but the recognition that the *average* progress of the universe tends to disorder remains intact. The tendency of certain systems to increase in complexity does not in and of itself contradict the second law of thermodynamics, if for every gain in local structuration there is a tithe of free energy to be paid in connected systems. The insistence that all systems are open amounts to a claim about the accounting system of nature with respect to the expenditure of free energy. Every phenomenon has associated with it both an endothermic and an exothermic, internal and external, entry in the cosmic ledger. If the system under scrutiny makes a gain in available free energy, there must be in the long term a consequent greater loss overall among the systems with which it is in contact. The structuration represented by convective cells in fluid requires a focused, prolonged heat source, while its own resulting exothermic reaction will be radiative, unable to furnish work with anything like the same economy. The energy bound into the chemical bonds in food is freed by enzymes in our gut to maintain and prolong our own metastable order, but what we take, what we can possibly take out, is less than that gifted by the ecosystem in the first place. The cost of maintaining order, or increasing complexity, against the disorder of equilibrium, will routinely be miscalculated without some double-entry accounting of the local and the global, then. Charles Lineweaver expresses this neatly: 'To answer the question, "is complexity increasing?" we need to disambiguate it. Are we talking about the average complexity of the universe or about the complexity of the most complex object?'[30] And Lee Smolin draws out the long-term consequences on a cosmic scale:

> The second law is doing its best to drive the solar system to equilibrium, but as long as there's a big star radiating hot photons into cold space, that equilibrium is postponed. While it's postponed, molecules can ride the energy flow to greater and greater states of organization and complexity.

And stars burn for billions of years, so there's lots of time for complexity to proliferate.[31]

In other words, while it is routinely acknowledged in contemporary physics that all systems are open, and that this allows an indefinite growth in relative order and complexity, away from disorder, it is illegitimate to conclude from this that the second law is superseded. It is true for certain systems under consideration, but *because* it is true for them, the reverse is true of those surrounding systems in contact. Indeed, we should bear in mind the principal criterion for *defining* an open system as such. An open system is one which enjoys a throughflow of energy (our Earth receives heat from the sun, absorbs, synthesises and radiates back out). This is another way of saying (as Deleuze does) that energy gradients are the precondition of any event at all, that order, structure and complexity are driven by that flow. Chaos theory stands squarely behind the Deleuze who speaks of 'flow', and even the 'liquid physics' he calls for in A Thousand Plateaus, yet cannot finally underwrite the details of his resistance to the second law.[32] Nor, as we shall see, does this definition of openness associated with chaos theory suffice for a Deleuzian Nature; a wider definition will be required. Chaos theory serves to chart the prevalent ways in which the route march to equilibrium is deferred, and in the process perhaps problematises the principle of least action, but finally must leave in the realm of conjecture whether this deferral can amount to anything more. Nevertheless, we shall have reason to explore the fruitful connections between the 'deferred equilibrium' of chaos theory and the concept of 'retardation' as it figures in Deleuze's work.

If Deleuze's resistance to the second law cannot be straightforwardly underwritten by either classical dynamics or chaos theory, what of the field of quantum physics, which supersedes classical theory every bit as much as the latter, but in markedly distinct ways, on a profoundly different terrain? Writing in the latter half of the twentieth century, Deleuze is familiar with and puts to use concepts germane to the field, such as 'superposition'. Yet the same caution is required as in any attempt to evaluate the compatibility or otherwise of any philosopher's work with the scientific-theoretical corpus. One passage where such caution is especially due concerns an argument Deleuze adopts, ostensibly from atomic theory, in support of his suspicion of the second law. On the face of it, the argument seems a ready-made point of entry into the task of aligning the philosophy of difference with the domain of quantum physics:

> The values of implication are centres of envelopment. These centres are not the intensive individuating factors themselves, but they are their

representatives within a complex whole in the process of explication. It is these which constitute the little islands and the local increases [*remontées*] of entropy which nevertheless conform overall to the principle of degradation: atoms taken individually, for example, even though they nonetheless confirm the law of increasing entropy when considered *en masse* in the order of explication of the system in which they are implicated. (DR, 255–6)

At the atomic scale, Deleuze maintains, entities are immune to the processes of degradation which afflict macroscopic entities. It is necessary to forgive Deleuze a little looseness of expression here. '[R]*emonter*' indicates a 're-ascending', a sense faithfully preserved in the translation, rather than a *descending* (more typically, decreasing) of entropic values. In context, the latter (descending, decreasing) would seem to be required; the decrease of entropy is inversely correlated to the decrease of order or complexity (or when entropy decreases, order increases and vice versa). Deleuze, however, intends to convey an *opposition* between the low entropy of 'intensive individuating factors' and the susceptibility to increasing entropy of macroscopic bodies (these bodies '*nevertheless* conform overall to the principle of degradation'). Deleuze is in effect referring to the process dubbed 'negentropy' after Erwin Schrödinger, which refers to the tendency of certain forms of organisation, including principally those associated with life, to form local pockets or islands of increasing order in apparent contradiction to the mandate of entropy.[33] *Nevertheless*, as Deleuze acknowledges, the concept of negative entropy does not violate the second law of thermodynamics; the gain in organisation for isolated 'islands' is balanced by a corresponding loss in the environment of the system, or (as Deleuze would insist) 'centre of envelopment'. The opposition is thus drawn between two scales: the macroscopic, which is susceptible to 'degradation', and the atomic, which is not. In this way, Deleuze is asserting that atoms, or more properly relations between atoms below the level of macroscopic assemblage, are exempt from the second law. He clearly intends to establish a correspondence between the intensive nature of the virtual ('intensive individuating factors'), which he asserts is likewise immune to degradation, and the energetic regime of the atomic scale. The example of the atom, in other words, is intended as an illustration of the claim that entropy is a transcendental illusion, applying only to the explicate, to large numbers of atoms in combination. While the generally accepted reconceptualisation of the atom away from the letter of atomist principles may offer some support here, this is not sufficient to make Deleuze's case. Modern physics no longer supports the idea that atoms are enduring ('eternal') entities – indeed, it is misleading even to talk of the 'path' of a particle. Such a path is not the route of an identical particle through space; as David Bohm puts it: 'The notion of continuity of existence is approximated by that of very rapid recurrence of similar forms, changing in a simple and regular way (rather as a rapidly spinning bicycle wheel gives the impression of a solid disc, rather than of a sequence of rotating spokes)'.[34] Although this picture affords some alignment with the notion of intensive unfolding or explication which Deleuze would favour (indeed, 'unfolding' is precisely the term Bohm adopts for the process described in the preceding quotation), it does not of itself secure the immunity from entropy Deleuze envisages on the terrain of quantum or atomic scale physics.

The point of contention comes with respect to the well-known wave/particle duality which informs quantum theory. Every particle, particulate ensemble and indeed macroscopic object alike are lent form, we are to understand, through an associated wave-form or wave-forms, each with a signature frequency. Over time, and acutely so over cosmic time-scales, all such frequencies will lengthen and hence weaken. This is an implication of the expansion of the universe, betokened by the red-shift of galaxies first observed by Hubble, which dilutes available energy, undoing structure, ultimately down to the atomic scale. Milič Čapek writes: 'If the law of dissipation of energy means a lengthening of the wave-length of every kind of energy, it must apply to matter itself, which means a gradual transformation of matter into radiation.'[35] The association of the intensive with the subatomic scale is rendered more plausible, however, by the tendency of contemporary theories to reconceptualise the nature of the atom in terms of entities at scales below that of atoms and even below that of their constituent components (protons, neutrons, electrons and quarks). For string theory, it is the way in which minute strings are shaped and folded amongst themselves that result in the signature energies of particulate matter, while for loop quantum gravity, these are the result of unlocalised loops of energy. If Deleuzian metaphysics is to be attuned to the advances of modern physics, it may be a matter of recognising that atomic and directly subatomic entities are in fact explicate, in a different but just as real sense as are macroscopic entities. If the intensive is to be located at a given scale, as suggested (though the suggestion is far from consistently maintained) by Deleuze's own example, that scale may be a level below the atomic. This line of argument, in my view a necessary corrective to the Deleuzian text, will be elaborated in the discussion of Bohm's own work below.

More generally, while the question of entropy does not typically occupy the foreground in quantum theorising, it would be untrue to say that it is generally contradicted or even unaccommodated in the history of the field. Von Neumann proposed, in an interesting parallel to Deleuze's own standpoint, that entropy takes effect at that point where the wave-function collapses. Once again, the specifics of Deleuze's resistance to the second law are required to see the connection fully. The colouring of entropy as a transcendental illusion rests on Deleuze's claim that entropy takes effect in explicated, actualised phenomena, but could not apply to the intensive, energetically incommensurable phenomena of the virtual domain. *Prima facie*, Von Neumann's formulation offers promising points of contact between the realm of the wave-function and the (precisely) *observed* world after collapse. The first is outwith the second law, which extends only over the second.

The concept of entropy has proven key to the intersection between quantum theory and cosmology, and in particular the high-energy physics of black holes. The Bekenstein-Hawking conjecture posits a remarkably direct correspondence between the level of entropy represented by a given black hole and its 'surface area'. This line of thinking has in turn been adopted to bolster a novel interpretation of quantum cosmology: the 'holographic' universe.

The preceding observations do not finally serve to establish Deleuze's resistance to the second law as incorrect, nor is it assumed that any scientific position implying the long-term heat death of the universe is ultimately correct (indeed, the empirical proof would require a perseverance equal to Poincaré's ironic 'patience', which might be called upon for several times the duration of the universe to date). Moreover, I hope to demonstrate to the contrary that there are resources in the scientific literature which strongly resonate with the philosophy of difference on this issue. Rather the exercise has been fourfold: to emphasise to what degree and in what senses the Nietzschean-Deleuzian resistance to the second law is iconoclastic; to demonstrate (*pace* Deleuze) the internal tensions of the argument from eternal return; the need to supplement that argument from other angles (and to give an initial indication of the ways in which Deleuze does this); and most importantly to interrogate the robustness of the Nietzschean superior principle of sufficient reason, which we can now see goes by the name of 'the necessity of chance'. In truth, while a necessary tactic to bring to the fore the above points of contention, it has been somewhat misleading to present the argument from eternal return without detailing two crucially related elements of the Nietzschean-Deleuzian corpus: the singular conception of chance itself common to both thinkers (this is profoundly distinct from that employed by Boltzmann, for example), and the dual regimes to which energetic phenomena belong. The first will be addressed in the chapter on the Ideal Game, the second with reference to the themes of Limits and Explication. Both are necessary to an understanding of Order and Disorder in the Deleuzian sense.

2. *Entropy and the Complete Concept in Leibniz and Deleuze*

If Nietzschean necessity is 'the necessity of chance', allied to a superior sufficient reason and key to the concept of Chaosmos, I hope to have shown that certain caveats apply in the course of establishing a common rubric between our metaphysics (so far) and the evolving history of thermodynamics. Over the rest of this book, I would like to demonstrate (*pace* Deleuze) the various ways in which the Leibnizian strand of Deleuze's metaphysics serves more productively to illuminate questions of order and disorder shared with scientific discourse. There are certain indispensable elements required of this Leibnizian reading: the primacy of divergence; disparity as the precondition of any event whatever; radical chance; a demonstrable relation to thermodynamics and the second law. The reading itself depends on a construal of Leibniz's principle of sufficient reason as a principle of *dissymmetry*, rather than one of symmetry. Its keystone is the novel form of a certain Leibnizian necessity, which governs the selection of events. The necessity in question is the necessary inclusion of all predicates pertaining to an individual in the complete concept of that individual.

Dan Smith systematically and insightfully explores the nuances of Leibniz's metaphysical logic and its relation to Deleuze's own in his essay 'Logic and Existence: Deleuze on the Conditions of the Real'. Of particular interest here is his demonstration that Leibniz's turn away from Aristotelian formal subject-predicate logic transforms the territory from abstract categorial reasoning to a logic of the event. He focuses on the formulation by Leibniz of the principle of sufficient reason as a reciprocal tenet to the principle of identity, often encapsulated in the shorthand example 'A = A'. In its most common sense form, this principle states that a thing is what it is – a tautology that represents a necessary truth. A more developed form of the principle is that whenever a given predicate is applied to a given subject, the resulting statement will be found to be necessarily true when it is shown that the subject itself contains the predicate by definition. Thus we cannot deny that a triangle is a three-sided shape when 'three-sidedness' is shown to be inextricable from the idea of 'triangle'. All we need do is analyse the notion of triangle to conclude the necessary truth of this statement; it is thus known as an analytic statement. This reasoning singles out a necessary relation. Leibniz rehearses this classical (Aristotelian) logic in the eighth section of the *Discourse on Metaphysics*, but notes that the definition of identity involved is merely a nominal, and hence insufficient one. We might illustrate this point with the observation that the concept of a unicorn necessarily includes the predicate 'horned animal', and in this way (and any number of others) accommodates the principle of identity. This feature goes to show, however, that the principle has no essential connection to existence or existents as such; it is merely nominal. This for Leibniz will not serve a productive investigation of truth, and he concludes:

> Now it is evident that all true predication has some basis in the nature of things and that, when a proposition is not an identity, that is, when a predicate is not explicitly contained in a subject, it must be contained in it virtually.[1]

Leibniz's pragmatic requirement, that predicates have some basis in the nature of things, is in some ways simply one example of the familiar assertion that abstract logical relations (here, the 'containment' theory of meaning) cannot in themselves assert anything true of the contingent world, as any proposition should if it is to be truly meaningful. But it is much more than this, due to Leibniz's very distinctive conception of 'the nature of things'. What form of predication is required for a Leibnizian metaphysics? It is one which must answer to the exigencies of some tightly dovetailed principles governing the nature of things. These include of course the principle of sufficient reason, the principle of the identity of indiscernibles, and other well-known elements of Leibniz's philosophy. I will argue in addition that the principle of least resistance, or principle of least action, belongs squarely among these with respect to the problematic to be addressed, in a way that is not immediately obvious, but which provides a bridge to the questions concerning thermodynamics treated here.[2]

Leibniz's proposal to ground predication in the nature of things is conveyed in the idea of 'the complete concept'. He illustrates his reasoning in correspondence with Antoine Arnauld, taking as an example of an individual the biblical figure of Adam:

> As if we should mean by Adam the first man, whom God set in a garden of pleasure whence he went out because of sin, and from whose side God

fashioned a woman. All this would not sufficiently determine him and there may have been several Adams separately possible or several individuals to whom all that would apply. This is true, whatever finite number of predicates incapable of determining all the rest might be taken, but that which determines a certain Adam ought to involve absolutely all his predicates. And it is this complete concept which determines the particular individual.[3]

It is clear from the phrasing that Leibniz's thought is motivated by his principle of the identity of indiscernibles here, which states that any two individuals that were wholly alike in every respect would in fact be the same individual. For Leibniz, this principle serves not so much to establish what it is for things to be identical as it does to delineate an absurdity, since for him it is a necessary truth that all actually existing individuals are differentiable, however minimally. In the last analysis, this differentiability may be due only to the single final term of all applicable predicates, yet this would be enough to differentiate two individuals. Why necessary? On account of the principle of sufficient reason, which states that there must be a reason why things are thus and not otherwise. This principle is taken to govern even God's selection from among the realm of possible candidates for existence; if there were no reason to choose between one possible entity and another, if they were wholly identical, God would lack sufficient reason to select one for actualisation rather than the other. The complete concept idea of predication is furnished to map faithfully onto these principles concerning the nature of things. It corresponds to the relationship which the possible bears to the actual; no definition for any individual can be complete until all its contingencies unfold, until all the reasons, both local and global, to which it is subject over the course of its existence are exhausted. In addition, these principles taken as a whole will furnish the basis for my claim that Leibniz's metaphysics, and in particular the principle of sufficient reason, grounds the world on a final, ineradicable dissymmetry. There can be no complete symmetry in a world where each existent is discernible.

What of the particular necessity which belongs to the idea of the complete concept? Leibniz tells us:

> we are able to say that this is the nature of an individual substance or of a complete being, namely, to afford a conception so complete that the concept shall be sufficient for the understanding of it and for the deduction of all the predicates of which the substance is or may become the subject.[4]

In short, to know the complete concept is to know what predicates belong, have belonged and will belong to any individual whatever. Again, necessarily? Yes, Leibniz tells us, this is known *a priori* to God. As we might put it, there is a necessary fact of the matter whether we know it or not.⁵ This feature is brought to the fore in another sense belonging to Leibniz's rationale, which Smith highlights with the observation that the complete concept is a reciprocal principle to that of identity. The necessity belonging to the complete concept, that all predicates of an individual belong to it necessarily, is in a sense the inverse necessity of the principle of identity. And this is so because of the consonance of the complete concept with the principle of sufficient reason. Smith comments: 'The principle of identity says that an analytic proposition is necessarily a true proposition, whereas the principle of sufficient reason says that a true proposition is necessarily an analytic proposition.'⁶

Taken at face value, as a statement about logical relations, this tenet has often been seen as a scandal at the heart of Leibniz's system, for it implies nothing less than that everything pertaining to a given subject belongs to its definition, not incidentally, but necessarily; the fact of being hit by this raindrop as opposed to that one is characterised as a necessary truth. Indeed, this is nonsense if taken as a statement of logical necessity. Yet it is not intended as such; it is intended as a statement about action, divergence, selection. According to Leibniz's complementary tenet that every action affects and is affected by the entire universe, the complete concept and its close correlate, the principle of sufficient reason, function as an injunction to us to bear in mind that description in terms of isolatable essences, of differentiable species and genuses in the Aristotelian fashion, will lead attention away from the interconnected web of series which are in constant process at a level below statements such as 'the rain fell on me'. The rain is composed of individual raindrops, some of which were taken up and condensed within one particular cloud rather than another, each of which has its history in turn necessarily connected to the rest of the causal universe. Yet, as Smith points out, the corollary of this is that the understanding of what it is to predicate something of something else ('I was soaked') becomes not a matter of 'predication' – of the attribution of a quality to a thing – but of the *event* as such ('there was a soaking'). The necessity in question is not one of the logic of identity or essence, but of the potentially infinite propagation of interconnected causes converging on the particular phenomena expressing themselves in and through a particular subject.

At this point, we may ask what, for Deleuze, is missing in the framework as presented by Leibniz; are we not in the realm of a temporal process of endless differentiation, presupposing not identity but constantly varying series which constitute difference as such? Is this not the basis on which to describe difference in itself? The answer is – almost.

Deleuze does commit without reserve to the event as a constant exchange of virtual and actual series, and to this dynamic as a principle of selection, yet he is concerned to identify a form of difference which will escape completely and utterly from any prior supposition of identity, of any explication of difference as relying on the opposition between stable, pre-given identities. His objection to Leibniz's necessity, the 'complete concept' represented by intersecting series of events in the Leibnizian world, is a measure of the radical nature of his own understanding of difference in itself, and serves to illuminate his stated rationale for seeking a superior sufficient reason in the eternal return. It is that Leibniz's 'complete concept', reliant as it is on differentiation extended indefinitely, differs from the Aristotelian framing of essence in terms of division by opposition (both of these subjects belong to mankind, but one belongs to the 'female' category, while the other belongs to 'male') only in one respect. While Aristotle maintains that at some level the division must end (or else we lose sight of meaningful differentiation), Leibniz effectively extends the process to infinity. For Deleuze, this is to reinstall identity at the outermost limit; to push individuation to its furthest reaches is nevertheless to retain identity as a precondition for differentiation. The superior sufficient reason he seeks must overcome this objection, and hence he turns to the radical open-endedness of the eternal return. This is the objection he offers to the Leibnizian metaphysics in *Difference and Repetition*. The non-essentialist account presented by Leibniz falls short of that required by the philosophy of difference, of the chaosmos. Yet here again, we might pause to parse the question differently. It is not finally the inadequacy of the complete concept idea which harbours the real incongruence, but Leibniz's account of possible worlds. The neat dehiscence of the Best world moment by moment from those lesser possible worlds, consigning all but one to inexistence, is the root difference. It is what constitutes the validity of the principle of non-contradiction on which Leibniz relies; contradictory elements, the 'incompossibles' of the metaphysics, are ontologically proscribed from actualisation within one world, but may occupy *separate* worlds indiscriminately, for they are outwith causal contact. It is that causal separation which ensures non-contradiction. The border between one possible world and another is the border at which the complete concept and the principle of sufficient reason must stop. Without it, there is nothing to prevent both propagating endlessly, among the proliferating multiplicities of the virtual and the paradoxical causalities of the chaosmos. In this light, Deleuze's argument misses its mark, for once the borders between incompossible worlds are relinquished, the complete concept is nomadically freed, just as is the principle of sufficient reason.

Indeed, it seems to be precisely such a liberation for those concepts that Deleuze intends when he insists in *The Fold*, against Leibniz, that there *is* a 'vague Adam', and when he describes Whitehead's Process God, who 'affirms incompossibilities and passes through them' (FLB, 81). Here it is not at all the notion of infinite predication which provides the source of contention with Leibniz. Quite the reverse: to insist on a vague Adam is to remove the borders between incompossible worlds, the borders at the edge of contradiction, and it is those very borders which prevent the truly infinite predication which Deleuze requires. For our purposes, and according to Deleuze's later viewpoint, the complete concept remains not merely intact, but requisite, if God is truly to affirm incompossibilities, if nature is to be attuned to all its potential, both actual and virtual.

DISSYMMETRY, ENERGY GRADIENTS AND 'THE ULTIMATE ORIGINATION OF THINGS'

It remains to establish in what sense the triple principles of the complete concept, the identity of indiscernibles and sufficient reason can respond from within the Leibnizian corpus to the exigencies of the thermodynamic energy gradients which Deleuze places at the heart of his philosophy of difference. All are mobilised in his assertion: 'Disparity – in other words, difference or intensity (difference of intensity) – is the sufficient reason of all phenomena, the condition of all that appears' (DR, 222). The question is intimately tied to a reading of the principle of sufficient reason as a principle of dissymmetry. In fact, there is one Leibnizian text which aligns these themes beautifully: 'On the Ultimate Origination of Things', where we find that the dissymmetry, the differential in question, is precisely that of an energy gradient.

Before proceeding, one significant obstacle to the proposed reading must be addressed. It is that Leibniz's principle of sufficient reason has been interpreted routinely in precisely the reverse sense: as an argument from symmetry. The classic example of an argument from symmetry might be taken from Anaximander, whose cosmology provides an account addressing the question, 'if the earth is not supported by anything, why does it not fall through space?' Aristotle reports in *De caelo*:

> There are some who say that the earth remains in place because of similarity [or symmetry], as did Anaximander among the ancients; for a thing established in the middle, with a similar relationship to the extremes, has no reason to move up rather than down or laterally; but since it cannot proceed in opposite directions at the same time, it will necessarily remain where it is.[7]

Leibniz's God would have no reason to choose one direction or the other to move this world, since the respective distances to the edge of the void (Anaximander's word is *apeiron*) are indiscernible; in other words, symmetrical. Charles Kahn comments, 'it is indeed the same reason which was glorified in modern times by Leibniz as his Principle of Sufficient Reason'.[8]

Indeed, there are passages in Leibniz's work which seem to settle once and for all, and in the *affirmative*, the question as to whether he viewed the principle of sufficient reason as an argument from symmetry. When Leibniz wants to convey to Clarke the pedigree of his Principle, the example he gives is drawn from Archimedes' *De aequilibro*, concerning the reason for the balance of weights; ''Tis because no reason can be given, why one side should weigh down, rather than the other',[9] clearly articulating one of the variants of this principle, known as the principle of insufficient reason. Ian Hacking references a brief note from 1678 in the Leibniz archive entitled '*De incerti aestimatione*', wherein Leibniz states the 'principle of indifference' holding that equipossible cases have the same probability (thereby reflecting a symmetry), and makes the claim that it may be justified metaphysically. Hacking concludes, as we might well, that this is an unspecified reference to the principle of sufficient reason.[10] The argument for sufficient-reason-as-dissymmetry would appear to falter at the gate. Notwithstanding Leibniz's own recognition of these variants, it is my contention that by far the greater deal of the force and drive of Leibniz's philosophy can best and most coherently be understood in terms of sufficient-reason-as-dissymmetry. For what is the final lesson to be drawn from the principle but that in cases where complete symmetry pertains, nothing happens? More emphatically, with respect to the realm of potential, if all entities were in a relation of perfect symmetry, perfect identity, nothing would originate at all. And if, as we have seen, Leibniz's motivation is to furnish a logic faithful to the 'nature of things', to the Event rather than to merely 'nominal' distinctions, then the principle of insufficient reason provides no traction; it serves only to identify a certain redundancy at the outer limit of phenomena. The incompossible symmetry which the principle of indifference identifies *precludes* any Event. As Deleuze has it, if God's calculations rounded out, there would be no world.

ON THE ULTIMATE ORIGINATION OF THINGS

In 'On the Ultimate Origination of Things', Leibniz broaches the idea of a 'certain dominant unity' which orders the world, or 'the aggregate of finite things'.

For the dominant unity of the universe not only rules the world, but also constructs or makes it; and it is superior to the world and, so to speak, extramundane, and it is thus the ultimate reason of things. For a sufficient reason for existence cannot be found in any single thing alone, nor in the whole aggregate and series of things.[11]

In pursuing the ultimate origination of things, then, we are indeed in search of sufficient reason. Leibniz sets out the task of God in terms of an analogy with a game with rules. The rules are extramundane, pertaining to the world of potential rather than the actual. The first is to do with essence:

We must first acknowledge from the fact that something exists rather than nothing, that there is in possible things, i.e. in possibility or essence itself, a certain demand for existence or (so to speak) a straining to exist ... all possible things strain with equal right for existence.[12]

The next consideration is the implications of this rule for maximising strategy (God's):

And the situation is like that in certain games where all the spaces on the board are to be filled according to certain rules, and where unless you use some skill, you will in the end be excluded from certain spaces and forced to leave more spaces empty than you would have wished.[13]

The skills required bear on the most elegant translation possible from the conditions above to the constraints pertaining to the progress of the game below. The most efficacious move will be the one that does not inadvertently (through lack of forward thinking) cut the player off from the end goal, the one which preserves the most productive long-term outcome. Sufficient reason is not an abstractly applied principle, but one which is acutely sensitive to conditions pertaining at each instant in the passage of nature. Equally, in maximising strategy: 'Assuming that a move is to be made from one point to another, although nothing further determines the path between them, the easiest or shortest way will be chosen.'[14] With this last step in the chain of reasoning, Leibniz is stopping little short of identifying the principle of least resistance, our principle of least action, with the principle of sufficient reason. This line of thought marries perfectly with the characterisation of entropy as a principle of selection; those phenomena will tend to be deselected which embody an energy state overreaching that readily available under local conditions, taking the balance sheet further than it 'need be' from equilibrium. 'Moves' (phenomena) which contradict this rule are not strictly forbidden, but will have to be paid back on the balance sheet by contributions of energy from elsewhere. Just as arbitrary or ill-thought-out choices made by God with respect to particular individual phenomena will produce distortions of the well-ordered fabric of the best world, so random fluctuations in energy state will ramify in the form of 'unnecessary' turbulence.

We always bear in mind, of course, that in all of this Leibniz is embellishing rather than moving away from the notion of actualisation as subject to God's choice, but all the particulars of that embellishment are aligned to a rounded sense of physical causality which cannot help but remind the modern reader of our science of thermodynamics:

> From these considerations it is now wonderfully evident how a certain divine mathematics or metaphysical mechanics is employed in the very origination of things, and how a determination of the maximum holds good, just as, of all the angles, the right angle is the determinate angle in geometry, and as liquids placed in other liquids organize themselves into the most capacious shape, namely the spherical; but especially in common mechanics itself, when several heavy bodies are struggling against each other such a motion finally arises through which occurs the maximum descent on the whole.[15]

The images Leibniz offers translate with some facility into the register of thermodynamics. His analogy of the 'several heavy bodies' suggests strongly a set of precariously balanced boulders on the brink of collapse, whose potential energy will be converted into kinetic through the operation of gravity should their precarious balance fail. The exchange between potential and kinetic energy (and indeed all energetic exchange) is governed by the first law of thermodynamics, which states that the total energy of the world is conserved, while the collapse of boulders toward a more stable plateau conforms to the second law, which requires that all systems seek their lowest energy state in the long term. At the same time, however, this image recalls the metaphysical 'straining of essences' for existence, as though compossibles were vying to fall through into the actual, to achieve 'maximum descent', to adopt the path of least resistance.[16] The model is metaphysical and it is not. More recent incorporations into the vocabulary of thermodynamic theory also allow us to recognise the image of the more viscous liquid immersed in the less, and adopting a spherical shape, as one example of the topological expressions for equilibrial energy distribution we come across in complexity theory; the example of a bubble's tendency to spherical shape is a close parallel (found in both Gleick and DeLanda).[17]

If Leibniz's 'compossibility' bears such a close relation to the existence of energy gradients, then, and with such close association to the principle of sufficient reason, it seems there is indeed much overlap with Deleuze's concept of the virtual, whereby differences in intensity are the sufficient reason of all that appears. As we have seen, the 'metaphysical mechanics' of the compossible straddles the two domains of the potential and the actual, just as do Deleuze's intensive relations; God's choice requires a minimal difference at every turn in this world below and in the world above. Genesis is a perennial process manifest in two regimes. Moreover, both the virtual and the compossible are construed not to entail any ultimate descent into disorder, or equilibrium. It would indeed require an aggressive psychoanalytic reading to confuse the final stasis to which Leibniz's theodicy tends, the Harmony, with the scientists' Heat Death. On both Leibniz's and Deleuze's part, it seems, the premises of thermodynamics are embraced, but not the conclusions.

We know the formula for Leibniz: things are selected, chosen by God from among the compossible candidates with a view to overall best functional fit for progress toward the Best world. Leibniz's text presents origination, or actualisation, by way of an extended analogy with dynamic processes: The reference to heavy bodies suggests a pile of precariously balanced boulders. The heavy bodies are seeking equilibrium, the world is seeking to collapse all gradients (of energy, of disharmony), to take the path of least resistance or steepest route. It is the world described by thermodynamics.

Moreover, Leibniz's principle of least resistance circles in lockstep with the idea of the complete concept, the principle of sufficient reason, the principle of the identity of indiscernibles, the breadth of his metaphysical system. A brief rehearsal demonstrates as much.

God's choice is not motivated between indiscernible entities;[18] those essences which are indistinguishable, identical, will not enjoy transition from potential to actual,[19] could not contribute to the progression of the world toward the Best. Yet should the essences considered by God differ in their *complete concept* by the merest scintilla, by any gradient whatever,[20] there is sufficient reason to decide.[21] The dynamic model mirrors the metaphysical system. The precariously balanced rock whose destiny it is to fall first, differs infinitesimally in balance from the others; if there were perfect symmetry of balance, there would be no sufficient reason to choose, nothing would happen. And that contingency is a function of its complete history, its complete concept: prior falls, angle, the relative proportion of minerals which cooled into its composition, future fractures. Any deviation from the history of the other boulders is a precondition for choice, discernibility. Nor will its complete concept, its 'essence', be exhausted until its history is over; for Leibniz, things accrue their own essence over a lifetime and all their contingencies belong to them necessarily. Essences strain for existence just as heavy bodies fall toward their complete concept down the steepest route, subject to the principle of least resistance. It is metaphysical and it is not; God's choice requires a minimal deviation at every turn in this world below and in the world of potential above. The boulder will slip and fall at a new angle. Genesis, Origination, is a perennial process devoted to coining a new world at each moment.

FROM MANY WORLDS TO CHAOSMOS

When Deleuze comes to make a break from the Leibnizian form of sufficient reason, it centres on a rejection of the many possible worlds scenario that ultimately underpins Leibniz's system. Deleuze insists rather on the existence of a single world which contains all compossibilities and incompossibilities within it; this one world he names the 'chaosmos'. This rejection of the many worlds hypothesis is entangled with a standpoint on the nature of energy and entropy, and should be interpolated into the extended discussion of energy and entropy in chapter 5 of *Difference and Repetition*.

Deleuze is conscious of the drastic distorting effect to Leibniz's system represented by his insistence that the unactualised states of affairs remain in one cosmos, the chaosmos. To revisit at greater length the quotation above regarding divergent series:

> Each series tells a story: not different points of view on the same story, like the different points of view on the town we find in Leibniz, but completely distinct stories which unfold simultaneously. The basic series are divergent; not relatively, in the sense that one could retrace one's path and find a point of convergence, but absolutely divergent in the sense that the point or horizon of convergence lies in a chaos or is constantly displaced within that chaos. (DR, 123)

The point of contention centres on the nature of series, and as we have seen, more particularly on the property of *convergence* or *divergence*. The claim effectively is that the neat dehiscence of events in Leibniz's cosmology reduces the radical displacements of chance, subordinating them to a linear flow of time. The series selected for actualisation cease to have any causal (or expressive) connection with those which remain unselected, due to incompossibility or incompatibility with the criterion of 'the best'. In Leibniz's scenario, divergent worlds are consigned to non-existence. At the end of the world, all troubling diversions have been left behind and all series converge to Harmony.

This process belongs equally to another register, at once both mathematical and philosophical, furnished from Leibniz's work and attended closely by Deleuze in all his discussions of Leibniz: differential calculus. The calculus as developed by Leibniz deals with the reciprocal determination of series in terms of the difference between two given values representing the degree of change in a given figure or system.

No final value may be reached for the rate of change, or indeed the rate of change of change, except by identifying a limit toward which the values converge. This, as is well known, is mathematically straightforward for linear functions, offering an integral value corresponding to the relation between the two initial differentiated values. Reiterations of the process can offer greater and greater accuracy, converging ever closer to the identified limit. Leibniz was never to solve the problem of integrating non-linear functions, though he recognised the importance of finding some way to do so. It is a small step to draw the analogy between this state of mathematics and Leibniz's metaphysics: the compossible is the actualisable, while the linear is the integrable; equally, the incompossible is unactualisable in this world, while the non-linear remains unsusceptible to integration. The analogy is all the more apt given that the differential calculus depends finally on the differentiation between two points at an ever more exquisitely proximate, *infinitesimal* remove, asymptotically approaching identity yet in the end theoretically discernible. The calculus seems poised precisely at the entry-gate to existence guarded by the principle of the identity of indiscernibles.[22] If integration and actualisation go hand in hand, then in the mathematical register Deleuze's point of departure from Leibniz effectively equates to an insistence that both linear and non-linear functions, both the ruly and the unruly, both the ordered and the disordered, figure in the selection of events. When Deleuze insists that divergent series are primary, this is at once a prioritisation of the non-linear mathematical function and the turbulent phenomena which resist simple integration. The linear world is a series of small islands in the preponderantly chaotic ocean of nature. To banish to another world that which threatens disorder is to ignore its properly productive role in this.

To follow the developments Deleuze makes from Leibniz's differential philosophy to his own full-blown philosophy of difference, then, is first and foremost to recognise the accommodation of productive disorder within one world. Leibniz's isolated worlds render them amenable to integration, to the balance of harmony, just as classical physics isolates the system and takes the result, equilibrium, to be the purest expression of nature. In fact, both were hunting down and caging the rarest bird. Deleuze's refusal of the particular form of disorder we call entropy stands squarely on the same ground as chaos theory. Phenomena we cannot integrate, energy which escapes mathematical taming, is too quickly written off as random disorder. This departure from the Leibnizian framework will come to be consolidated and embellished by the coining of the notion of disjunctive synthesis, and the substitution of the (Leibnizian) notion of 'divergence' for the more subtly nuanced interplay of complication, implication and explication.

THE CALCULATING GOD

It is entirely in keeping with his project that Deleuze should begin the chapter following his extended discussion of Leibnizian themes with a figurative image of cosmological entropy inspired by the nature of the mathematical continuum: 'God makes the world by calculating, but his calculations never work out exactly [*juste*], and this inexactitude or injustice in the result, this irreducible inequality, forms the condition of the world' (DR, 222). This complex image resonates throughout what is to follow in Chapter 5 of *Difference and Repetition*, encapsulating numerous aspects of the equally complex argument. Ultimately it is intended to serve as a marker on the way to the conceptual appropriation of Nietzsche's eternal return as a superior sufficient reason.

The image of God the calculator on a denotative level makes reference to the history of mathematics: specifically the serial invention of various different types of number, each intended to fill in a gap left by the preceding regime. Thus the Natural or counting numbers are supplemented by the Whole numbers including zero, then the Rational numbers allowing us to express number values as fractional, followed by the Irrationals which are incapable of expression by fractions, the Complex numbers which are composites of imaginary and real numbers, and so on. In each case the type of number in question was conceived as a way of addressing complex problems which extended beyond the capacity of the existing range of types. Ultimately, the conjecture is that there is a 'space' of number which may be smoothly and completely filled by a full range once this is discovered – this space is known as 'the continuum'. Deleuze's God, then, on a denotative level, is working through the continuum. The crucial implication of this metaphor, though, is that for Deleuze, the continuum will never be exhausted; the space of number will always retain something of the incommensurable, the unequal, within itself inherently – if the intention of God the calculator is to equalise everything out once and for all, he may succeed provisionally on one level, but only at the expense of having to pursue this inequality, this disequilibrium, ever onward into the next regime of number. This is in contrast to Leibniz's God, who supersedes the incommensurable, the incompossible, through consignment to non-existence, and who finally resolves the disharmony of troublesome series. This extended metaphor is laid out with the conclusion:

> Finally, God has not defeated the unequal in itself, but only separated it from the divisible and enclosed it within an outer circle, *kuklos exothen*. He has equalised the divisible in this extension, which is the extension of the Soul of the world, but underneath, at the deepest layer of the divisible, the unequal still rumbles in intensity. (DR, 233)

It is on the *connotative* level, though, that this image connects with physical action, and in particular with entropy: 'The world "happens" while God calculates; if the calculation were exact, there would be no world' (DR, 222). The first half of this assertion (that the world 'happens' while God calculates) echoes a marginal note Leibniz made to himself on his own copy of the 'Dialogus'.[23] The second half is Deleuze's own elaboration, in effect distancing the claim from the principle of indifferent reason. What counts in the world is the unequal, the dissymmetrical, difference, which are always prior and resist any tendency to homogeneity:

> The world can be regarded as a 'remainder' and the real in the world understood in terms of fractional or even incommensurable numbers. Every phenomenon refers to an inequality by which it is conditioned. Every diversity and every change refers to a difference which is its sufficient reason. (DR, 222)

We are to understand, then, that the nature of the physical world is such that action, just as with the domains of number, sweeps ever on past itself without attaining an ultimate fulfilment; the 'remainder' is no transitory inequivalence in God's calculation, it is rather an ineradicable component of nature, without which existence itself would terminate. '[I]f the calculation were exact, there would be no world.' We should note too, that diversity and indeed all change in the chaosmos which Deleuze is outlining have their own sufficient reason, inherent in an ineradicable inequality or heterogeneity, a disparity between forces. Further, for Deleuze, following Nietzsche, the very inequality of the remainder itself, of any given moment with itself, renders nonsense the idea that a terminus may be reached; 'permanence and fixity' rule out becoming.

In other words, any arrival at equivalence or equilibrium, or what amounts to the same thing, identity, is strictly out of the question, since this identity in itself is an epiphenomenon of the difference which underlies it. Deleuze goes on to develop God's calculation in more explicitly physical terms through the course of Chapter 5; intensity and extensity are said to maintain just such a relation of calculation to remainder; intensive multiplicities express themselves in actualised occasions, in extensive quantities, but retain an irreducible tendency therein: 'Intensity is difference, but this difference tends to deny or cancel itself out in extensity and underneath quality' (DR, 223). Yet:

> We cannot conclude from this that difference is cancelled out, or at least that it is cancelled in itself. It is cancelled insofar as it is drawn outside itself, in extensity and in the quality which fills that extensity. However, difference creates both this extensity and this quality. (DR, 228)

In the transition from many worlds to chaosmos, then, there are a number of correlated distinctions arising between Deleuze's position and Leibniz's, all of which bear on the character of the principle of sufficient reason. Differentiation assumes priority over integration, divergence over convergence; the status of 'the remainder' is turned on its head, transforming from the disharmony over which Leibniz's God will ultimately prevail to the productive precondition of all that appears; compossibility and incompossibility remain imbricated within one chaosmos. Sufficient reason can no longer serve to balance the books; it is rather the law which ensures that no final balance could in principle be reached, just as the continuum will never be exhausted. In the end, however, it would be misleading to suggest that such a clean distinction can delineate the boundaries of Deleuze's debt to Leibniz, or that the argument so far conveys the full 'superiority' of his sufficient reason; we shall return to these themes later with respect to the topics of symmetry and the identity of indiscernibles.

MATHEMATICAL THOUGHT, THE PROBLEM AND THE COSMOS

As we have seen, mathematical thinking plays a productive role in philosophical thought for Deleuze; we commonly find the two intertwined in his work. This aspect of his philosophy donates its own contribution to the picture of an evolving cosmos which we are developing here, in ways that are not immediately obvious. Some elaboration at this point on the specific nature, value and creative potential of mathematics for Deleuze will serve to foreground why this is so, and provide an initial waymark toward a specific form of dialectic which is so important for Deleuzian natural philosophy; specifically a dialectic which circumvents any form of negation. This in turn will illuminate the key role of the concepts of 'limit' and 'constant', which will increasingly come to the fore in the later stages of this cosmological reading of Deleuze's work.

From the start, let us identify three motivations which play no role in Deleuze's adoption of mathematical concepts. Firstly, there is no subscription to mathematical truths as in any sense more rigorous than other claims, as somehow representing a closer approximation to Ideas in the Platonic sense, and thereby as capable of underpinning any more sublunary, contingent truths which he may wish to treat. Indeed, if there is any 'truth' to mathematics at all for Deleuze, it belongs to the *sense* of mathematics rather than to particular statements or propositions, and that sense must enfold paradox, ambiguity, uncertainty and contradiction every bit as fully as the sense of spoken and written language. This much is evident from, for example, his paradoxical conception of 'the ramifying series' in *The Logic of Sense*, or the profoundly multivalent nature of singularities and multiplicities in his work generally – both ideas derived from mathematics and commandeered to speak of the world. Secondly, he does not require from mathematics any enduring, unchangeable objects or entities. For Deleuze, inspired by the work of the mathematician Albert Lautman, mathematics is an adapting, mutating and mobile field which expands through its own exigencies, its own self-determination. Lastly, while mathematical concepts are frequently adopted to illuminate Deleuze's argument, they should not be taken as metaphorically *representative* of processes in the world; this would be to ignore the broadside and extended attack on representation as a mode of thinking as such which occupies so much of *Difference and Repetition*. Rather, they serve as a particularly direct example of the differential processes to which all phenomena – natural, social, psychological – are subject. In an unambiguous sense, it is eminently possible for problems prompting a mathematical response to express themselves in altogether different domains – natural, social, etc. The problem is, so to speak, a common root of all domains.

Albert Lautman's work provides a model of dynamic structuration which speaks at once to Deleuze's sense of thought and to the passage of nature as he presents it in his own work. On the level of scientific thought, it provides the basis for him to parse between two basic approaches, the axiomatic and the problematic, and to valorise the latter over the former. The axiomatic method was first consolidated by Euclid, in his *Elements*, which deals with plane geometry. An axiom, or postulate, of a given mathematical system is understood to be a fundamental truth of the system from which further secure inferences may be elaborated, something akin to an *a priori* truth. Thus, armed with the axiom that the angles of any triangle add up to 180 degrees, we are able to specify without measurement the magnitude of a third angle given the magnitudes of the two adjacent. The axiomatic method is essentially a method of deduction from a small set of postulates.

The axiomatic method has its own inherent limitations, however. The axioms of plane geometry will not automatically generalise to encompass other geometrical systems. In the geometry of curved spaces, it is not true that the angles of a triangle will sum to 180 degrees.

On a curved surface, the triangle figure is 'inflated' outward convexly or deflated concavely, augmenting or diminishing the degrees of the respective angles. The mathematician who is engaged in enlarging the descriptive (or perhaps functional) capacities of the discipline will serially encounter difficulties, whereby the axioms of one field (plane geometry) will fail to transfer to another (the geometry of curved surfaces). The problem encountered will force solutions, but in the course of arriving at those solutions the terms of the method may require transformation. The relative concavity or convexity of curved surfaces have no correlate in plane geometry, yet must clearly be factored in; the problem has (in this case) forced a bifurcation of possible solutions and a corresponding differentiation of approach. We encounter not only a previously inapplicable question – is the surface concave or convex (and hence the angle more oblique or more acute than for a triangle on a flat plane)? – but each case presents its own set of possible solutions, corresponding to the degree of concavity or convexity encountered. There is a set of solutions specifying the degree to which the angles are augmented, predicated on the degree of convex curvature of the given surface, and another set ranging over the concave. The problem serves to redistribute the conditions dictating solubility. At the time the problem is discovered, the axioms already established for the simpler case of plane geometry will no longer serve, while those governing the more complex case are yet to be established. An enforced period of explanation and discovery is required at such junctures, which may lead to the adoption of a fresh set of axioms more adequate to the enlarged domain. There is a 'problematic' phase. The example of projective geometry serves to illuminate this movement. Projective geometry can be understood as the study of three-dimensional figures 'projected' onto a flat plane. A circular figure with a light behind it casts a shadow onto a flat surface. As we turn the circle perpendicularly to the light source, it casts increasingly slender ellipses until, fully perpendicular, it becomes a straight line; the projection registers only the two-dimensional aspect of the circular body. As such, the axioms serving projective geometry must allow for the treatment of straight lines as special cases of curves or ellipses. More generally, projective geometry 'can be defined as the study of those properties of plane figures that are unchanged during central projection'.[24] It serves as a bridge between plane geometry and more full-blown forms of curved surface geometry. Its axioms subsume those of plane geometry, but in the course of this generalisation a different perspective is conveyed on plane figures themselves; a physical meaning comes to underpin the treatment of the straight line as 'merely' a special case of the curve. The structural mutation between sets of axiomatics belonging to related fields is complex; it is a shift of sense, a reconfiguration more than simple addition.

In the axiomatic and the problematic, then, we have two methods or modes. Daniel Smith characterises the distinction as follows:

> The fundamental difference between these two modes of formalisation can be seen in their differing methods of deduction: in axiomatics, a deduction moves from axioms to the theorems that are derived from it, whereas in problematics a deduction moves from the problem to the ideal accidents and events that condition the problem and form the cases that resolve it.[25]

The two modes relate to each other dialectically – a period of exploration followed by the resulting period of axiomatisation. Deleuze recognises both modes and their respective utility, but for his philosophy the problematic mode is by far the more important. Moreover, he is content to identify the tension between the two modes as dialectical, albeit in a sense which avoids any suspicion of the negative inherent in Hegelian-style dialectic. To recognise the motivation for valorising the problematic over the axiomatic, and to understand how this can contribute to framing the movement of evolutionary cosmology, it is useful to examine briefly Deleuze's debt to Lautman and the profound connections to the Idea and the Event which Deleuze attributes to the mode of the Problematic.

In 'Introduction: On the Nature of the Real in Mathematics', Lautman writes:

> Mathematics is constituted like physics: the facts to be explained were throughout history the paradoxes that the progress of reflection rendered intelligible by a constant renewal of the meaning of essential notions. Irrational numbers, the infinitely small, continuous functions without derivatives, the transcendence of e and of π, the transfinite had all been accepted by an incomprehensible necessity of fact before there was a deductive theory of them.[26]

For Lautman, then, the 'real' of mathematics (after Brunschvicg) is a kind of 'matter' which offers 'resistance' to those theoreticians who are engaged with it. He adds: 'This matter is neither simple nor uniform, it has its folds, its edges, its irregularities, and our conceptions are never more than a provisional arrangement that allows the mind to go further forward.'[27] The elements of the real which Lautman offers for example are not the well-regulated and simply deployed foot soldiers of the mathematical field such as the cardinals. They are each in some way intractable, enigmatic and paradoxical, existing seemingly beyond the world of biddable number in some eminent realm whose powers and nature we can only glimpse at one remove. The parallels with Platonic Ideas are more than suggestive; Lautman regularly and explicitly draws the connection. On the face of it, this Platonist aspect should place in question the appeal for Deleuze's philosophy of difference, when so often Platonic Ideas or Forms are read as the metaphysical guarantors of identity, sameness and resemblance; perfect eternal types to which sublunary tokens may only aspire. Indeed, Deleuze himself is concerned to 'overturn' Platonism on exactly those grounds, for instance in the first Appendix to *The Logic of Sense*, where he presents the argument that the only reality lies with the token, the simulacrum, rather than the type. Lautman's own investment in Platonism, however, is expressed in ways that circumvent this reading. For Lautman, the Idea at the heart of mathematics, the 'matter' which resists, is not 'simple nor uniform', not self-same, but rather has its 'folds, edges and irregularities', never more than 'provisional' in form. He explicitly distances his reading of the Platonic Idea from the type/token model: 'By Ideas, we do not mean models whose mathematical entities would only be copies, but in the *true* Platonic sense of the term, the *structural schemas* according to which effective theories are organised.'[28] Not simple, not self-same, not immutable, Ideas are rather expressed in structural schemata. Lautman elaborates: 'If qualitative distinctions exist in mathematics, they characterise the theories rather than the entities.'[29]

In other words, then, the paradoxical, problematic elements of mathematics such as π and e remain as such, remain intractable, until they are situated within a given theory. We might think here of the notion of infinity, which remains chimeric until expressed within some relevant field such as Cantorian set theory. Here again, though, it is no small feature of Lautman's vision that the paradoxical element comes to be expressed *integrally* within the structure of the explanatory framework, the structural schema: the Cantorian innovation which renders infinity tractable is the bifurcation of the concept into 'countable' and 'uncountable' forms of infinity, a function of the deduced viability of mapping the elements of one set (e.g., the natural numbers) onto another (say, the primes). It is the structural schema of the theory by which the Idea is to be understood, the distribution of the paradoxical elements within its own particular field. Without this structure, without the acceptance that exhaustive mapping between sets constitutes a form of 'counting', the mathematical entity remains intractable. One further aspect of Lautman's thought should be noted if we are to appreciate its value for Deleuze: when Lautman asserts that effective theories are organised according to structural schemas, we should hear alongside this a corollary: the structural schemas are not arbitrarily conceived, but motivated to accommodate enduring paradoxical forms in ways as yet not foreseen. This is certainly the case with Cantorian set theory;

the problematic at hand, the imperative (in this case) to render infinite series amenable to mathematical procedure, informs the novel structural schema. Thus Lautman's philosophy entails a dialectic; a dialectic comprised of the movement of Ideas. While a given theory may achieve the desired tractability of the paradoxical element in question, this can only be the provisional resolution of the problem. This does not imply that the paradoxical element is in itself resolved; it retains its disruptive powers, its 'remainder' within the explanatory framework, which will itself once again redistribute, redeploy, in an inevitable encounter with the next explanatory framework. In this sense (a sense which Deleuze embellishes), the 'problem' and the 'solution' are profoundly different in kind to question and answer. Whereas an answer might be understood to put a question to rest, the solution cannot resolve the problem finally. The problem retains the power to force movement onward beyond the solution; any given solution remains merely one among a set of possible solutions. Lautman writes: 'facts consist of the discovery of new entities, these entities are organised into theories and the movement of these theories embodies the schema of the connections of certain Ideas'.[30] Hence, 'Ideas are not immobile and irreducible essences of an intelligible world, but ... are related to each other according to the schemas of a superior dialectic that presides over their arrival.'[31] It is this sense of the dynamic movement of mathematical structural schemas which Deleuze adopts and broadens into his own metaphysical real under the sign of the Problem. He specifies: 'true problems are Ideas and ... these Ideas do not disappear with "their" solutions, since they are the indispensable conditions without which no solution would ever exist' (DR, 168). Just as Lautman likens the mathematical real to problems in physics, Deleuze does not restrict the paradoxical movement to the realm of mathematics: 'Problems are always dialectical; the dialectic has no other sense, nor do problems have any other sense. What is mathematical (or physical, biological, psychical or sociological) are the solutions' (DR, 179). As one aspect of the Event, Problems are ubiquitous and unceasing: 'The event by itself is problematic and problematizing' (LS, 54). Differently put, the distribution of singularities and problematic elements pertaining to one event is the result of, is informed by, the prior event from which it evolves, and equally serves to inform the event into which it will morph: 'The moment that the two series resonate and communicate, we pass from one distribution into another. The moment that the two series are traversed by the paradoxical agent, singularities are displaced, redistributed, transformed into one another, and change sets' (LS, 53).

In all that Deleuze writes of the problem, then, he is concerned to preserve the sense of structural movement and dynamic which Lautman attributes to the development of mathematics. This, the most signal characteristic of mathematical thought for Deleuze, is unrelated to any search for some superior rigour, much less an attempt to ground truth on the basis of eternal entities. Rather, we can see in outline in the mathematical model, and the Problem more generally, the same internal motor of evolution which governs the passage of nature in Deleuze's philosophy. The tension between problem and solution is there in that same tension he names disparity. In light of Lautman's analogy, the world itself, 'matter', offers its own 'resistance', its own retardation, complexification and folding. The world in effect is a dialectical movement between problems and solutions; in the constantly shifting redistributions of singularities in the event, the world endlessly raises problems and proposes solutions in response. The event is 'by itself problematic and problematising', it does not wait for judicious formulation in the mind of an engaged thinker; the problem determines itself, just as complex mathematical entities present their own particular intractabilities. 'In fact', Deleuze asserts, 'the domains of resolvability are relative to the process of the self-determination of the problem' (LS, 122). All of this line of reasoning underwrites Deleuze's metaphor of the calculating god on the cosmological scale. Deleuze's cosmos is a problematic cosmos. In the end, the aspect of problematics which will prove to be most significant for the project of orientation to modern scientific cosmology, and most illuminating in squaring the contentious circle of entropy, is articulated as follows: 'The negative, under its double aspect of limitation and opposition, seemed to us in general secondary in relation to the instance of problems and questions' (DR, 106).

Among the complex values attributed to the Problem for Deleuze, the most valuable is its capacity to overcome the negative. This is its particular form of dialectic. As we shall see, this is due to a sense of 'limit' and 'constant' in nature as provisional and in constant deployment and redeployment, as caught up in perpetual evolutionary movement.

THE COMPLETE CONCEPT AND DISJUNCTIVE SYNTHESIS IN SUFFICIENT REASON

Leibniz's consignment of less fit worlds to inexistence can be characterised as an exclusive disjunction. No element of a world so consigned may have causal influence on any element of the world selected in the line of progress toward the Best, nor even on its most adjacent partner in rejection. All are *causally disjointed*. The logical term 'exclusive disjunction' is for this reason inapplicable in the chaosmos Deleuze paints for us. All relata are for him rather *expressively complicated*; the unactualised state of affairs may be incompatible, counterfactual to the one which takes place, but it is not thereby excluded from the realm of expressive relations. It remains in the folds of the *Eventum Tantum*, as the secret power of the Event. This is the meaning of Deleuze's term 'complication'. It is for this reason that Deleuze is brought to coin his most challenging concept: disjunctive synthesis, or inclusive disjunction. An inclusive disjunction, Deleuze claims, 'does not close itself within its own terms. On the contrary, it is non-restrictive.'[32]

François Zourabichvili, one of Deleuze's most perceptive students, calls disjunctive synthesis, 'the principal operator of Deleuze's philosophy, his signature concept above all others'.[33] At the same time he acknowledges its 'monstrosity' with respect to the history of philosophy. This monstrosity is firstly entailed by the disregard the concept implies for the mainstays of traditional logic: the law of excluded middle and the principles of contradiction. If the chaosmos is to have its 'superior sufficient reason', then it must abandon these logical foundation stones. Indeed, as philosophical concept, disjunctive synthesis is proposed with the explicit intent of obviating these overly restrictive principles, as Deleuze sees it, reliant as they are on the exigencies of identity and sameness; equally, as philosophical concept, it is intended to overcome the mathematical shortcomings of the differential philosophy – the Leibnizian dependence (perforce) on integration and its correspondent principle of selection/actualisation. Moreover, with respect to Leibnizian philosophy more broadly, we need only note that Leibniz includes amongst his principal tenets that the first marker of incompossibility is the logical relation of non-contradiction, or excluded middle (this logical relation understood as a constraint on God, who may not act in a self-contradictory way), and that prior to any Leibnizian investigation of multiplicity as such is the belief that in order to satisfy logic an irreducible unity must first be found, albeit one of a very singular kind – the monad.[34] The underpinnings of Deleuze's 'superior sufficient reason' are different in terms of the principles of logical relation to those of Leibniz. To understand the import of disjunctive synthesis, then, we should begin with the formulation of the law of excluded middle: an individual may not at the same time and in the same respect be both A and not-A. This is a law of subject-predication, assigning the rule of 'either-or' to the valid application of predicates; a law of exclusive disjunction, in effect asserting a non-relation between the individual and the excluded term (A is a rational animal, and thus not a non-rational animal). Inclusive disjunction comprehends the set of possible relations in a markedly contrastive manner: 'the non-relation becomes a relation, disjunction becomes a relation'.[35] Alongside this transposition, we should note that the predicative function of the law becomes merely secondary; the inclusive disjunction is no longer intended to preside over subject-predicate logic, but represents a causative, or rather, expressive relation. Deleuze's chaosmos knows no either-or; contradictory phenomena remain linked through the complexities of expression.

To appreciate this more fully, we should note the parallels between this formulation and Leibniz's term 'the complete concept'. Leibniz's term is equally scandalous in context of the history of logic, since it too represents a reversal of subject-predicate logic. Leibniz's argument was that all predicates associated with the lifetime and context of a given individual should be included as 'necessarily' belonging to the complete concept of that individual; all contingencies in effect becoming necessary. This is a direct result of his tenet that all phenomena in any given moment are causally connected to all others, more or less distinctly, just as is true for Deleuze. But as we are now in a position to see, the need to found this principle on the law of excluded middle disappears with the removal of boundaries between the actual and virtual worlds. It was the law of excluded middle that kept the gate between worlds, without which the complete concept may propagate indefinitely; to assert that all phenomena in the chaosmos are related, whether actual or virtual, compatible or not, is the precise meaning of Zourabichvili's phrase, 'disjunction becomes a relation'.

Let us recall that when Deleuze wishes to give a positive example of the momenta he seeks to set free from Leibniz, it is to Whitehead he turns, whose God 'affirms incompossibilities'. No reader of the two thinkers can fail to be struck by the correspondences between them (we shall focus on several), and it is certainly true that Whitehead's nature offers strong parallels with Deleuze's chaosmos. And while Whitehead famously characterised the whole of philosophy (his own included) as 'footnotes to Plato', there is nevertheless a significant common root for Deleuze and Whitehead in their reading of Leibniz. Indeed, Whitehead's arrival at this 'affirmation of incompossibilities' should be read less as a schism with Leibniz than an astute development of his metaphysics. For Whitehead, the route to 'inclusive disjunction' is through an extension, rather than a contradiction, of Leibniz's logic. The key is his refinement of the Leibnizian term 'appetition', which refers to the tendency of the monad to seize its own future, to shape its own composition from among the phenomena in its world – an appetite or desire for self-organisation, understood without necessary reference to conscious decision. The body of water breaching the damn and flowing to lower ground will serve as an example of appetition equally well as the animal seeking food or social reinforcement.

The word 'appetition' occurs not infrequently in Whitehead's work, though his own coining is 'prehension'. Both words convey essentially the same import. All individuals 'prehend' all others – the entire universe is expressed through the relations pertaining to any given individual therein.[36] Prehension belongs equally to the event as to the conscious decision. The 'nexus' or 'actual occasion' is the outcome of prior appetitive or prehensive enfolding for Whitehead as it is for Leibniz, and the aggregate of past prehensions shapes the future of the individual. The crucial refinement comes with the term 'negative prehension'.

For Whitehead, accepting those same tenets that characterise Leibniz's metaphysics, the interconnection of all things and the tendency of systems to enfold elements from their total situation, negative prehension is a necessary corollary to positive appetition. It belongs to the 'principle of limitation' which Whitehead saw as a necessary supplement to Spinozist metaphysics, and which we shall encounter in some detail in following chapters. It is that form of prehension which annuls the influence of a given phenomenon from within the individuated nexus under consideration, due to distance or causal neutrality of each with respect to the other. In a very real sense, in coining this term, Whitehead is recognising the need for a certain reversal of viewpoint demanded by Leibniz's conception of nature. Instead of 'How is it that all things are interconnected?' the question becomes, 'Given that all things are interconnected, how is it that individuation is possible?' In a more Leibnizian vein, 'How is it that the mirror universe prevents itself from becoming an infinite hall of mirrors without point of view?' Our account must comprehend not merely the selection of adjacent possibilities incrementally through the appetition of the given monad (or nexus), but the affirmative refusal of others. This affirmative refusal of necessity embraces all phenomena which are of no significance to the nexus in its evolution, and counts with as much weight as those phenomena positively prehended. Indeed, infinitely more so, since all phenomena at whatever remove throughout the universe figure in this exchange more or less distinctly, more or less obscurely; all may come to figure more clearly for the nexus in question through positive prehension, or be demoted to obscurity through negative prehension. In this way, Whitehead is free to agree with Leibniz that, 'Every present state of a simple substance is a natural consequence of its preceding state, in such a way that its present is big with its future',[37] while insisting that that future is a reciprocal exchange between what is adopted and what is refused. In a sense, Whitehead displaces the God governing Leibniz's selection of compossibles to the scale of individual systems; prehension at once selects the elements to combine and those to relinquish. Each nexus at each moment is a world adopted from a myriad of others left unactualised.[38]

We have taken a step toward Deleuze's Chaosmos, along a more ostensibly Leibnizian path, but other factors in Whitehead's metaphysics are required to bring the full correlation into view. Most importantly, prehension is not to be conceived as a (dual) relation pertaining solely between actualised phenomena. Both the actual and the non-actual shape the landscape of prehension: 'in the becoming of an actual entity, the potential unity of many entities in disjunctive diversity – actual and non-actual – acquires the real unity of the one actual entity; so that the actual entity is the real concrescence of many potentials' (PR, 22). Potential in the Whiteheadian passage of nature is a real factor in its evolution. Systems, nexūs, work through *disjunctive diversity*. Counterfactuals figure in the total situation, just as they do for Deleuze in a much-quoted passage: 'A stranger knocks at his door. Fang makes up his mind to kill him. Naturally there are various possible outcomes. ... In T'sui Pen's work, all possible solutions occur, each one being the point of departure for other bifurcations' (LS, 114). The garden is full of forking paths. For Whitehead, incompatibility and contradiction have their place in logic, but, he says, 'It will be observed that logical notions must themselves find their places in the scheme of philosophical notions' (PR, 3). In fact, he claims, contradictions and incompatibilities are not only rare in nature, and most merely apparent, but it is part and parcel of the work of prehension to transform and overcome such negation: 'the heightening of intensity arises from order such that the multiplicity of components in the nexus can enter explicit feeling as *contrasts*, and are not dismissed into negative prehensions as *incompatibilities*' (PR, 83). Here, the idea shares much with Deleuze's *centres of envelopment*: the channelling of heterogeneous series more or less stably into attunement. Finally, Whitehead does not stop short of relegating the status of logical contradiction, of negation, in light of these insights:

> A physical pole is in its own nature exclusive, bounded by contradiction: a conceptual pole is in its own nature all-embracing, unbounded by contradiction. The former derives its share of infinity from the infinity of appetition; the latter derives its limitation from the exclusiveness of enjoyment. Thus, by reason of his priority of appetition, there can be but one primordial nature for God; and by reason of their priority of enjoyment, there must be one history of many actualities in the physical world. (PR, 348)

We are doing no violence to the respective thought to substitute 'explicate' for 'physical pole' and 'implicate' for 'mental pole'.[39] It is only in extension, the explicate domain, says Deleuze, that negation supervenes on the difference in itself of the implicate. Only the physical pole, claims Whitehead, knows contradiction. The implicate and the mental pole are blind to the distinction between factual and counterfactual, to contradiction. For both, disjunctive diversity, disjunctive synthesis, is the vibrant signature of natural process.

Each philosopher finds a productive bifurcation from Leibniz's metaphysics, and both for the sake of overcoming negation, the excluded middle, the traditional bedrock of identity. Deleuze erases the barriers between possible counterfactual worlds, at the furthest reaches, while Whitehead locates the movement of those worlds in the prehensive appetites of nexūs in process, at the least physical scale. Cosmology is at once a micro- and a macro-phenomenon. Scientific cosmologists themselves would assert the same. To estimate the total mass of the universe we first need to evaluate the relative mass and relative preponderance of each natural kind within it, the weight of the proton and the electron. To understand the characteristics of the early cosmos, we must understand the characteristics of plasma fields. The quantum nature of vacuum energy must be factored into estimates of the capacity of the universe to expand. The local and the global are entwined. Whitehead's evolutionary cosmology takes pains to adhere to this tenet. Evolution is ingrained in each sub-whole, each Blakean grain of sand.

Thus, to the picture of the chaosmos we have developed so far, we may add the co-presence of contradictory logical elements, understood in terms of the relations of contingent phenomena, alongside a commitment to the world and physical action as at root based on the play of incommensurable forces. Disjunction becomes a relation. Deleuze's adoption of the term disjunctive synthesis can be seen in this light as a key conceptual tool underpinning the superior sufficient reason he seeks. The logical relation outlined in the law of excluded middle cannot apply in the philosophy of difference, which must define itself independently of the concept of identity. The same must be true of the superior form of sufficient reason. Deleuze favours a certain Leibniz: not the Leibniz who claims of the monad that it secures for the world an isolatable point, unsusceptible to infinite division as are all merely spatial points (and thereby the Leibniz who champions the law of excluded middle), but the Leibniz who shows us that the world is multiplicitously enfolded within each monad. As for the interrelation of the local to the global, Deleuze explores this theme through the work of Gilbert Simondon.

PHYSICAL SYSTEMS, DISPARITY AND DISJUNCTIVE SYNTHESIS

A sizeable proportion of the fifth chapter of *Difference and Repetition* is devoted to discussion of physical processes – biological individuation, speciation and evolution in particular – but the important figure of Gilbert Simondon, and the interpretation he offers of both organic and inorganic processes within the same framework, is decisive in developing Deleuze's line of argument with respect to disjunctive synthesis. Deleuze also draws on Simondon's work in *The Logic of Sense* and, much later, in *What Is Philosophy?*. Energy gradients and thermodynamic processes, intimately associated with the principle of sufficient reason, remain central to the argument.

First and foremost, Simondon's work in the natural sciences – an attempt to provide an account of the genesis of individuals without recourse to pre-existing forms – reflects a concern that motivates Deleuze explicitly and underlies his treatment across the corpus of memory, identity, time, extension, etc. The goal is to find a form of immanence which is not 'immanent to' anything.

As such, Simondon's critique of Aristotelean 'hylomorphism', an account which is formulated in terms of the union of matter (*hyle*) with form (*morphē*), is entirely consonant with Deleuze's own. The association with chaos theory is unmistakeable here too, since Simondon is unmistakeably furnishing an account of self-organisation, a factor in natural systems which has, according to Ilya Prigogine and Isabelle Stengers, greater explanatory power than previous paradigms: 'We are tempted to go so far as to say that once the conditions for self-organization are satisfied, life becomes as predictable [in terms of its emergence from the inanimate] as the Bénard Instability or a falling stone.'[40] Deleuze adopts or adapts terms from Simondon's work to illuminate the business of genetic explanation. Simondon's 'Disparity' is in effect the intensive form of intersecting heterogeneous series with respect to the operation of forces, while his 'pre-individual singularities' remain with Deleuze those elements in a given system which catalyse individuation. Sean Bowden defines the shared confluence of ideas between Deleuze and Simondon with reference to a quotation from Simondon's *doctorat*:

> As he puts it, 'the individual is the reality of a constitutive relation', a constitutive relation which does not depend for its existence upon already given terms, but rather refers only to other relations. Granting primacy to relations over individuals 'all the way down' is a consequence of Simondon's commitment to an anti-substantialist approach to individuation.[41]

Indeed, when Deleuze introduces the term 'disparity' in *Difference and Repetition*, it is in the context of an insistence on the infinitely regressive nature of differential intensities in relation:

> [T]he expression 'difference of intensity' is a tautology. Intensity is the form of difference in so far as this is the reason of the sensible. Every intensity is differential, by itself a difference. Every intensity is E-E', where E itself refers to an e-e', and e to an ε-ε' etc.: each intensity is already a coupling (in which each element of the couple refers in turn to couples of elements of another order), thereby revealing the properly qualitative content of quantity. We call this state of infinitely doubled difference which resonates to infinity *disparity*. (DR, 222)

And it is at this point too, that we are referred back to the engagement with Leibniz; we are being offered a key to the nature of the 'superior sufficient reason' which must be adequate to the chaosmos: 'Disparity – in other words, difference or intensity (difference of intensity) – is the sufficient reason of all phenomena, the condition of that which appears' (DR, 222). Our understanding of the principle of sufficient reason, then, is directed toward, if not identified with, the operations and processes associated with intensity; intensity as 'the condition of that which appears' is the chaosmotic version of the 'reason why things are thus and not otherwise'. This is evident too in the visible parallel between Leibniz's insistence that the difference between analytic and contingent truths is that the perceived necessity of contingent truth entails following an infinitely regressive chain from the phenomenon under consideration to its furthermost conditions in the state of the entire cosmos. Here, the infinite regression in question is that pertaining to intensity, closely identified with difference; it is the asymmetrical, non-equilibrial intersections and divergences of intensive series which will lead us by series on series of reasons to infinity. Two things are equally clear: the functional fit for the argument of the notion of intensity with the refusal of equilibrium, since intensive infinite regression admits of no quantitative final balance between forces; and the consequent co-existence in one chaosmos of the compossible and the incompossible, of the convergent and the divergent.

If thus far the Simondonian notion of 'disparity' is consonant with Deleuze's direction of argument, there is one further factor which clarifies the signal importance of the term; it is that, like Deleuze, Simondon explicitly construes forces and their interaction as incommensurable, non-equilibrial and beyond quantification as such, locating rather the capacity for novelty in the world as issuing from the realm of the 'metastable', far from equilibrium. As Brian Massumi points out, discussing the term in the register of 'information':

What differentiates Simondon in general from the cybernetic and information-theory traditions out of which Bateson was working (in particular, what differentiates him from Wiener and Shannon/Weaver) is that, for Simondon, this differencing process can in no way be understood in quantitative terms and is not susceptible to any kind of stable formalization.[42]

Moreover, the term as used by Simondon is within a distinctly thermodynamic register, connoting first and foremost the energetic *differential between* forces inhering within a milieu, an energy gradient. Just as did his mentor Georges Canguilhem before him, Simondon placed emphasis on the reciprocal determination of individual and milieu in the process of individuation.[43] Prior to the emergence of any given individual, there is a matrix of uncoordinated differential heterogeneous forces inherent in the chemical and thermodynamic make-up of this 'mother-liquor', as Anne Sauvagnargues expresses it.[44] The mother-liquor is in an initial (and continuing) metastable state in which the forces are brought to bear on one another by the introduction of a singularity. In the case of a crystal, that singularity is a 'seed', an impurity akin to the grit which initiates the growth of a pearl in an oyster. The forces de-phase around the singularity and converge on a threshold by dint of which they enter into communication; they achieve 'disparity' or disparition, and their initial incoherent heterogeneity 'concresces' into a system with its attendant 'regime of functioning'. The important feature of such processes is that they emphasise the reciprocally determinative relations between the individuating entity and the milieu. As Massumi points out, addressing a common misinterpretation of Simondon:

> The associated milieu is often wrongly understood to be synonymous with 'environment'. It is interpreted as referring to the space surrounding the boundary of the technical object (or the membrane of an organism), considered from the point of view of the elements contained in that space that are liable to fuel the technical object's functioning. In fact, the associated milieu is not fundamentally a spatial concept. Simondon defines it as the 'regime' of energy transfer *between* the technical object and its environment, across the boundary.[45]

For artefact ('technical object') and naturally occurring individual (membrane or crystal) alike, this 'regime of energy transfer' is subsumed under the title 'transduction', which serves to name the ongoing process of reciprocal determination between milieu and emergent individual. For every incremental 'concrescence' (Deleuze's term is 'enfolding') in the formation of the individual itself, there is a correlative variation of the constitution of the milieu; while series of salts and minerals accrue, converge at the surface of the crystal, and are subsumed into the depths, other series of elements are rejected, diverge; the consequent chemical and energetic variation of the crystal is matched by the variations in the milieu. Individuation is improperly understood, for Simondon, without taking into account the transductive, reciprocally determinative nature of all physical processes. Nor can we fail to recognise the deep correlation of this account with the Whiteheadian account of positive and negative prehension detailed above.

What Simondon offers, then, is a mechanism of individuation which must be pictured from another point of view than that of the individual coming-to-be (conjunctive synthesis); the 'deselection' of the other elements which remain outside (or, more accurately, are thereby constituted as 'outside') the individual are equally important in the process as a whole. The synthesis is disjunctive. The process must be recognised as reciprocal; the chemical constitution of the milieu, too, is coherently altered, along with its overall population of 'pre-individual singularities', the tenor of its intensities. What happens, happens between, diverging as well as converging, as Deleuze reflects, echoing the Simondonian notion of disparity as communication:

> Every phenomenon flashes in a signal-sign system. In so far as a system is constituted or bounded by at least two heterogeneous series, two disparate orders capable of entering into communication, we call it a signal. The phenomenon that flashes across this system, bringing about the communication between disparate series, is a sign. (DR, 222)

And we are to understand the importance of the notion in its wider context for Deleuze when he writes:

> There is indeed a unity of divergent series insofar as they are divergent, but it is always a chaos perpetually thrown off center which becomes one only in the Great Work. This unformed chaos, the great letter of *Finnegans Wake*, is not just any chaos. It is the power of affirmation, the power to affirm all the heterogeneous series. (LS, 260)

The key notion here is that of affirmation; in this light, Simondon's account of individuation offers precisely that affirmation which is demanded *en passant* throughout *Difference and Repetition* and in *Nietzsche and Philosophy* – a demand for affirmation of divergence, of chance, of chaos – a form of affirmation which does not presuppose a pre-existing subject to affirm, a form of immanent affirmation which does not presuppose anything to which it is immanent.

Simondon's vocabulary is placed firmly within this context once again in *The Logic of Sense*, when Deleuze analyses the synthetic relationship of divergent and convergent series together in terms of ontological genesis, though in this case the term 'singularity' conveys at one and the same time the connotations it possesses in calculus and geometry:

A world already envelops an infinite system of singularities selected through convergence. Within this world, however, individuals are constituted which select and envelop a finite number of the singularities of the system. They combine them with the singularities that their own body incarnates. They spread them out over their own ordinary lines, and are even capable of forming them again on the membranes which bring the outside and the inside in contact with each other. Leibniz then was right to say that the individual monad expresses a world according to the relation of other bodies to its own, as much as it expresses this relation according to the relation of the parts of its own body. (LS, 109–10)

Here then is Simondon's individuation as 'the prolongation of a singularity' made to march in tune with a conceptual distinction in geometry. A geometrical figure is said to possess both ordinary and singular points; the difference between the two is that the singular point is ambiguous with respect to the surrounding series with which it is in contact. An example Deleuze discusses is that of the apex of a pyramid, which is a singular point for several ordinary lines – those forming the vertices which converge upon it.

The two very different senses of 'singularity' – the Simondonian catalytic element (the grit in the pearl) which brings series into communication and the mathematically ambiguous sign – are reconciled here in a very complex act of conceptual synthesis intended to characterise the process of selection and individuation. The point at the apex of the pyramid is at one and the same time the final point in a series of points belonging to several lines; so to speak, it puts them into communication just as does the grit in the pearl. Equally Deleuze is reconciling Leibniz's divergent sense of the compossible and the incompossible with his own chaosmotic disjunctive synthesis: the world is expressed through each individual, in accord with Leibniz's monadic world, yet in a very different sense. Each local system is in contact with its neighbours through lines of convergence, which it expresses clearly through contiguity, as do Leibniz's monads, yet these lines extend up to and beyond those points where they diverge, the singular points. Each individual is in contact with, expresses, all individuals in the world, but obscurely, again, as with Leibniz, through infinitely ramifying lines of divergence. For Deleuze, all series intersect and diverge in communication with other series. Ultimately, no given point is simply self-same with respect to its identity within any given series, all are singular, belonging to a multiplicity of series. No longer is the Leibnizian distinction between compossibility and incompossibility put into communication through a God operating as a telephone exchange, a centrepoint ensuring harmonious exchange, but through aleatory points and ambiguous signs extending off indefinitely. Each individual, then, remains necessarily the sum of all its predicates, but in the same sense as a singularity contains its own power of expressing innumerable contradictions; here is Deleuze's 'object = x', the concept which overcomes the idea of world understood merely as the circle of convergence.

> We are now faced with the aleatory point of singular points, with the ambiguous sign of singularities, or rather, that which represents this sign, and which holds good for many of these worlds, or, in the last analysis, for all worlds, despite their divergences and the individuals which occupy them. There is thus a 'vague Adam,' that is, a vagabond, a nomad, an Adam = x common to several worlds. (LS, 114)

Deleuze acknowledges the resonance of this picture with Whitehead's work:

> For Leibniz, as we have seen, bifurcations and divergences of series are genuine borders between incompossible worlds ... For Whitehead (and for many modern philosophers), on the contrary, bifurcations, divergences, incompossibilities and discord belong to the same motley world. (FLB, 81)

The discussion above goes some way to establishing that for Deleuze processes such as those exemplified in the work of Simondon at the scale of individuating (partially isolated) systems are to be understood also at the scale of the chaosmos as a whole; that the chaosmos is a non-totalising aggregate of endlessly ramifying convergent and divergent series. This speaks of an attunement of the local with the global. Undoubtedly both Deleuze and Whitehead subscribe to such an attunement, but it would be wrong to conclude that the global is simply the aggregate of systems such as those described by Simondon. For both philosophers, it would be wrong to say that nature begins with the local and propagates out from myriad local centres like the countless interacting ripples in a lake under rainfall. The Event operates also through non-local means; modern science tells us this no less than our philosophers. This aspect will be treated in detail in a subsequent chapter.

Paradoxically, then, the chaos Deleuze seeks to identify – chance as the only necessity – can be found in utero within the well-ordered harmony of Leibniz's system. Leibniz's short, dense essay on 'Origination' (of which Deleuze was aware; he cites it in *Difference and Repetition*) seems to allow for such a development, in a way which avoids, perhaps, the difficulties of orientation attached to the argument from eternal return. We find the elements required: the primacy of divergence is of one piece with the principle of the identity of indiscernibles; the disparity of energy gradients is underwritten by the dissymmetrical nature of the principle of sufficient reason; the principle of least resistance entails direct dialogue with the field of thermodynamics. And the necessity of chance is the same necessity that belongs to the complete concept, conjoined as it is with these tightly interrelated principles. A complete concept adapted to include the vague Adam of the virtual chaosmos, accruing to each individual with every breaking of symmetry (the boulder falls toward its complete concept), but sweeping ever on past itself along both diverging and converging series, unchained from essence or identity, toward the *Eventum Tantum*.[46]

The foregoing serves not so much to restore to the displaced prince Leibniz the crown of superior sufficient reason, as to foreground features of Deleuze's chaos which allow a great deal more traction (I don't say agreement) with the discourse of physics. To champion *this* Leibniz is to champion a principle of dissymmetry. Ultimately, I will argue, it allows us to specify what it is that constitutes an open universe for a philosophy of difference.

Deleuze resists both the lessons of thermodynamics and the faith in symmetry which is prevalent in much of the history of physics. These are connected elements; disparity is dissymmetry. While it is possible to recast questions relating to the former in terms of the latter, this in itself cannot remove genuine difficulties in orientating the metaphysics to the physics. Firstly, let us make a brief examination of symmetry and its importance to modern physics, then address a telling question: 'can the Leibnizian-Deleuzian philosophy of difference coherently dismiss the heat death of the universe?'

CHAOSMOS AS COSMOLOGY

If energy gradients are the sufficient reason of all that appears for thermodynamics, symmetry is to most intents and purposes the sufficient reason from which modern physics draws its rationale. Mathematical relations of symmetry have come to take the place of 'law' in classical physics: where there is symmetry, science identifies an underlying order. As we shall see, however, the point of contention between Deleuze and the prevailing scientific consensus is by no means so black and white, and far from universally upheld among the scientific community. Once again, it is in the particularities of this tension that productive exchange may be found.

Let us return to the paradigm image Deleuze offers for physical action at the beginning of chapter 5 of *Difference and Repetition*: the image of the calculating God. If the internal disequilibrium, incommensurability (and dissymmetry) of the regimes of numbers through which God passes is first and foremost cast in terms of number theory, fated to advance toward a completion of the continuum which will ever and again recede, remaining 'problematic' in Deleuze's terminology, we should nevertheless not forget that ultimately we are being offered a metaphor for physical causation/expression. Moreover, there is a dual aspect to this image. It is in play on the scale of individual systems such as those treated in Simondon's work, which redistribute ever anew the internal and external ('pre-individual') singularities in transductive exchange, just as the Lautmanian structural schemata reconfigure in the transition from one regime of number to another. It is also unmistakeably to be taken as applicable (metaphorically) on the level of the cosmos: if God's calculations were exact there would be no world; the very term chosen to designate this ever-unfolding continuum, the 'chaosmos', is in itself calculated to connote a (non-)totality on a cosmological scale; Nietzsche's concept of the eternal return, which Deleuze adapts to underpin the temporality of God's calculations, remains in Deleuze's hands a tableau of cosmic dimensions, of eternity. Dissymmetry and disequilibrium are to be understood as universally applicable. Disparity is intensity. To grapple adequately with the cosmological scale, and tensions remaining between Deleuze and scientific discourse, it is first necessary to outline the universal application of symmetry in key scientific frameworks and the ways in which Deleuze's philosophy points in other directions.

There are clear instances in the history of science and mathematics where the notion of symmetry plays a fundamental part. It represents an unequivocal cornerstone in the conceptual apparatus of special relativity, in the form of the group theory established by Évariste Galois; group theory is intended to identify invariants under transformation of a given group of elements, and its use by Einstein represented a radical new conception of what it was to solve a problem relating to physical action.[47]

In the formulation of the Standard Model of particle physics, the equation which bears the name of Dirac is an iconic case in point. According to Nicholas Mee, symmetry lay at the heart of Paul Dirac's intuitions of nature. The Dirac equation was an attempt to address an anomaly which had arisen by 1928 between the nascent disciplines of relativity and quantum theory; for quantum theory, the behaviour of wave-like forms, specifically electricity and magnetism, grew intractable at speeds approaching the velocity of light, disagreeing with the formulations of relativity. In an effort to reconcile the two theories, Dirac found a solution in the form of an equation which contained within it a singular implication: that there was a 'previously unsuspected symmetry at the heart of matter'.[48] Specifically, this was subsequently to serve as the prediction of the existence of a symmetric counterpart of the electron, the positron. More generally, the Dirac equation predicts that for every given kind of particle there must be a mirror-image particle; for the proton, the anti-proton, for the neutron the anti-neutron. As a mark of the equation's prodigious influence too, later developments in the Standard Model have generalised this initial insight into a 'zoo' of particles, including among them such exotic pairings as the quark and the squark, an increasing range of which have been confirmed to exist under experimental conditions (the anti-proton confirmed in 1955, the anti-neutron in 1965, the Higgs boson most recently in July 2012).

In 1979, the Nobel Prize was awarded to Weinberg, Glashow and Salam, who had, following the example of Dirac, posited a resolution to the unification of the electromagnetic force and the weak atomic force in terms of a fundamental symmetry between them, under conditions achievable only under extreme high-energy states:

> Just as the magnetization of a piece of iron can be wiped out and the symmetry between different directions restored by raising the temperature of the iron above 770 degrees, so also the symmetry between the weak and electromagnetic forces could be restored if we could raise the temperature of our laboratory above a few million billion degrees.[49]

Peter Woit, in *Not Even Wrong*, considers at length the extent to which mathematical formulations of symmetry have been incorporated into physical theories, citing not least the influence of the mathematician Hermann Weyl in this history, with respect to the mathematical underpinnings of quantum mechanics represented by group theory and the Lie groups in particular. For quantum mechanics (and less directly so for classical mechanics), when there are transformations of a physical system which do not change the physical regularities governing the system, these transformations are said to be 'symmetries' of the system: 'Some of the most basic aspects of physics follow from looking at symmetries. The symmetry under translations in space implies the conservation of momentum, symmetry under translation in time implies the conservation of energy.'[50] Weyl himself wrote a monograph on symmetry, in which he makes clear just how fundamental the concept is to his philosophy: 'As far as I can see, all a priori statements in physics have their origin in symmetry.'[51] Bernard d'Espagnat sums up the significance of symmetry and invariance in twentieth-century physics as follows:

> we must emphasize how right Largeault was in stressing the importance present-day physicists attribute to symmetries. To claim that this concept (and perhaps even more its 'offspring,' the notion of the symmetry-break) dominated the whole of twentieth-century physics would hardly constitute an overstatement.[52]

It is with respect to two factors here that we can bring into focus the potential conflict between Deleuze's philosophy of difference and the conceptual foundations of physics. Firstly, we note that 'symmetry' for physics denotes more than mere spatial relationships; translations in time (for which we might read 'evolutions' or 'phases' of a system), for instance, are understood to be of equal significance. Each is understood to capture the 'invariants' of a given system. An invariant is simply that which remains constant under translation; the simple translation of rotation in a two-dimensional plane, for instance, can be characterised as that translation which preserves the distances of all elements on the plane from the centre of rotation. Secondly, we note that symmetry bears a close conceptual relationship to physical principles of conservation; the conservation of momentum inherited from Newton and the conservation of energy as formulated in classical thermodynamics by Clausius are prime examples. Richard Feynman draws this connection: 'It is extremely interesting that there seems to be a deep connection between the conservation laws and the symmetry laws. This connection has its proper interpretation, at least as we understand it today, only in the knowledge of quantum mechanics.'[53] This association of symmetry with conservation laws was ultimately to be codified by Emmy Noether into a series of equations which effectively represent the translation of the idea of 'law' in classical physics into the idea of symmetry for modern physics. Symmetry is Law.

Deleuze, on the other hand, could not be more clear on his resistance to the idea of symmetry: 'The negative expression "lack of symmetry" should not mislead us: it indicates the origin and positivity of the causal process' (DR, 20). And: 'Curie commented that it was useful but misleading to speak of symmetry in negative terms, as though it were the absence of symmetry, without inventing positive terms capable of designating the infinite number of operations with unmatched outcomes' (DR, 234). The translations by now are apparent. We can equate Deleuze's 'origin and positivity of the causal process' arising from 'lack of symmetry' with the notion of disparity, or disequilibrium, which he calls the 'sufficient reason of all that which appears'; dissymmetry and disequilibrium are cognate terms. It is interesting to note, however, that Deleuze cites a scientist, Pierre Curie, for support on this line; an initial suggestion, which I shall develop later, that the contrasting viewpoints here may be as much a matter internal to science as a point of contention between the philosophy of difference and scientific discourse as a whole. Differences of opinion internal to scientific discourse notwithstanding, in context of the connections between symmetry and equilibrium, and the parallel between symmetry and conservation laws more generally, it is clear that any serious treatment of Deleuze's philosophy and its relation to science must address the detail and the implications of his resistance to the idea.

Finally, it would be misleading to claim that Deleuze's emphasis on disparity, incommensurability and dissymmetry amounts to a complete dismissal of the concept and indeed the value of symmetry as such. As with the concept of entropy, there are caveats to observe. For in truth, the concept of symmetry has had many different instantiations in the history of science and mathematics; the transformations and symmetries with which group theory deals can in no way be likened straightforwardly to simple spatial or geometrical symmetries, subsuming as they do non-commutative relationships and vectorial transformations. Moreover, as Manuel DeLanda points out, Deleuze was quite aware of the role of symmetry in group theory, and quite prepared to embrace the tenets thereof for the greater explanatory potential of a genetic rather than an axiomatic account.[54]

ABSOLUTE ZERO, LIMITS AND THE INFINITE

To work through what is at stake, let us take a salient example; an example at once of symmetry and equilibrium, underpinned, as all things are in physics, by conservation laws. The concept of absolute zero. This state is an implication of the third law of thermodynamics, most familiarly described in terms of final equilibrium for an isolated system, a system lacking any differential energy gradients, any free energy. On a cosmological scale, this is heat death. Walther Nernst, an experimental chemist who helped clarify the law, proposed in 1905 a specific physical meaning for the notion: absolute zero is that temperature at which the entropy of a perfect crystal is exactly equal to zero. Why might only a crystal attain this state, and a perfect one at that? It is a requirement of symmetry. Of all forms in nature, crystals enjoy the highest order of symmetry due to their lattice structure. Any deviation from perfect symmetry by definition introduces an energy gradient. Surface tension, for example, or frangibility within the crystal body (as with flaws in a diamond), and on a big enough scale, gravitational differentials. The balance of the properties of a material body depend on its measure of symmetry.

Deleuze is aware of the entailments involved in resisting symmetry and equilibrium; he does not flinch from denying the scientific concept of absolute zero. This refusal is itself nested within a further context; his rejection of conservation laws and natural constants. Deleuze's rejection of the concept of absolute zero and its bearing on the nature of symmetry and equilibrium are intertwined themes; at its broadest, the question for him is one of the nature of limits. Discussion of these broader themes will be taken up again in a subsequent chapter, in conjunction with the thought of A.N. Whitehead and David Bohm.

To focus on our example, the assignment of the value of absolute zero is woven into an order of discourse that is imbricated throughout the modern scientific corpus. Absolute zero is calibrated with respect to Planck's constant, which, as a corollary to assigning a least quantum of energy, furnishes the calculation of a 'ground state' for a system under which no exchange of free energy may be possible. This explicitly rules out material or energetic phenomena of any kind below this scale.[55] This is rendered in quantum mechanics by the concept of 'zero-point energy', or 'zero-point motion', which describes not the total arrest of movement, but a state of minimum motion from which no further energy can be removed. Nernst's formulation of the third law contains within it the implication that no amount of cooling of any body will achieve absolute zero in a finite number of steps. It is a graphic demonstration of the degree to which questions of symmetry are intertwined with questions of energy gradient in thermodynamics.

The value of the constant absolute zero is significant for the fate of the cosmos with respect to another constant identified initially by Einstein, known as the cosmological constant, which represents the ratio between the speed of expansion of the universe and the sum total of mass therein; the exact value of the ratio (the subject of some sharp debate and equivocation, even on Einstein's part, from the very first, and especially since the discovery of dark matter and energy) is taken to determine the long-term tendency of the cosmos toward endless expansion or the potential recontraction. If there is sufficient mass in the universe, the reasoning goes, gravity will in the long term prevail over expansion, in which case the universe will recontract, whereas the reverse will be true should overall mass fall short. In other words, the cosmological constant is taken to determine whether the cosmos will end up in a 'Big Freeze' near absolute zero, or a 'Big Crunch'. Consequently, there are far reaching consequences for any attempt to find the productive exchange between the philosophy of difference and scientific frameworks with respect to this question. Absolute zero may be a number, but it is not dismissably 'simply' so, as Deleuze claims in *What Is Philosophy?*; it is arrived at through deliberation, experimentation and intertwined theoretical necessity. So much is also true for other constants, limits and conservation laws.

We have arrived at a similar juncture to the one outlined with respect to the argument from eternal return above. It seems that in order to subscribe to the philosophy of difference, our reading of Leibnizian sufficient reason as dissymmetry is left with no choice but to affirm that dissymmetry against the scientific corpus. In the long run, there is no inherent reason why such a bold move should be illegitimate; in the history of science, after all, we have seen the earth unhinged to circle the sun, and the force of gravity recast as the warping of spacetime. And it may prove equally fruitful to recast constants, limits and conservation laws in terms of the dissymmetry favoured here. This is in fact the conclusion I will defend. But as with the argument from eternal return, it is no straightforward matter for the Leibnizian variant of the philosophy of difference to contradict the well-established tenets of science; it is legitimate to question whether it can coherently uphold such a contradiction in its own terms, whether Deleuze's philosophy succeeds in giving us the necessary vantage point to critique the science wedded to the closed, sterile, moribund universe of maximum entropy.

I would contend that there are potential inconsistencies within the philosophy of difference as a whole which might give us pause here. It is deployed in favour of a fundamentally creative nature, of an open universe. And *prima facie*, the condition called heat death represents the very antithesis of that creativity. Yet the very principles adopted to support this characterisation of nature introduce a tension. Is the philosophy of difference able coherently to dismiss the physicists' heat death as uncreative?

The questions above abut on two closely related tenets of Deleuze's philosophy of difference: the relational nature of time, and the refusal of difference to vanish between even the most closely related terms. Both tenets maintain us on Leibnizian territory. Briefly, relational accounts of time hold that there is no elapse independently of events; the passage of time is a function of what happens, each event with its own characteristic time-signature, which may vary substantially from one type of episode to another. The modern statement of this idea belongs to Leibniz, in his anti-Newtonian confrontation with Clarke. The refusal of difference to vanish may be seen as a consequence of our trio of Leibniz's principles: the identity of indiscernibles, essence as 'complete concept', and sufficient reason.

It is part and parcel of Leibniz's philosophy that no two existents may be identical; if two things are found to be indiscernible, we can only conclude that they are one and the same thing. We note as a corollary, that the difference between any two given individuals may be as small as imaginable in Leibniz's world, since what distinguishes the individuals ultimately is the 'complete concept', which includes the entire contingent history of that individual. Deleuze formulates his own

Entropy and the Complete Concept 63

version of this principle in *Difference and Repetition*, in the context of a discussion of 'the dark precursor':

> It is well known that in certain cases (in certain systems), the difference between the differences brought into play may be 'very large'; in other systems it must be 'very small'. It would be wrong, however, to see in this second case the pure expression of a prior requirement of resemblance ... For example, it is insisted that disparate series must necessarily be almost similar, or that the frequencies be neighbouring (w neighbour of wo) – in short, that the difference be small. If, however, the identity of the agent which causes the different things to communicate is presupposed, then there are no differences which will not be 'small', even on the world scale. (DR, 120)

However, it is precisely the 'identity of the agent' (here 'the dark precursor') which is contested. Deleuze continues:

> We have seen that small and large apply badly to difference, because they judge it according to the criteria of the Same and the similar. If difference is related to its differenciator, and if we refrain from attributing to the differenciator an identity which it cannot and does not have, then the difference will be small or large according to its possibilities of fractionation – that is, according to the displacements and disguise of the differenciator ... The important thing is not that a difference be small or large, and ultimately always small in relation to a greater resemblance. The important thing, for the in-itself, is that the difference, whether small or large, be internal. (DR, 121)

What is at stake here is a notion of difference in itself, which knows no prior measure or metric, but which produces its own in the very process of differentiation.[56] In the footnote to this passage, Deleuze enlists the work of Léon Selme to round off his point: 'Léon Selme showed that the illusion of an annulment of difference must be all the greater the smaller the differences realised within a system (and therefore in thermal machines), in his *Principe de carnot contre formule empirique de Clausius*' (DR, 318, n25). Deleuze later returns to Selme in chapter 5 of *Difference and Repetition* to reinforce this tenet; in sum, we might say that for Deleuze any difference at all between series or phenomena is all that is 'required'; any difference is all the difference in the world, since there is no pre-set scale by which to measure series, phenomena, events. To assume there were would be in some measure to accept essence at a fundamental level, strictly out of keeping with Deleuze's anti-hylomorphic stance. It is this strand of thought which explains Deleuze's preference for non-metric forms of mathematics (as found for example in Riemannian multiplicity) as more adequate to the realities of the event. The general principle here, of difference in itself, is moreover directly in tune with the rejection of predicative logic on Leibniz's part in favour of 'the complete concept'. All things are discernible ultimately only by reference to the sum total of events which comprise their entire history. In the end, for Deleuze, even particles of the same spin, weight, element, etc., may be discerned by reference to the series to which they have belonged in their individual histories; even the least quanta of being are differentiable not by quality but by the nature of the event.

The two principles addressed above – that of the relational nature of time and the full existence of difference in itself regardless of qualitative similarity – may be put into the cosmological context of the Big Freeze, in which all matter approaches absolute zero. Martin Rees, illustrates these themes:

> The interval between 10^{-15} seconds and 10^{-14} seconds is likely to have been just as eventful as that between 10^{-14} seconds and 10^{-13} seconds, even though the former is 10 times briefer (and likewise for even earlier intervals). It is therefore more realistic to give equal weight to each power of 10. In this perspective there is plenty of action even at earlier stages – to ignore these early eras is a severe omission indeed.[57]

We might gloss the above insight in terms of 'epochs': for any given epoch it is the passage of nature – at root the sum total of energetic interactions – which provides the better yardstick for appraising the passage of time, rather than the grid of a given mathematical metric, here fractions of a second expressed in powers of minus ten. Time is relational. As a corollary, we might insist as a broad principle that each epoch is to be distinguished by a characteristic number, large as it may be, of energetic interactions. Thus, apparently even minimal temporal divisions may in themselves count as epochs, given the vastly 'greater rate' of interaction pertaining to one epoch in comparison to another. This 'greater rate' deserves quotation marks in this context, since it is precisely the interactions themselves, which constitute 'rate' and 'speed' of elapse as a function of the vastly greater levels of free energy available at even minimally earlier epochs. To imagine an observer notionally transported from the cooled-down era of the universe which we occupy (an era formidably longer in terms of seconds elapsed, dating arguably from 38,000 years into the history of the 13-billion-year-old universe) to the very early conditions of the nascent universe, is to confront the impossibility of transporting a clock regulated by our own regime to that very different one. Any clock we might furnish, any yardstick of time, any conscious appraisal of the passage of time, would be subject to the 'greater rate' of the passage of nature. Such a scenario illustrating the relational nature of time is explicitly at the heart of the account furnished by general relativity. All things being equal, the passage of a unit of time, however defined, is indistinguishable under the initial conditions to those pertaining under later. The challenge is to conceptualise for ourselves a passing of time which genuinely (subjectively?) corresponds to this equivalence over such vastly different scales, or 'rates'; to imagine the virtually instant (for us) elapse of 10^{-15} seconds as if it were equivalent to the epoch, with its own attendant regime, through which we are passing on the scale of billions of years. It is a challenge which applies alike to the cosmological physicist and to all those who subscribe to the relational nature of time.[58]

So much must be true, then, for the scenario pertaining to the Big Freeze; in the moribund state, whereby free energy is close to minimum, the presumably final epoch, we are once again challenged to conceive the sheer difference in scale which would allow the equivalent number of energetic interactions to characterise the epoch; trillions of years certainly rather than billions.

Moreover, in the sense in which I am using the term here (whereby the transition from an early cosmos composed of plasma, in which protons and electrons remain too energetic to combine, to a cosmos of atomic natural kinds, should be considered to mark two distinct regimes), there is a potential change in the *regime* of nature conjectured in speculative physics which bears on the range of possible complexity 'reachable' at the Big Freeze. That epoch may count as qualitatively distinct from our own, over and above the quantitative distinction in terms of the flat numerical counting of energetic interactions. Rees outlines the implications of eternal expansion, the motor of the freeze for the Big Freeze scenario:

> Most of the atoms that went into the making of galaxies will eventually get trapped in black holes or inert stellar remnants; each galaxy will become just a dark swarm of cooled white dwarfs, neutron stars and black holes. But eventually the atoms will themselves decay; if the baryons of which they are made were absolutely immutable (as we believe the amount of charge in our universe is), the excess of matter over anti-matter would never have emerged in the ultra-early universe. The eventual decay of protons restores the symmetry between matter and anti-matter with which our universe began ...
>
> If even the heaviest black holes eventually evaporated too, nothing would be left but radiation, and electrons and positrons. A direct hit is highly improbable; electrons and positrons could nevertheless be brought together by forming a bound pair, orbiting around each other, and then spiralling together. So immensely dilute does everything become that there would eventually, on average, be less than one electron in a volume as large as our present observable universe. Immensely wide binary pairs could form; an electron's motion could be controlled by the electric field of a single positron ten billion light years away, and after enough aeons had passed the radiation drag would have brought them closer together.[59]

This is precisely the moribund state which Deleuze is refusing, a minimum state of order or complexity. Yet I would argue that there is nothing in the *letter* of the Deleuzian law which cannot at least countenance such a scenario. The objection takes its source rather from the *spirit* of Deleuze's work.

We may ask, 'what novelty remains in the cosmos at the Big Freeze?', and start by noting that in the picture Rees paints for us, the energy gradient, Deleuze's disparity and intensity, impoverished as it is, remains the motor of physical action, the asymmetry of which provides the 'origin and positivity' of all causal processes. Nor yet in the lights of this scenario do we attain the universal equilibrium which would mark the disappearance of the world as such. In subscribing to the relational nature of time, we might insist on the implication for Deleuze's philosophy of difference that the sheer scale of time required for any sufficient number of energetic interactions to take place would not mark out this epoch as in any sense essentially different than those preceding; the principle behind the notion of difference in itself, that any difference at all is all the difference required, renders it illegitimate to refuse the moribund picture of the Big Freeze as simply too exhausted to constitute novelty. Finally, the incommensurability of energy, in the form of energy gradient, remains not merely *de facto*, but in principle, in the canonical book of physics, in the shape of Nernst's third law of thermodynamics:

> We saw that the coefficient of performance of a refrigerator depends on the temperature of the body we are seeking to cool and that of the surroundings ... the coefficient of the performance falls to zero as the temperature of the cooled body approaches zero. That is, we need to do an ever-increasing, and ultimately infinite, amount of work to remove energy from the body as heat as its temperature approaches absolute zero.[60]

The message is clear, in Peter Atkins's discussion of the third law above, that absolute inactivity, a ground state applying to the universe as a whole, cannot be reached in a finite number of steps, since by definition a superior amount of energy would be required from the environment to extract energy from the body in question than is contained in that body. Technically, absolute zero is an asymptotic limit. And of course, the notion of an environment in which the universe is placed is at best problematic and perhaps self-contradictory.[61] Consequently, the expanding universe of the Big Freeze scenario would be fated to expand forever, unable to cease, just as is true for the Event in Deleuze's philosophy. The existence of a differential which constitutes the path by which the actual and the virtual are exchanged persists *ad infinitum*.

The particular necessity we have identified as belonging to the Leibniz-Deleuze principle of sufficient reason and the complete concept goes some way to displacing the argument from eternal return, then.

It broadens the enquiry outward from the key idea of the incommensurability of forces to the notion of symmetry (or rather, dissymmetry) more generally, and in doing so brings the points of connection and contention between the philosophy of difference and the corpus of physics into sharper focus. Yet in both cases, there is genuine aporia in the attempt to square the circle. The problem turns out not to be that the philosophy is in too great an antagonism to the thermodynamics, but that it is rather too much in agreement, too little able to place distance. If we take seriously both the principle that time, the rate of elapse, is a function of what happens, and the principle that any difference in the world makes all the difference in the world, then we cannot consistently dismiss the scenario of a high-entropy, moribund universe as devoid of creativity. Rather, we are forced to grant that creativity acquires its own time-signature dependent on whatever conditions prevail, however massive the difference in scale. Defence for Deleuze's position on the second law requires support from elsewhere, which will be proposed in the final chapter; a certain kind of 'openness' is required for a Deleuzian cosmos. We are, however, in a position to recognise from the above discussion just how indispensable is the *continuous* nature of the event to Deleuzian metaphysics. It is not amenable to hibernation, nor to exquisite attenuation, nor indeed to the punctuation of phase shifts. A certain indispensable level of order, complexity and creativity must be true of Deleuzian nature, or it cannot count as such. Martin Rees's moribund universe cannot count as such. This is as much as to identify a tension between the letter and the spirit of the Deleuzian text. A mismatch between the inexhaustible creativity of nature to which Deleuze subscribes and the limit case at the edge of his metaphysics. When he speaks of the world as a plenum, devoid of negativity, or a continuum, or a ceaseless *Eventum Tantum* (by lights of which the exhausted cosmos may be found wanting, and ruled out), when he evokes the sublime force of volcanic pressure to characterise the creative power of nature, this is the spirit investing the Deleuzian philosophy of nature, endlessly self-renewing, eternally returning. It may be that he countenances only the productive potential inherent in the complexities of our own epoch, with its own calibrative time-signatures, neglecting the extent to which the two principles in question are interlinked. If time is *in principle* relational, if it lacks the absolute universal measure of which Newton speaks, then the only way to judge the fullness and vigour of nature is by reference to some clock naturally arising within the epoch in question (rotation of the earth, revolutions of the caesium atom, the dissipation of a black hole through Hawking radiation). But equally, if *in principle* the difference in play at any step in the passage of nature may not be thought of as large or small in itself, then what is to distinguish in novelty between the incremental pull between electron and positron billions of miles distant in the far future and a flash of lightning today? Yet there seems something inherently unequal between these two phenomena; the lightning flash, let's say, depends on a greater range of energetic factors than the electron path. It depends on the relative density of conducting humidity in the atmosphere, and the relative height of the nearest earthing structure to determine its path; it conjoins at once the activity and exchanges of a whole population of electrons and ions. We might say, then, that for sake of comparison, we should rather take as many 'electron-positron' exchanges in the far future, ever further flung though they may be, as it takes to equate to the lightning flash. Even then, we have nothing by the principle of internal difference (which is neither great nor small) to distinguish the greater or lesser rate of activity in the two scenarios, since that rate is itself a consequence not of relatively confined location nor of absolute duration, but of what happens, of the principle of relational time. The two principles are interlinked. Moreover, in the attempt to balance out more equitably the scenarios under consideration, we are falling foul of the Deleuzian-Nietzschean tenet which assigns incommensurability to energetic phenomena; all forces are multiple forces in tension, disparity is the sufficient condition of all that appears.

Yet for all the difficulties revealed for the philosophy of difference at this cosmological scale, we are not yet forced to any final capitulation on the issue of the second law. These difficulties serve rather to identify underlying points of contention which will be addressed with resources from elsewhere in Deleuze's work. If a certain minimum level of order is the key, what is it that constitutes order in the Deleuzian philosophy of nature? And what is there to assure us that that minimum will pertain without fail?

SIMPLE ORDER

Gregg Lambert offers a treatment of the notion of order as it pertains to Deleuze's philosophy in his work *The Non-Philosophy of Gilles Deleuze*. He seeks to show that order for Deleuze is an inextricable part of the passage of nature, which at first sight seems to be what is required: a certain minimum level of order or complexity. It conforms to the Deleuzian tenet 'order without law' and it draws, as Deleuze himself so often does, on the philosophical fiction of Jorge Luis Borges.

The Borges piece in question is the famous short story 'The Library of Babel', from the collection *Labyrinths*. For Lambert, the 'order

Entropy and the Complete Concept 69

without law' represented by this library is pertinent to a particular period of questioning for Deleuze; one which lasted from the publication of *Difference and Repetition* to the publication of *The Fold*. He encapsulates Deleuze's problematic in the following way: 'How does one live in a world in which all principles have been shattered to bits?'[62] I will argue, against Lambert, that Deleuze is best understood precisely to be adhering to an overarching principle in his natural philosophy, rather than purely divining the grain of each phenomenon as it is encountered. The Borgesian library is a claustrophobic yet infinite world formed from interlinking identical cells containing the same number of volumes, on the pages of which are found works of dizzying variety in no apparent order, and in varying stages of completion. The protagonist spends his life attempting to make his way through this world, trying to glean anything of its sense or overall pattern, to converge on the original principles of its constitution which seem irreparably to have degraded in sense and organisation, the original principles of which have been 'shattered to bits'. Ultimately, Borges divulges that: 'If an eternal traveller were to cross it in any direction, after centuries he would see that the same volumes were repeated in the same disorder (which, thus repeated, would be an order: the Order).'[63]

Lambert fixes on the analogical similarities in Borges' remarks here to Deleuze's own concept of the fold; the fact of the library's unlimited and cyclical nature implies that it might be compressed into one volume containing an infinite number of infinitely thin leaves, whereby each page folds into the next. As such, Borges' work prefigures, claims Lambert, the solution which Deleuze draws from Leibniz in answer to the loss of principles, citing from *The Fold*:

> The Baroque solution is the following: we shall multiply principles – we can always slip a new one out from under the cuff – and in this way we will change their use. We will not have to ask what available object corresponds to a given luminous principle, but what hidden principle corresponds to whatever object is 'given', that is to say, to this or that 'perplexing case' ... a case being given, we shall invent its principle. (FLB, 67)

So, Lambert concludes, 'the principle of the fold becomes inseparable from the species of repetition that is deployed by a process of reading'.[64] The analogy is a neat and developed one, rallying together common themes in Deleuze and Borges respectively; the 'principle' becomes a function of the 'reading' of cases, a mobile and adaptable process responding to the passage of nature, to the state of progress through the permuting library. It thus joins hands with Deleuze's figure of the 'reading' or 'calculating' God who reads through all the diverging series of the world, whose selection of a path through the library creates fresh principles ever anew, a new set of salient divergent paths. While Deleuze is acknowledging here the human condition, so to speak, whereby to properly appreciate newly encountered phenomena, we must resist the impulse merely to appropriate them *sub specie aeternitatis*, nevertheless, there is a prevailing principle which subsists beneath this attitude, whose existence is signalled by the word 'perplexing' in the above quotation: 'folding' with its multiple cognates includes 'perplication' or problematisation, which in itself governs the attitude to nature that Deleuze insists is necessary; the potential for explication, implication or complication is inexhaustible for nature as a whole, together comprising its essential form of order, complexity, yet provisional for any creature confined to a point of view, any of nature's monads, seekers in the labyrinth and the library. As Nicholas of Cusa would have it, the world explicates God, while God implicates the world. In short, the Baroque, proliferative solution to a world in which 'all principles are shattered' in truth rests on the situated nature of the observer; any 'reading' of phenomena is external, we may at best exhaust as much of the library's contents as time permits, seeking patterns, recurrences, repetitions. In the explicated world only the external order is accessible. Yet just as surely there is the other, internal principle suggested in the analogy of the Baroque; the proliferation and thirst for exhaustion of form is *creative*; the 'Baroque solution' which Deleuze valorises does not seek to remain faithful to the proliferative *forms* of nature so much as to apply nature's own tactics, seeking its internal order. Which is to identify the overarching principle in question: novelty, or creation. For purposes of the present argument, I will favour the word 'evolution', since this will serve to bring the thought more directly into orientation with Whitehead, and this in turn gives more directly onto developments in the physics of the twentieth and twenty-first centuries.

The essential point of contention here rests in the characterisation by Borges-Lambert of order from repetition: 'after centuries he would see that the same volumes were repeated in the same disorder (which, thus repeated, would be an order: the Order)'.[65] In a sense, this is a refusal of disorder.[66] Yet of course not all demurrals from the notion of disorder are equivalent. While in my opinion Lambert is absolutely correct to say that for Deleuze there is nothing but order in the world, nevertheless the order that counts does not rest on any simple index of contingently discovered consistencies; his 'order without law' is rather generative and evolutionary in nature. This distinction between indexical and generative order will be taken up again later, in connection with the work of the quantum physicist David Bohm, whose work presents a universe in evolution.

3. Order

> Chaos appears there, spontaneously, in the order, order appears there in the midst of disorder. We will assuredly some day have to abandon this so negative label, which implies that we are thinking only in terms of an order.
> Michel Serres[1]

In his work *Creative Evolution*, Henri Bergson was concerned to establish a distinction intended to definitively dispel an illusion relating to order, and its inverse, disorder. An illusion which bore directly on the remit of science as it had developed over the long course of its history since the Greeks, an illusion fostered by the mathematisation of physical processes and the concomitant spatialisation of time. The distinction intended to dispel this illusion was to be understood as subtending all other criteria for differentiating order from disorder, and indeed to collapse that very distinction itself.

> So there arises the problem how order is imposed on disorder, form on matter. In analysing the idea of disorder thus subtilized, we shall see that it represents nothing at all, and at the same time the problems that have been raised around it vanish. (CE, 23)

Bergson's contention was that disorder possesses no substantive existence in nature, and that all we may ever encounter are instances of two distinct yet related forms of order. He acknowledges, however, that we are nonetheless habitually given to posit the existence of disorder and indeed to recognise instances thereof in the phenomena of nature. Moreover, he notes the presence of sophisticated conceptions of disorder in science; a key example is the tendency to 'degradation' represented by entropy, which he dates from Clausius and Carnot.

The source of this illusion, according to Bergson, is simultaneously a conflation and a misrecognition:

> Now it is only order that is real; but, as order can take two forms, and as the presence of the one may be said to consist in the absence of the other, we speak of disorder whenever we have before us that one of the two orders for which we are not looking. The idea of disorder is then entirely practical. It corresponds to the disappointment of a certain expectation, and it does not denote the absence of all order, but only the presence of that order which does not offer us actual interest. (CE, 289)

While we recognise the two forms of order as distinct in everyday life, Bergson claims – the examples offered are those of the mathematical ordering of astronomical bodies and the originality of order in a Beethoven symphony – we nevertheless are led to conflate the two by superficial similarity; broadly speaking, both are taken to consist essentially of similar structures which repeat, likenesses which lead to possible generalisation, and hence a *'general order of nature'* (CE, 239, emphasis in original). With this conflation inured in our habits of thought, we habitually misrecognise and indeed fail to understand our true object in searching out order within phenomena in any given instance; to identify the presence or absence of *either one* of these two kinds. The failure to encounter the one expected leads to the misguided conclusion that order *tout court* is absent. For Bergson, this failure is in reality of a converse kind: the failure to recognise that we are in fact in the presence of the other sort of order. The apprehension of disorder can only ever be illusory. As we shall see, Deleuze accepts and endorses this diagnosis, yet not in its given formulation. We shall examine the detail of Deleuze's development of this line of argument below, but for the meantime let us note the affinity between the two thinkers on this matter:

> Instead of starting out from a difference in kind between two orders, from a difference in kind between two beings, a general idea of order or being is created, which can no longer be thought except in opposition to a numbering in general, a disorder in general, or else which can be posited as the starting-point for a deterioration that leads us to disorder in general or nonbeing in general. In any case, the question of difference in kind – 'what' order? 'what' being? Has been neglected. (B, 47)

We note the intimate connection between 'disorder' in general and 'nonbeing in general' maintained here as they are in Bergson's text. Deleuze goes on to link these aspects with an overarching theme in Bergson – the critique of negation: 'We see, therefore, how all the critical aspects of Bergsonian philosophy are part of a single theme: a critique of the negative of limitation, of the negative of opposition, of general ideas' (B, 47). These associations (of order and being intertwined at root) do not merely represent Deleuze's gloss of Bergson's work, however; they reappear elsewhere: 'Chaos does not exist; it is an abstraction because it is inseparable from a screen that makes something – something rather than nothing – emerge from it' (FLB, 76–7). 'Disorder' is illusory, 'non-being' is illusory, each in turn because of their common dependence on negation as such. It is this essential insight which furnishes the basis of Deleuze's claim that entropy is a 'transcendental illusion'. I will argue that to fully appreciate the significance of the issues at stake, it is important to spotlight a certain reading of Deleuze's notions of temporality, a reading once again deriving from Bergson: time as retardation. In turn this reading leads to intriguing questions about the relationship of order to complexity in the Deleuzian corpus.

MECHANISM AND VITALISM, ORDER AND COMPLEXITY

Bergson maintains a resistance to the idea of substantive disorder, based on the assertion that only order pertains, in two forms. What is the nature of these two forms, and how are they to be distinguished? In short, for Bergson, there is a 'mechanistic' order and a 'vitalistic'. Much of *Creative Evolution* is devoted to laying out the distinctions between the two.

Mechanistic order governs the operation of inert matter. If much of what Bergson has to say of it echoes well-known critiques of the Newtonian clockwork universe, this is no accident; Bergson firmly identifies the object of science with this type (and this type only) of order. This affords him a critique which is intended to demonstrate the shortcomings of the scientific enterprise as such: '[The mechanistic order] may be defined as geometry, which is its extreme limit; more generally, it is that kind of order that is concerned, whenever a relation of necessary determination is found between causes and effects' (CE, 236). In Bergson's account, the tendency of human thought to encounter mechanistic order first and foremost is an anthropological (indeed evolutionary) one – our first relation to the world is pragmatic, identifying things, patterns or states of affairs which are useful and which may be manipulated predictably to our advantage, hence a tendency to orientate to a spatial order.[2] Ultimately this tendency becomes hypostasised or reified into increasingly sophisticated concepts and frameworks exceeding the exigencies of bodily necessity or want, but retaining the same essential root; it is in this sense that 'geometry' (or spatial order) is the extreme limit of this tendency. In essence, for Bergson, all that science fails to address in its approach to nature (and this is a great deal) is a function of its focus on the mechanistic order and the misplaced assumption that this form of order can and does furnish an exhaustive description of material action; a description that is for this reason incapable of transcending determinism.

Most tellingly, and in retrospect most influentially, he maintains that a unique focus on the mechanistic order elides the very notion of time.[3] Bergson demonstrates that this elision is a consequence of a certain form of scientism, which effectively rules out of court any sense of the open-ended nature of time:

> What does it mean to say that the state of an artificial system depends on what it was at the moment immediately before? There is no instant immediately before any other instant; there could not be, any more than there could be one mathematical point touching another. The instant 'immediately before' is, in reality, that which is connected with the present instant by the interval dt. All that you mean to say, therefore, is that the present state of the system is defined by equations into which differential coefficients enter, such as ds/dt, dv/dt, that is to say, at bottom, present velocities and present accelerations. You are therefore really speaking only of the present – a present, it is true, considered along with its tendency. (CE, 23)

The scientific account, therefore, for Bergson, ruled out any genuine understanding of duration as becoming:

> When the mathematician calculates the future state of a system at the end of time t, there is nothing to prevent him from supposing that the universe vanishes from this moment till that, and suddenly reappears. It is the t-th moment only that counts – and that will be a mere instant. What will flow in the interval – that is to say, real time – does not count, and cannot enter into the calculation. (CE, 23)

It is evident, then, that science is to be condemned when it subscribes to absolute time in the Newtonian manner: 'All motions may be accelerated and retarded, but the true, or equable, progress of absolute time is liable to no change.'[4]

It is well acknowledged, not least by Deleuze himself, that Deleuze's position on the nature of time and duration is drawn heavily from that of Bergson.[5] In short, as does Bergson, Deleuze subscribes to a relational account of time; the passage of time is captured in reciprocally determinative relations in action. Moreover, any virtue attached to the calculus must be insofar as it is able to encompass precisely the reciprocally determinative nature of systems. For Deleuze, the event has no existence outwith the *exchange* between virtual and actual, just as the rate of change indicated by the calculus has no existence outwith its differential terms.

Bergson pursues this line of thought to its ultimate, cosmological implications in a section entitled 'Modern Science'. Because it is 'of the essence' of science to handle signs, it is therefore 'tied down to the very condition of the sign, which is to denote a fixed aspect of reality under an arrested form' (CE, 347). In other words, the representations of science amount to a 'virtual stop' in the continuous passage of nature:

> To each virtual stop of the moving body T at the points of division T_1, T_2, T_3... we make correspond a virtual stop of all the other mobiles at the points where they are passing. And when we say that a movement or any other change has occupied a time t, we mean by it that we have noted a number t of correspondences of this kind. We have therefore counted simultaneities; we have not concerned ourselves with the flux that goes from one to the other. The proof of this is that I can, at discretion, vary the rapidity of the flux of the universe in regard to a consciousness that is independent of it and that would perceive the variation by the quite qualitative feeling that it would have of it: whatever the variation had been, since the movement of T would participate in this variation, I should have nothing to change in my equations, nor in the numbers that figure in them. (CE, 356)[6]

Nor does Bergson shy away from pursuing the final ramifications:

> Let us go further. Suppose that the rapidity of the flux becomes infinite. Imagine, as we said in the first pages of this book, that the trajectory of the mobile T is given at once, and that the whole history, past, present and future, of the material universe is spread out instantaneously in space. The same mathematical correspondences will subsist between the moments of the history of the world unfolded like a fan, so to speak, and the divisions T_1, T_2, T_3, ... of the line which will be called, by definition, 'the course of time.' (CE, 357)

Thus: '[Science] takes account neither of succession in what of it is specific nor of time in what is of it that is fluent' (CE, 357).

It would be a mistake, however, to conclude that this critique, associated as it is here with 'signs', is merely one example of the oft-maintained objection that an unbreachable disparity pertains between logical entities and the physical world, whereby logical entities exist outwith time and cannot therefore be taken to characterise its movement. On the contrary, for Bergson there *is* a substantive mechanistic order in matter, and science does truly treat of this aspect and is able to capture its correspondences, its translations. It is merely that by definition any universe in which this were the *only* form of order would exhaust its 'course of time' instantaneously.

The second form of order is 'the vital', and it is the relationship, the dynamic, between this form and the mechanistic that is responsible for the observed fact of duration, of the passage of nature. On its first introduction in *Creative Evolution*, Bergson characterises 'the vital' in the following fashion:

> it is with the vital that we have to do, and the whole present study strives to prove that the vital is in the direction of the voluntary. We may say then that this ... kind of order is that of the vital or of the willed, in opposition to [the mechanistic], which is that of the inert and the automatic. (CE, 236)

It was precisely with respect to this strand of thought, elaborated throughout the work, that Bergson encountered robust objection from the philosophical and scientific community: vitalism was taken to imply that nature itself possesses an innate form of sentience; the very term 'will' employed to characterise the vital seemed to impart an anthropocentric viewpoint to this account of physical action, distinguished by orientation to final cause, purpose, teleology. As such, it could not but be at loggerheads with the paradigm of natural selection which had taken root and held sway since the time of Darwin and Huxley. For many, vitalism was tantamount to a form of mysticism. It is not my intention here to pursue the niceties of this matter of contention; Bergson does much to delimit these implications in *Creative Evolution*. The 'willed' character of the vital, finally, bears more relation to Nietzschean Will, devoid of sentience, than to any form of panpsychism, and I would submit that at the very least that there is no violence done, and perhaps a great deal of clarity to be gained, in taking Bergson's 'vital' to signify 'complexity'.[7]

Of far greater significance to the argument at hand is the nature of the dynamic relation which, according to Bergson, holds between the two forms of order. Frequently he asserts that it is of the essence of the vital to introduce an 'interruption' into the irrevocable onward rush of the mechanistic order, to delay this rush through 'hesitation' and more particularly through 'retardation'. This aspect is central to the reading to be offered here of 'the vital' as 'complexity' and merits a number of citations from *Creative Evolution*. Firstly, 'hesitation' is most clearly linked to consciousness and thus life as such, and appears in context of a discussion of the distinction between instinct and consciousness, serving as the distinguishing moment between the two. While unconscious actions are taken to be merely those wherein consciousness is *nullified* (as opposed to the action of a falling stone, where consciousness is absent), it is hesitation which serves to introduce a gap between the automatic action and the performance thereof. While 'the representation of the act is held in check by the performance of the act itself', consciousness resumes when the automatic action is interrupted:

> If we examine this point more closely, we shall find that consciousness is the light that plays around the zone of possible actions or potential activity which surrounds the action really performed by the living being. It signifies hesitation or choice. (CE, 152)

We encounter this same line of argument again in the first chapter of *Matter and Memory*; here Bergson likens the neuronal centre of the brain to a (now obsolete) kind of telephone exchange, wherein the progress of a message is interrupted by the process, conscious on the part of the operator, of allocating its proper channel. The essential element here is that the 'automatic' or the 'mechanistic' is interrupted or retarded by 'the vital'.[8] As with consciousness, so with 'life' more generally:

> All our analyses show us, in life, an effort to remount the incline that matter descends. In that, they reveal to us the possibility, the necessity even of a process the inverse of materiality, creative of matter by its interruption alone. (CE, 259)

Here, as throughout *Creative Evolution*, the phrasing and terminology reveals a certain ontological primacy attached to life or the vital for Bergson; 'life' is identified at root with the interruption which retards the 'descent' of inert matter. Moreover, this interruption associated with life is accorded a strikingly preconditional role in the genesis of matter itself:

> The life that evolves on the surface of our planet is indeed attached to matter. ... But everything happens as if it were doing its utmost to set itself free from those laws. It has not the power to reverse the direction of physical changes, such as the principle of Carnot determines it. It does, however, behave absolutely as a force would behave which, left to itself, would work in the inverse direction. (CE, 259)

It is a descent linked explicitly to the cosmic regime of order and entropy, then, as the reference to Carnot reveals, and the immediately following passage consolidates: 'Incapable of stopping the course of material changes downwards, it succeeds in retarding it' (CE, 259).

Hesitation, interruption and retardation are part and parcel of this dual interpenetrating order. Nor is this notion confined to *Creative Evolution* and *Matter and Memory*; it reappears in *Duration and Simultaneity*, wherein Bergson claims there is 'a certain hesitation or indetermination inherent in a certain part of things'.[9] We cannot help but note that the great Bergsonian themes revolve intimately around this nexus of terms, not least in that 'hesitation' takes its place alongside 'indetermination', or the possibility of the new, in this last citation. But the notion achieves its most distilled formulation, the one most integral to the Bergsonian project, in an essay from 1920 entitled 'The Possible and the Real', later included in *The Creative Mind*:

> Some fifty years ago I was very much attracted to the philosophy of Spencer. I perceived one fine day that, in it, time served no purpose, did nothing.

> Nevertheless, I said to myself, time is something. Therefore it acts. What can it be doing? Plain common sense answered: time is what hinders everything from being given at once. It retards, or rather, it is retardation.[10]

We are in the presence of that self-same vital principle here, 'hindering everything from being given at once', or in other words preventing the mechanistic order from instantaneous exhaustion of its every possibility, which would constitute the collapse of 'the course of time'. Correlatively, retardation is revealed in its most fundamental manifestation: time itself. Finally, then, this line of reasoning arrives at a paradoxical and counterintuitive sense of what time or duration must be: whereas we typically associate the movement of time with an onward march, in Bergson this notion is reversed, precisely in terms of the dynamic between the two forms of order (this dynamic to be heard with our provisional gloss under the term 'complexity', to be developed) whose mutual implication leaves no room for substantive disorder. To be more precise, the onward march of mechanistic time, were it unhindered by vitalistic duration, would result in a null universe. Far from representing the idiosyncrasies of a particular terminology, I will maintain that this insight allows us to identify an important underground channel feeding paradigms of physical action and order across the history of philosophy and science, and in particular in the twentieth and twenty-first centuries; a channel that brings together the thought of Bergson, Michel Serres, Gilles Deleuze, advocates of supersymmetry such as Steven Weinberg, and the cosmology of Lee Smolin. The nexus of terms 'hesitation', 'interruption' and 'retardation' alone will not serve to locate the starting point; we will need to take account of the link Bergson furnishes between these and 'descent'.

For the present, though, we should first note that Deleuze's own philosophy of difference is attuned to the Bergsonian insights above. Like Bergson, Deleuze takes *disorder* to be illusory, an abstraction; chaos, he tells us, 'does not exist'. He takes up and glosses the notion of *retardation* or *hesitation* in *Bergsonism*:

> But the fact that real space has only three dimensions, that Time is not a dimension of space, really means this: there is an efficacity, a positivity of time that is identical to a 'hesitation' of things and, in this way, to creation in the world. (B, 105)

And puts it to use in *What Is Philosophy?*:

> Philosophy proceeds with a plane of immanence or consistency; science with a plane of reference. In the case of science it is like a freeze-frame. It is a fantastic *slowing down*, and it is by slowing down that matter, as well as the scientific thought able to penetrate it with propositions, is actualised. (WP, 118)

For both thinkers, then, retardation or slowing down is inextricable from the very process of material becoming – for Deleuze, as for Bergson, tied to the novel, the new, and creation.

But in what way does this throw light on the critique of limits, and in particular on the 'limit of opposition' and the 'limit of negation', both of which Deleuze valorises in Bergson? As we shall see, the key here is the link which Bergson established between the ubiquity of this dual order, the illusion pertaining to disorder and the illusion of non-being. We are approaching the central Deleuzian theme of immanence.

Bergson rejects as a badly posed question the philosophical conundrum, 'why is there something rather than nothing?' It is based on an illusion; an illusion at once due to negation as such and constituting the direct corollary of the illusion of disorder:

> Thus the problem of knowledge is complicated, and perhaps made insoluble, by the idea that order fills a void and that its actual presence is superposed on its virtual absence. We go from absence to presence, from the void to the full, in virtue of the fundamental illusion of our understanding. (CE, 289)

Bergson is not merely aware of the implications of the line of reasoning here; he has left no other route to arrive at the conception of the void other than as a negation of the given; this is moreover the self-same negation by which the idea of disorder is furnished from that of order. Each is a different aspect of the same illusion:

> existence appears to me like a conquest over nought ... In short, I cannot get rid of the idea that the full is an embroidery on the canvas of the void, that being is superimposed on nothing, and that in the idea of 'nothing' there is less than that of 'something'. (CE, 291)

It is precisely this idea that Bergson is concerned to reverse, for in truth, he maintains, the idea of nothingness cannot be a kind of default over which all that exists is draped. Rather, the default, the more basic idea, is the given, from which we conjecture its negation, nothingness. There is a certain parsimony of thought which Bergson urges on us here; to opt for the idea which presumes less, which entails least, is to privilege order over disorder. He devotes some space to outlining the character of this illusion, invoking the thought experiment necessary to approach a conception of the void: 'I am going to close my eyes, stop my ears, extinguish one by one the sensations that come to me from the outer world.' Nevertheless, this approach, according to Bergson, is destined to undermine itself:

> When I no longer know anything of external objects, it is because I have taken refuge in the consciousness that I have of myself. If I abolish this inner self, its very abolition becomes an object for an imaginary self which now perceives as an external object the self that is dying away. (CE, 294)

It is clear from the above line of reasoning that Bergson leaves no possible gap between the fact of existence and the fact of order. Any mere existence entails automatically the expression of some order, and the illusion that it may be otherwise is the by-product of our innate tendency to grasp the world pragmatically.[11] And for Deleuze, once again, we may read off the persistence of these interconnected themes of order and being in the late work on Leibniz, *The Fold*; disorder does not exist, because the screen brings about *something* rather than *nothing*.[12]

Deleuze's valorisation of Bergson's resistance to negation (negation of 'limits', negation of 'opposition') speaks of an intuition of becoming which is indissociable from an affirmation of order. If to limit is to negate, we find some grounds for Deleuze's later resistance to the constants of nature, indeed to principles of conservation as such, in *What Is Philosophy?*

Yet this excavation of Deleuze's debt to Bergson raises in its turn a number of productive questions.

1. Is there not some high level of caution due in response to this close association of being and order; after all, is it not much more customary to consider material nature as distinct from its organisation? Whitehead, a close philosophical spirit to Deleuze as we have seen, nevertheless holds open at least some minimal distinction of this type: 'Now the correlative of "order" is "disorder". There can be no meaning in the notion of "order" unless this contrast holds. Apart from it, order must be a synonym for "givenness". But order means more than "givenness", though it presupposes "givenness", and each totality of "givenness" attains its measure of order' (PR, 83). In short, can we allow that Deleuze does enough to warrant skipping the step from Whitehead's 'givenness' to 'order' by way of 'attainment', however inevitable and summary? In what way is this to be squared with Deleuze's commitment to 'genetic' accounts in preference to all others? Ultimately, I shall suggest, it is more productive to read Deleuze in a way which prioritises complexity rather than any simple notion of order as such.
2. If we are to understand Deleuze's characterisation of entropy in terms of 'transcendental illusion' as a corollary to Bergson's refusal of substantive disorder, equally on the grounds of 'illusion', this leaves in question what is at stake in Deleuze's use of the term 'transcendental' in this context, left underdetermined by the Bergsonian text. Is Bergson's association of being with order a transcendental deduction or an empirical induction? In light of Bergson's suspicion of Kant's philosophy, we may conclude the latter – but are we not

forcibly reminded of Kant's dove in section five of the A deduction in the *Critique of Pure Reason*, illustrating those who for Kant remain subject to a transcendental illusion: the illusion that flight remains possible outwith its conditions of possibility, that our wings will carry us beyond the stratosphere? Is not Bergson's diagnosis of the illusion of disorder attendant on our ignorance of the conditions by which the given is given (that insofar as this form of order pertains, it is due to the absence of the other form, or if they comingle, the comingling is at once a co-exclusion)? Or by another reading, can it be an empirical matter? A matter of recognising just what kind of order is given in the phenomena confronting us here and now? What bearing might these questions have on Deleuze's scandalous synthesis – in his transcendental empiricism – of these two irreconcilable strains of philosophical method?

To attempt an answer to these questions, to bring into focus nuances underlying the question of order, and to convey their pertinence to the Deleuzian concept of immanence, it will be useful to examine the analogy of the game. Ultimately, our focus will be on the Ideal Game Deleuze describes in *The Logic of Sense*, but this in itself is best understood through comparing and contrasting a number of texts in our orbit which employ their own game analogies.

THE GAME ANALOGY #1: LEIBNIZ AND KANT

First, let us recall the terms in which Leibniz lays out the game of nature in 'On the Ultimate Origination of Things'. Selection is cast as a decision from among possible moves. Each selection leaves indeterminate the possibilities for each player for the rest of the course of the game, and indeed the permutations of relations between the pieces as a whole, the possible states of the ensemble.[13] Needless to say, each move is constrained by the past evolution of the game, whereby the relative strategic importance of each piece has differentiated from its mere nominal character. The pawn which blocks a knight's progression is no longer merely the pawn it was at the game's commencement, the initial conditions. The game is thus a branching process, successively predicating all future ranges of possibilities on the degrees of freedom remaining after those moves already taken have reduced the maximum. *In medias res* it is no longer a matter of free choice; the particularities of each move are potentially a matter of sacrifice, victory or defeat. One can only do the Best given the state of evolution of the game; each next move is predicated on those that have gone before, and a function of the last most of all. For Leibniz's game-playing deity, a complex state of affairs evolves from a relatively minimal set of constraints. Logical contradiction, the excluded middle, is the constraint Leibniz uses to illustrate God's limitations, and indeed, for all intents and purposes, the Best is a logical (in the sense of definitional) constraint, since God is unable to act counter to his own excellence, though Leibniz does not rule out contingent constraints on God's action. We might add on Leibniz's behalf that each piece is (or mirrors) the entire game from its own point of view. We have already examined the close affinities the game as Leibniz presents it bears to the notion of entropy and the associated principle of least action.

Firstly, let us mark out what is put in play by the metaphor as Leibniz presents it. There are on the face of it two fundamental elements in the organisation of the game: the pieces, the stuff, the matter; then there are laws, rules, translations. On the face of it, these two elements enjoy ontologically distinct, albeit interdependent, forms of existence. Matter may be subject to the laws, may translate or transmute according to their dictates, but the laws themselves remain independent of such mutability. On the other hand, the laws themselves are effectively null, would enjoy no purchase, without the stuff on which they operate. As Leibniz would have it, constraint is what 'comes from the outside', the 'extramundane'; laws and matter are external one to the other. If we were to accept Whitehead's assertion that 'order' means more than 'givenness', with respect to this reading, then we would have to stipulate that the order in question may refer only to the 'attainment' inherent in the evolution of a specific game; there is unquestionably already a form of order implicit in the design of the game itself, in the valences of each piece and the initial setup on the board, its own 'givenness'. No less of course, does this apply to the valences of matter and initial distribution, a cosmological 'givenness'. All of which is to broach the issue of Platonism, and perhaps by the perils of metaphor to import into our paradigm of physical action the unwelcome division of nature into the timeless, ideal form and the individual particular (the design of the game, in which each particular game participates, the forms of basic matter along with the immutable laws which govern them). No less is it to countenance the Newtonian Paradigm, for which time flows equably and for which space abstractly locates matter.

The readings of the game metaphor offered both by Michel Serres and Deleuze are explicitly fashioned to avoid this implication. I would argue that, for both, the crucial distinction is the degree to which Leibniz's own principle of reciprocal determination is applied.

There is a certain impasse, a certain reduction to absurdity, to which the division in principle between 'law' and 'matter' leads, exemplified in the work of Immanuel Kant. In both the *Critique of Pure Reason* and the introduction to the *Critique of Judgement*, Kant broaches a fundamental difficulty with respect to the very possibility of transcendental reasoning, and moreover the transcendental unity of apperception:

> Appearances might very well be so constituted that the understanding should not find them to be in accordance with the conditions of its unity. Everything might be in such confusion that, for instance, in the series of appearances, nothing presented itself which might yield a rule of synthesis and so answer to the concept of cause and effect.[14]

This, for Kant, bears on the question of the relationship between the intuition and the understanding, between appearances presenting in the manifold and the *a priori* categories themselves. For, he says, even in that case where grounds for synthesis in thought were lacking (i.e., where the manifold lacks any structure), nevertheless, the role of intuition continues unfettered: 'But since intuition stands in no need whatsoever of the functions of thought, appearances would none the less present objects to our intuition.'[15] There is nothing, in other words, in things-in-themselves, in the *noumenon*, to guarantee any conformity between the manifold and results of synthesis. There is, on the face of it, the possibility that the manifold is subject to no law but that of accident, and that any repetition, pattern or correspondence emerging from phenomena in synthesis may carry none of the weight of necessity which Kant insists belongs to the causal relation proper. Thus, for Kant, the question is essentially how conditions of thought can have an 'objective ground'.[16] His answer, which sets the transcendental apart from the empirical, is 'affinity'. In short, it is not only necessary (as a condition of cognition) that we associate elements of the manifold, but that they be inherently *associable*, that they bear some prior affinity. Alastair Welchman remarks:

> It appears that 'affinity' is Kant's name for the *capacity* of the manifold to undergo synthesis, and be unified in a single consciousness. This capacity – that appearances be *assoziabel* – is however, not a function of any formal properties that might be introduced by the subject. It is not a result of synthesis, but rather a property of the *content* of the manifold ...[17]

He proceeds to draw out the dangerous entailment behind this thought for transcendental reasoning, and indeed Kant's critical philosophy as a whole. Citing the introduction to the *Critique of Judgement*, where Kant acknowledges that 'the manifoldness and heterogeneity' of empirical laws may ultimately be so 'infinitely great' as to present only a 'raw, chaotic aggregate', Welchman spells out the consequences:

> Kant comes to acknowledge that the arguments of the first Critique do not prove the necessity for any particular causal law. Every event could therefore be in principle deemed to have a cause, in fact necessarily to have the cause that it in fact has. But this is compatible with every instance of causation being the unique representative of its own law: that there could be as many laws as there are events.[18]

While we cannot but recognise the paradox presented under the phrase, 'unique representative of a law' (which while not Kant's own, plausibly translates his inference) and recall Aristotle's warning over the descriptive opacity of the singular event, it is nevertheless just such a paradox around which the third Critique revolves. Indeed, it is the insistence on Kant's part in the *Critique of Pure Reason* that the sole object of the understanding is such *laws of genera*, without which there would be no understanding, which renders the plausibility of Welchman's glossing formulation.[19] This conjecture, of course, does not commit Kant to anything other than a particular conception of what might constitute disorder. He proceeds to identify the transcendental condition which rules out the substantive existence of this form of disorder: since those very conditions which are required to produce a coherent cognitive experience are the self-same conditions which he has dubbed 'affinity', pertaining to the manifold itself, the manifest experience of coherent cognition establishes its substantive correlate in the manifold. Welchman goes on to problematise the distinction Kant introduces to finesse the argument here – the distinction between 'constitutive' (and even with respect to this line of reasoning replayed in the third Critique, 'regulative') judgement and 'reflective' judgement – arguing that the distinction can only collapse through the logic of Kant's own architectonic.[20] We might conclude with Westphal, nevertheless, that the positive thrust of Kant's argument establishes at most the caveat that 'if there is experience, then nature must have whatever regularity it takes to constitute experience'.[21] Thus far, Deleuze asserts his agreement with Kant; there must be a prior order which allows cognition.

Let us align the Kantian deliberations above with the analogy of the game. The speculative diminishment of the applicability of rules as such to the bare domain of the singular instance in each case amounts to a kind of atomisation of the playing board, whereby no 'move' has any further potential latitude than the very ground it occupies – no 'rule' instantiated in any given phenomenon bears any meaningful collocation with the rule instantiated in any other singular phenomenon. As we shall see, there is a paradoxical adjacency to Deleuze's own version of the game analogy here, whereby each move is irreducibly singular. In the Kantian schema, therefore, we seem to have encountered that limit case which strays closest to the Deleuzian tenet, frequently brandished against Kantian transcendentalism itself, that 'the conditions should be no broader than what it condition'. For the latter, Kant, of course, this notion of disorder is branded with a negative sign, while on the Deleuzian side of the fence between this abutting territory, the sign is wholly positive; chaos is to be affirmed. And it could be argued that the various engagements Deleuze undertakes with Kant consist in a series of disarticulations of this boundary: the status of genera, the categories, the nature of conditions, etc. For Kant, the specific form of disorder envisaged here is in truth the final remnant of a powdered necessity, there where the minimal reduction of the antagonism between the transcendental and empirical methods subsists (for, as Welchman points out, Kant's aim in the above line of reasoning, the rationale for positing the affinity of the manifold, is to establish a fatal insufficiency of Humean 'association', which admits no prior affinity in things). As such, it may be subject to the critique offered by Bergson encountered earlier with respect to the very prospect of conceiving disorder; a critique which is levelled against just such phenomenal pulverisation: 'First we think of the physical universe as we know it, with the effects and causes well proportioned to each other; then, by a series of arbitrary decrees, we augment, diminish, suppress, so as to obtain what we call disorder' (CE, 246).

Moreover, we find motivating the Kantian argument a division maintained in extremis and expressed in its most stark form, which by implication disallows the operation of reciprocal determination between the two regimes of the game as set out above: the division between law and the manifold, necessity and material phenomena, the rule and the piece. For Kant, these two levels may never determine each other in kind. Even when the rules are powder, each a singular instance, they are rules nevertheless.

The following two versions of the game analogy are counterposed in significant and illuminating ways with respect to this division.

THE GAME ANALOGY #2: CLAUDE SHANNON AND MICHEL SERRES

Michel Serres, in the first volume of his ambitious *Hermès* series, *La communication*, introduces the book, and the series as a whole, with a paradigm of order intended to serve as a model both for physical action and for all entities of any degree of structure whatever, mythology, biology and human knowledge included. 'Communication' is understood here to encompass much more than meaningful exchange; all phenomena 'communicate'. As such, Serres construes physical action and the promulgation of ideas alike, under the extended analogy of the network, or *'reseau'*. Serres' paradigm can be seen in the context, then, of the wave of structuralist thought which had gained ascendence in the academy by the early 1960s, but equally it may be situated within the increasing purchase of information theory. Above all, however, as so often in Serres' work, the debt is most directly to Leibniz – the analogy of the network is modelled in the image of Leibniz's game in 'Ultimate Origination'. Its importance for the present argument lies in its broadening of the remit for reciprocal determination; as such, it instructively throws light on the application of this principle in Deleuze's own thought, and indeed his own interpretation of 'the game' as paradigm of physical action. Before examining the detail of Serres' extended analogy, we should recognise that the contribution of information theory itself motivates toward a greater emphasis on reciprocal determination, if not couched explicitly in those terms by its founders, Claude Shannon and Warren Weaver.

GAME #2.1: CLAUDE SHANNON'S 'A MATHEMATICAL THEORY OF COMMUNICATION'

Claude Shannon's paper 'A Mathematical Theory of Communication' was published in 1948 as a result of his technical work on maximising capacity for transmission over the Bell telephone networks; the theoretical breakthrough far exceeded its ostensible target and is now generally recognised to represent the single-handed creation of an entire scientific discipline. This discipline enjoys a breadth of application in the physical sciences, and indeed theoretical physics, by dint of the adoption of entropy as an index of information, content and capacity. It forms the basis of subsequent theoretical work such as the Hawking-Penrose Conjecture and Max Tegmark's 'Holographic Universe'.

As such, it is clear that for the purposes of this discipline 'information' connotes at a much more physically profound level than, say, 'data', just as 'communication' does for Serres. Weaver explicitly makes this clear in his 'Introductory Note' to Shannon's paper: 'communication' is to connote 'the procedures by which one mechanism ... affects another mechanism'.[22] He notes:

> In particular, information must not be confused with meaning. In fact, two messages, one of which is heavily loaded with meaning and the other of which is pure nonsense, can be exactly equivalent from the present viewpoint, as regards information.[23]

Shannon and Weaver partition the elements of any communication into an information source, a transmitter, a channel along which a signal is sent (and which is subject to potential interfering sources of noise), a receiver and a destination. A key parameter of the capacity of any such assemblage to convey information, and the one which renders the theory so amenable to incorporation in accounts of physical action, is that any significance derivable from information received can only be indexed in relation to the possible degrees of freedom available to the source, and against the degree of noise the channel may suffer. Theoretically, then, these aspects are closely analogous to the Hamiltonian or Lagrangian functions in physics, which map the degrees of freedom enjoyed by a particular system or ensemble into a representative state space. Universally, any such system is subject to entropy, or 'noise'. Indeed, entropy as such, with its associated mathematical formulae, is an index of the degrees of freedom available to the system; a system of a highly entropic state enjoys fewer degrees of freedom than those in lower entropic states.

An illustration of this close collusion of physical event with 'information' may be taken from the history of cosmology in the form of the classification of the 'Cepheid variable' type of star. This was a crucial step in the history of mapping the size of universe and it owes its place in that history to the conviction of Henrietta Leavitt at the Harvard College Observatory in the early 1890s that the observed variable luminosity of a certain class of stars (the 'Cepheids') were of key significance to establishing objective distance. Prior to this breakthrough, an inherent ambiguity had dogged cosmology: brighter stars may be so because they are closer but less luminous than equivalently bright stars, which in turn may be further away yet more luminous. Leavitt's work in resolving this problem is particularly notable in that it took place in the context of a debate in cosmology between those who believed that the universe consisted only of one galaxy (by default our Milky Way) and those who argued that there were many. For the former, observed diffuse emissions of light were all to be labelled 'nebulae', since they were to be distinguished from individual stars or star formations. Contemporary cosmology distinguishes between sources of diffuse light, which represent signature traits for separate galaxies. It reserves the term 'nebula' for massive, diffuse, cosmic clouds of gas.

This obstacle of apparently inherent ambiguity associated with relative luminosity represented a barrier to any realistic evaluation of the size of the universe, and hence the plausibility of the case for one or many galaxies. Since this ambiguity pertained to all solar objects, no fixed point of triangulation could be established.

What Leavitt recognised was that the regularly periodic variation of intensity of Cepheid variable stars between a lower and an upper bound was a key to their mean, 'real' luminosity. With the pragmatic assumption that a subset of the class (those found within the Magellanic cluster) were approximately the same distance from earth, she was able to show a close (logarithmically mapped) correlation between the cycle of luminosity and the relative intensity of any given star within the Cepheid class. While the length of cycle for individual stars varied, it did so in good consistent proportion to their objective luminosity.[24]

Why do Cepheid variables behave in this way? One mechanism currently proposed is that Cepheids over the course of a cycle are switching between a preponderance at the surface of one particular isotope of helium and another; a switch both prompted by and subject to the uptake and subsequent expulsion of energy flows arising from the core. One of these isotopes (doubly ionised helium) can occur only under extremely energetic conditions such as those found at the core of the sun; this form has a heat/energy absorbing character and will retain energy influx. This has the consequence of heating up the core and forcing bodies of this isotope toward the surface. Once at the surface, the accumulated energy has the opportunity to dissipate, and the helium will tend to cool to the point where it can re-acquire electrons, thereby resuming a singly ionised form. This form of helium isotope, however, will resist the influx of energy and recede back inwards toward the core, no longer compelled to expand. This recommences the higher-energy phase; the doubly ionised form begins once again to preponderate and the cycle begins again. The upper and lower limits of luminosity correspond to the relative preponderance of the two isotopes with their contrasting thermodynamic characteristics.[25]

In information theoretic terms, the various elements of this particular model would map out as follows: the star is the source (transmitter); electromagnetic fields (more specifically in modern telescopy, radio waves) are the channel, subject to distortion or 'noise'; our radio telescopes are the receivers. Most importantly, it is the reduction or expansion of the degrees of freedom pertaining to the system, the star, as its thermal expansion subsides or augments, which makes it possible to index the information it transmits against its physical significance for the state of the star; we determine its intrinsic luminosity and thereby its distance.

The signature pulsation of the Cepheid variable, dependent as it is on the thermal expansion and subsequent contraction of the star's outer layers, is a dramatic cosmic-scale example of the thermodynamic character of Shannon's theory of Information. But the scope of the theory, due to its close identification with the ubiquitous phenomenon of entropy, extends in principle to systems at any scale whatever.

Of most interest in the development of the game analogy here is the assertion regarding the interrelation of 'rules' and 'pieces' implied in this framework. Weaver's Introductory Note identifies three levels of salient action, associated with three sets of problems:

> Level A. How accurately can the symbols of communication be transmitted? (the technical problem).
> Level B. How precisely do the transmitted symbols convey the desired meaning? (the semantic problem).
> Level C. How effectively does the received meaning affect conduct in the desired way? (the effectiveness problem).[26]

With respect to the analogy of the game thus far, it would be natural to associate Level A, the technical aspect, with 'the rules', while Levels B and C might more naturally equate to 'the pieces' – to the individual symbols. On this reading, the individual elements of Level B are those individuals to which the 'rules' of Level A apply. Level C, it may be assumed, belongs 'merely' to the cultural realm, to the level of coded human behaviour. This would be to oversimplify, however, for at least three reasons. Firstly, information is not to be confused with 'content' here, except in the extended sense dealing with the conditions of its transmission ('channel', 'signal', etc.). Secondly, what is transmitted (symbols) may not be straightforwardly identified with discrete units of meaning as such, but must also encompass continuously varying signals (such as those emitted by the Cepheid variable, but also by television or telephone transmission). Thirdly, Weaver explicitly puts the reader on guard against this oversimplification:

> So stated, one would be inclined to think that Level A is a relatively superficial one, involving only the engineering details of good design of a communication system ... [But] part of the significance of the new theory comes from the fact that Levels B and C, above, can make use only of those signal accuracies which turn out to be possible at Level A.[27]

In short, Weaver is claiming here that the 'rules' do not stand apart from the 'pieces'. There is no Platonic form of order governing the essence of 'signal', much less 'symbol'; rather, the capacity of each system to display order, to transmit meaning, is irreducibly a function of the individuals in which it is instantiated. More particularly, it is a matter of degrees of freedom pertaining to the system in question, which will vary over time (for example, as a star reaches the point of collapse), and between different systems considered; gases near equilibrium have a different, lesser capacity for the new, the unexpected, the signal, than do gases far from equilibrium.

In terms of understanding the implications for interpretation of physical systems, there are certain significant principles here which bear on reciprocal determination:

1. The rules may change, develop, or, in the appropriate vocabulary, the degrees of freedom may alter.
2. There must be sufficient repetition, a threshold so to speak, for the unexpected divergence therefrom to stand out, to count as signal; there must be redundancy.
3. The nature of the channel is as important as the nature of the source; nor indeed should the nature of the receiver be neglected – a consideration which is at its most starkly evident when we consider the role of recording devices in quantum experiments.

The rules are reciprocally determined by the state of the system and vice versa; the signal is not in itself significant until distinguished against the background redundancy; the source itself cannot be known other than by the channel through which its information propagates; the star which emits the signature via electromagnetic radiation will potentially suffer the noise of lensing as the photons make their way across the intervening gap to the receiver.[28] At root in all these considerations lies an irreducible tenet of information theory: that information, and physical action, may be understood only in terms specific to the systems in which they are instantiated. Determinations are to be understood as singular in this respect, inextricable from a given phenomenon as a whole, 'rules' and 'pieces' alike. The Levels which Weaver identified are not self-contained, a significance which does not escape him: 'But a larger part of the significance [of the theory] comes from the fact that the analyses at Level A disclose that this level overlaps the other levels, more than one could possibly naively suspect.'[29] From the very beginning of his ambitious series of books under the title *Hermès*, Michel Serres advances a model of communication which at once rallies the conceptual resources of information theory and cybernetics and couples these to a post-Leibnizian programme recognisable from its scope: a *mathesis universalis* of networks. Unequivocally, too, he fashions the model under the regime of reciprocal determination, in a manner much more emphatic than Shannon and Weaver.

The influence of information theory is evident both explicitly and implicitly in Serres' formulation of the model: Shannon and Weaver are cited, as is Norbert Wiener, who collaborated with Shannon in the development of his work,[30] while precursors of information theory such as Brillouin and Fechner receive acknowledgement in the second volume. The preface to the first volume at once conjoins Serres' programme with the founding problematic of information theory (the ideal conditions for communication), marries this with the Leibnizian system, and gestures toward the overarching explanatory power this marriage promises. Serres intends to demonstrate 'the rigour of the principal Leibnizian organization: the communication of substances. The highest abstraction is born from the acute necessity for the best communication possible.'[31] The model is to accommodate not merely the nature of physical action, but the sum total of knowledge (Serres' adopted shorthand is '*l'Encyclopédie*'), the interrelation of disciplines, and the enduring power (à la Bachelard) of mythology. Serres adopts the vocabulary of information theory – the central concept, *réseau*, can both mean 'channel' and 'network'; problematic 'noise' (the loss of information through the channel) is granted its own volume in the series under the title *L'interférence*.

What, then, are the features of the network Serres proposes, and in what ways does it represent a more wide-ranging deployment of the principle of reciprocal determination than Weaver claims for information theory? Once again, as with Leibniz's analogy in 'Ultimate Origination', Serres takes pains to illustrate the dynamics of his model by analogy to a board game. He invites us to imagine the diagram of a network, comprised of nodes ('*sommets*') and channels ('*chemins*'), each point representing say a proposition ('*une thèse*') or a 'definable element of a determined empirical ensemble'. The channels are to represent the liaison between two or several elements. No point is to be considered inherently subordinate to any other, though each has a contingent zone of influence, just as the developing strategies of a game allot relative powers to pieces.

For Serres, this model implies at once a principle of reciprocal determination and a kind of duality between nodes and channels: 'two nodes may in fact share between them relations of reciprocal causality, of reversible influence, of equivalent action and reaction, or even simultaneous effect [*action en retour*] (the feedback of the cyberneticists)'.[32] This 'reciprocal causality' is identified more closely with 'reciprocal determination' as such in a footnote: 'When we say determination, we mean relation or action in general.'[33] Serres makes clear that the model is intended to overcome the simplifications of both linear and dialectic reasoning in favour of the order he dubs 'tabular'. This form of reciprocal causality is not in itself so distinct from the territory of information theory. Nevertheless it is in the movement from Shannon's single channel to Serres' network model that the potential explanatory reach expands exponentially; networks express complex interaction, while single channels invite constant recursion to linear accounts, treating non-linearity (an excellent case in point being feedback) as an anomaly to be tamed. As such, Serres is pointing forward to the nascent discipline of chaos theory; we may interpret the network model versus Shannon's focus on the channel as the difference between systems considered ultimately in terms of their interconnections and those considered in isolation.

Linearity has no final pre-eminent place in a network which sustains feedback, which escapes integration, where 'any flux whatever' may enjoy any speed of propagation. Nor on this level of reciprocal determination does Serres fail to draw implications which place us once again in touch with the theme of retardation or delay:

> Let's consider any subsystem whatever of our network: we see immediately that any flux whatever over one (or several) channel(s) is able to go from any node whatever to any other (or from several to several) in any time whatever: that depends on the delays [*retards*] encountered.[34]

The concept of retardation is reinforced in the footnote: 'This notion of delay in communication is a capital notion which will be developed independently elsewhere.'[35] The formulation is markedly close to that of Bergson: if action may be instantaneous, then what prevents everything from happening at once is retardation. We shall return to this line of reasoning in a discussion of Serres' later work *The Birth of Physics*, but in order to establish the extent and nature of reciprocal determination inherent in this model, and to further raise salient connections with Deleuze's philosophy of difference, let us first note the 'duality' of nodes and channels written into Serres' account.

Serres is specific; the reciprocal determinations of which he speaks are not confined to the 'pieces' alone: 'finally there exists a profound reciprocity between the nodes and the channels, or, if you like, a duality'.[36] This duality is to be understood aspectually:

> A node can be regarded as the intersection of two or several channels (a proposition may be constituted as the intersection of a multiplicity of relations or a situational element appearing all at once from the confluence of several determinations); correspondingly, a channel can be regarded as a determination constituted by the coming into correspondence of two preconceived nodes.[37]

This profound reciprocity or duality underlying the order Serres is laying out here already carries strong resonances with the 'singular' and 'ordinary' points in topology and the differential calculus on which Deleuze places so much emphasis; what is constitutive of the individual (object = x) for Deleuze are the series which converge and diverge around it. Further, the network of the board varies globally over the course of time; its regular Cartesian lines denatured to 'scalene' form in keeping with its faithfulness to the relations between pieces and channels rather than mere position as such. What is more, it is apt to reconfigure momentarily: 'For example [when] a point or node of the network abruptly changes place (like a piece of relative importance – king, queen, knight, etc. – on a chess board), and the network ensemble transforms itself into a new network.'[38] For James Williams, in *Gilles Deleuze's Philosophy of Time*, this sort of instantaneous restructuring is the key to understanding Deleuze's syntheses of time. When Deleuze claims that everything returns anew, that what returns is difference itself, we are to understand this in terms of the novel ways in which the event of each 'instant' palpably refigures the distribution of potential, virtual relations; the past, without changing its pastness, becomes what it was for this present now, in the way long-term tendencies vary, bringing elements to the fore which were previously of less central importance. These processes are subject to ever further reconfiguration as novel elements, novel instants, contribute to this continuous variation. Tellingly, Williams adopts the analogy of the game to illustrate this point:

> Deleuze is not referring to instants but to plays, to a process more like a move in a game. These do not take place in an instant, like the crossing of a threshold on a line, but rather spread through a structure and a system immediately.[39]

Clearly for both, what is at stake is a form of immanence that escapes the underlying presupposition of a static causality which operates undeviatingly from the past to the future in favour of a more supple, 'expressive' understanding of action and temporality; a precondition in both cases is the radical contingency attached to events; the network at each instant is a new network, the event recasts everything anew; further, for Deleuze, there is a certain reciprocal determination of the past, present and future. Williams writes:

> a variation in intensity changes past and future relations through all series stretching out from the living present. For instance, when a wine creates a singular delight or disgust, this novel intensity carries through all the series coming together in the present singularity expressed on the palate of the taster.[40]

It should be noted, however, that while Serres embraces this notion of *instantaneous* universal reconfiguration, he does not infer from this any reciprocal determination of past, present and future *per se*. This distinction between the two will be further pursued in the discussion of

Deleuze's analogy of the game below, but for now I wish to mark only that for both thinkers what is significant in the evolution of a given system is not that which registers as continuous, nor persistent, but the process of continual reconfiguration, continuous variation itself.[41]

We are now in a position to see in what ways the respective frameworks of Deleuze and Serres mark a step beyond the reciprocal influence between 'Levels' of communication/action envisioned by Shannon. It is the insistence of the focus on continuous variation itself and the dual aspect of the 'rules' and 'pieces' which so dramatically extends the scope of the principle of reciprocal determination. The 'levels' themselves disappear, are *only* aspectual. Rules determine the distribution of pieces, yet the distribution of pieces determines the rules; a flat ontology.

GAME #2.2: MICHEL SERRES' *THE BIRTH OF PHYSICS*

> Nothing is exterior to things themselves, a physics of immanence.
> The governance of the rudder is enough.
> Michel Serres (BP, 75–6)

We have seen the importance Serres attributes to the notion of 'delay' or retardation in physical systems; here I would like to explore the way this notion contributes to the principle of reciprocal determination in his 1977 book *The Birth of Physics*, and in turn to examine the contrastive ways in which this trope plays out in the development of Deleuze's own philosophy of immanence.

In *The Birth of Physics*, Serres investigates the work of the Roman atomist Lucretius (Titus Lucretius Carus), *De rerum natura* (*The Nature of Things*), thought to have been written around the fifties of the first century BCE. Serres uses the text as a locus to offer a wide-ranging account, both chronological and conceptual, of the emergence of complexity or turbulence from the natural order. He performs a *post facto* synthesis of the mathematical resources offered by Archimedes with the atomist model to outline a nascent physics ingeniously allied to a proto-calculus. In the process he valorises the power of Lucretius' model to prefigure the paradigm shift in recent physics from accounts centring solely on carefully isolated linear systems to those which encompass the non-linear. In Serresian terms this represents the shift from the dynamics of the 'solid' to fluid dynamics, the flux of turbulence which figures so prevalently and strikingly in Lucretius' imagery throughout, and which represents the real *explicandum* to which science should aspire.

In the beginning, according to Lucretian cosmology, there was the void through which atoms fell in perfect parallel, an ideal laminar flow, unable to interact or combine, until the appearance of a minimal angle, as small as may be imagined, the *clinamen*, inclining the path of one atom from the true, leading to collision with its neighbour, and by chain reaction to combinations of atoms, to recombinations of unstable forms, all deviations from the initial equilibrial state of strict downward fall. Turbulence. Our world, initially and perpetually out of true.

Serres encourages the reader to recognise in this paradigm the antagonistic relations of order, complexity and entropy. The maximal fall represented by the true downward path of each atom is the unhindered path to and from eternal equilibrium. (It is here that parallels begin to suggest themselves with Bergson's mechanistic order.)

By the logic of this first state in the void, Serres argues, there is no time. If time is relational, if it is 'what happens', then perfectly isolated, laminar, parallel movement or fall is equivalent to no movement at all, equivalent to rest. What surrounds the body of falling atoms is void; there is nothing by which to calibrate the fall, and equally no evolution of the system internally. The world begins and is forever set in the moribund state of inactivity which represents maximum entropy, stasis and equilibrium instantaneously, with infinitely short elapse. It is only through escape from the deterministic operation of maximal fall that space and time may arise. This escape is in and through the *clinamen*, the swerve leading to collision. As Serres puts it:

> All movement is in this way related to stability and takes place more or less easily. In the first physical model [he is referring to atoms falling through the void], this signifies the encounter of an element with another atom, with other atoms, which impede the first in its journey to rest. Collision is nothing but a check, a brake, a difficulty, on the precipitous rush towards the base. (BP, 68)

Here then are two suggestive parallels to the mechanistic order and the vitalistic, to the entropic and the complex, outlined above. Firstly, time is null in the void; the speed of the fall escapes all measure; it is the same as absolute rest, as terminal equilibrium, since there is an absolute lack of relation to anything beyond the atomic ensemble. Secondly, there is in the world a counter-principle to that of the maximal fall, a hindrance, a brake, which is as much as to say a retardation. It appears with the *clinamen*, and is generalised, Serres informs us, in the form of the *thalweg*. The term *thalweg* refers to those cross-currents of physical interactions which everywhere and immediately deflect atoms from the pure downward path; Serres' repeated example is of the tributary which joins the larger river, whose established bed defers arrival at the lowest point sought by the flux in obedience to the principle of maximal fall. Maximal fall in the world is relative always to the inclines offered by cross-cutting flows or turbulence, retarding from the very first. The vertical right-angled fall becomes an ideal thwarted by contingency, the simple rule everywhere confused by complexity. And Serres does not shy away from crowning this principle of complexification in the same manner as had that other Lucretian scholar, Bergson: 'Time is the interruption of rest' (BP, 69). The term 'rest' here we may gloss in light of the above as that absolute speed in the void which escapes measure; the same speed to which Bergson's mechanistic order is subject, along with the same interruption, the same hesitation. It is time itself which is at stake.

It would be the work of a different book to follow the mappings Serres makes from this mythological scenario, this cosmogony, to modern physics, the alignment of Lucretius' poetic register with terms such as bifurcation, metastability or self-organisation. The language of chaos and complexity theory allows Serres to identify the *clinamen*, this deviation from equilibrium, as present not merely at one creationary instant in the Lucretian first void, but here, there, in 'uncertain times and uncertain places', emerging from and accounting for the myriad of systems, stable and metastable, which constitute the fabric of nature: 'There is no time zero, no origin. The instant of birth is proper to each vortex, here and there, once, tomorrow, long ago, this is how the *clinamen* functions' (BP, 166). Finally, there is a certain character to the model offered by Serres through Lucretius, which is shared in turn by the Bergsonian schema in *Creative Evolution*. It is to do with the intricate interconnection of order with disorder, or rather, since neither thinker acknowledges the substantive existence of disorder, of entropy and complexity. The two are presented together in each case; the cause of one is the cause of the other, and in the same way. It is a question in each case of a certain immanence. For Serres, it is the *clinamen* and the *clinamen* only which is at the origination of things. While maximal fall is the regime under which all nature operates, it is nevertheless never achieved, since it is the ever-present resistance (retardation) of turbulence itself, of the *thalweg*, which defers it. As Serres puts it:

> The stream is its own dyke, the river its own wharves ... Everywhere in fact, only temporary, provisional, standstills form that defer the standstill. Obstacles, atoms, bodies, world, are in their turn just stabilities, but transient. The dynamics of force, unknown, introduces, by the minimal angle, collisions, interlacings, fabrics. It is reduced to friction. Far from being motive, it slows. (BP, 69)

This theme of retardation is not merely explicitly present in Serres' work, then – 'far from being motive, it slows' – but as we see it is intertwined with the very idea of the genesis of complexity – 'collisions, interlacings, fabrics'. In Bergson's case, as noted, all action would exhaust itself infinitely quickly in a (putative) world in which the only form of order were mechanistic; space, matter, 'arises' through the retardation of the vital order, or complexity. Serres and Deleuze both thematise this tenet in their respective ways.

A secondary underlying text (to that of Lucretius) in *The Birth of Physics* is one we have treated already: Leibniz's 'On the Ultimate Origination of Things'. For Leibniz, one discernible entity 'falls through' into the actual world as if through a gap opened by its differentiation, deviation, from another given compossible. By this light, it becomes by association much more clear that what is at stake for Serres is the genesis of the material world itself, rather than its deviation from simplicity into complexity, from atoms in the void to turbulence. Serres' presentation of the argument is often explicitly orientated to stipulating the structural analogies between Lucretius' paradigm and that of Leibniz: 'Things', he says, 'are drawn into existence along the steepest route'. Like Lucretius' atoms in the void, actualising phenomena are subject to maximal fall, or in less Lucretian terms, to the maximum unfolding of their potential, which may be chemical, electromagnetic or indeed gravitational, given local conditions. Serres takes pains to make explicit the same insight regarding Lucretius' world as does Bergson for his mechanistic order:

> Without declination, there are only the laws of destiny, that is to say the chains of order. The new is born of the old; the new is just the repetition of the old. (BP, 133)

> Repetition is redundancy. And identity is death. Everything falls to zero: the null point of information, the emptiness of knowledge, non-existence. *The Same is Non-Being.* (BP, 134)

Once more, space, 'Being', 'arises' through a counter-principle to this 'nullity', the *clinamen*. Serres' equation ('The Same is Non-Being') refers first and foremost to the stasis or equilibrium of atoms in the void, but may easily be mistaken for a quotation from Deleuze's work. As we have seen, Deleuze adopts the Nietzschean line that the world, had it ever attained stasis, self-sameness, equilibrium, would thereby blink out of existence. We have also examined the difficulties this presents for any orientation to physics. Yet finally we might conclude (on behalf of all our thinkers, Nietzsche, Bergson, Deleuze and Serres alike), that it is not existence as such which is at stake with mechanistic equilibrium, but the Event. In Deleuzian terms, the Event would indeed cease at equilibrium. The positive inverse, that Being is essentially the Becoming of differentiation, the difference that precedes identity (Serres' 'nullity'), is the central message of Deleuze's philosophy of difference. We should not fail to note, what is more, that for Serres just as much as for Deleuze, what is in play here is the idea of reciprocal determination; 'the stream is its own dyke, the river its own wharves'.

GAME #3.0: DELEUZE'S IDEAL GAME

As does Serres, Deleuze mobilises the ancient thought of Lucretius in characterising the play of chance, necessity and complexity. There is an accompanying suspicion at the heart of each of these authors about the opposition between order and disorder, and a desire to cast the paradigm of physical action in terms of immanence and its close correlate, reciprocal determination. These themes intermingle once again in Deleuze's own analogy of the Game as physical action, in ways that both differ interestingly from Serres' account and remain somewhat obscure unless we bear in mind the place of Lucretius in his argument.

To begin, we should note that it is by no means the case that *De rerum natura* has been read uniformly as a treatise for a world of novelty and contingency against determinism; indeed opinion has been historically divided between the two understandings.[42] Most closely to home, no less an influence on Deleuze than Bergson plainly presents Lucretius as a pessimistic fatalist and determinist:

> Thus on every page of the poem and in a thousand varied aspects, we rediscover the same idea, that of the fixity of the laws of nature. This idea, which obsesses the poet, saddens him; it explains his melancholy, melancholy of a completely new kind, and which finds in itself, so to speak, something of its own consolation. Unable to find in the universe anything other than forces which combine or compensate each other, persuaded that all that exists results naturally, inevitably from that which came before, Lucretius takes pity on humankind.[43]

Indeed, it is clear from Bergson's phrasing in this commentary on *De rerum natura*, his first published work, that Lucretius will come to represent exactly that spirit which he wishes to reproach in science, its redundant combinatorial and mechanistic framing of the world: 'everywhere forces which combine or compensate each other, causes and effects which couple mechanically ... laws of nature, fateful laws, force these elements to combine and separate; and these combinations, these separations, are strictly and for all time determined'.[44] Moreover, in a letter to William James of 1908, Bergson complains retrospectively of being completely steeped in mechanistic theories arising from his reading of Herbert Spencer during this period.[45]

What is it in Lucretius' text that Deleuze finds so at odds with Bergson's reading, and how does it feed into the radical contingency he places at the heart of the Ideal Game? In fact, as we shall see, his conclusions are more in the service of Bergsonism than otherwise. To draw them out requires a kind of Cortázarian hopscotch through *The Logic of Sense*.

The first hop places us in the chapter 'Tenth Series of the Ideal Game', where Deleuze contrasts his conception of the Ideal Game to that of the more rule-orientated mundane games with which we are familiar; the Ideal Game is one in which both the pieces and the rules themselves are in constant variation. We immediately find an apparent bar to the interpretation of Deleuze's Ideal Game as an analogy for physical action; this is Deleuze's assertion that the Ideal Game can only be thought. The implication seems to be that his version is not intended to be mistaken for a paradigm for physical action: 'The ideal game of which we speak cannot be played by either man or God. It can only be thought as nonsense' (LS, 60). This alignment with Thought is confirmed repeatedly in quick succession:

> But for precisely this reason, it is the reality of thought itself and the unconscious of pure thought ... If one tries to play the game other than in thought, nothing happens; and if one tries to produce a result other than the work of art, nothing is produced. (LS, 60)

There is a *prima facie* meaning to this assertion, with the attendant implication that 'life' is the real 'game' or 'work of art' in question; in this first sense, the analogy of the game of life that Deleuze is offering us here is one that adds its own connotations to a fairly common trope in moral philosophy and, from a reverse perspective, in the theory and practice of art: that life is a form of *poesis* which is best embraced or affirmed along with its own contingencies, this approach positively setting the individual free from delusions of control which stifle potential creativity, sweeping away habits inculcated by a positivist (Western) history. Equally in this sense, we are at the Nietzschean end of the Deleuzian spectrum, in the realm of *amor fati*. Art movements and individual artists have shown overt sympathies with and manifestly incorporated this message into their own practice: the Dadaists and Surrealists with respect to unruly unconscious impulses; Jackson Pollock and the Action Painters who sought to subtract as far as possible all but accident and contingency from their making. Art approaches life in relinquishing the classical verities of mastery over, and preconceived outcomes through, the materials and techniques of a given discipline (e.g. painting), while life may learn from art its own vital connection to the accident and the open. Perhaps the quintessential exemplar of the work of art suggested through this reading would be the performance piece by Alexander Calder in collaboration with Earle Brown entitled *Chef d'orchestre*, premiered in Paris in 1967, in which a custom-made 'mobile' (the form for which Calder was famous) was to serve as an instrument for a small team of percussion musicians. The rubric for the performance was that as far as possible the random movements of the mobile itself were to invite or suggest percussive acts from the players, ramifying along with the movements of the instrument themselves generated by those acts; the 'score' resembled more than anything a Mondrian rectangular composition whose elements recede from each other in water, having bled all colour and favouring no direction of reading. The players were instructed to interpret this score from the intuitive closeness of the instrument's configuration to any given (diagrammatic) aspect thereof; they were discouraged from driving the movement of the mobile to conform to the score.[46]

In many ways, this piece captures the essential structuration of Deleuze's Ideal Game, in that no two performances would ever resemble each other or could be rerun in the same way; the rules themselves mutate as the piece unfolds, and contingency is allowed to dominate, rather than being left to peek between the trammels in a note bent or a paintbrush flourished.

Yet while this is entirely within the import of the analogy of the Ideal Game, I would argue that it *is* first and foremost an analogy of action in the physical world, prior to life-as-poesis, to thought. Deleuze's caveats point us to the next hop: 'But precisely for this reason, it is the *reality* of thought itself ...' (LS, 60, emphasis added), and later in the 'tenth series', 'The Aion is the ideal player of the game; it is an infused and ramified chance' (LS, 64). Unless we were to take these as rhetorical flourishes, rather than statements intended to elaborate the characteristics of this paradoxical game, it becomes rather more difficult to locate the Game as such within the finitude of thought or the work of art, even in the most allusive reading, for the Aion is a form of time indifferent to the costless permutations of the imagination. The key is in the connection of this tenth series with the appendix to *The Logic of Sense* entitled 'The Simulacrum and Ancient Philosophy', and the link therein with Lucretius' text and the nature of time and contingency.

Aligned, then, to the virtual time of the Aion, which it is so much the work of *The Logic of Sense* to establish as the time of the event, this 'thought' of the Game is more than it seems. In fact, as we shall see, it is to be read more in the vein of a 'thinking God', much as elsewhere we encounter a 'reading God' (*The Fold*) or a 'calculating God' (*Difference and Repetition*), where, as in these cases, what we are being offered is (also) a figure of physical action. What is at stake both in the appendix and in the discussion of the time of Aion is the infinite divisibility of time, which serves to explain the immunity of the Event from actualisation in states of affairs; the Event, by dint of this infinite divisibility, is always either just about to arrive or just having taken place.

What are the features then, which distinguish this Game, and how do they tie in to the appendix on Lucretius? Deleuze sets out four descriptors which serve to distinguish his concept from our usual notion of games, of which the first two are relatively brief:

> 1) There are no pre-existing rules, each move invents its own rules; it bears upon its own rule. 2) Far from dividing and apportioning chance in a really distinct number of throws, all throws affirm chance and endlessly ramify it in each throw. (LS, 59)

Here we might note both the shape of the Nietzschean will to power, the dice throw with its power of constant creation, and a concomitant distinction between the 'chance' of the Game and more domesticated forms of probability. The phrasing ('apportioning chance in a really distinct number of throws') suggests Deleuze has in mind the classic Bayesian formalisation of probability, which proceeds by enumerating the entire range of outcomes, each with a salient weighting; in the case where each outcome is equally likely (say, fair dice), the probability of each is represented by the fraction in which the numerator is unity (1), and the denominator the number of possible outcomes (in the case of fair dice, 1/6). This being the case, it is clear that one important feature of the chance that Deleuze is valorising here (against Bayesian formalisation) is that it may not be subsumed under unity, since the mutating rules of the Ideal Game refuse a determinable, identifiable range of outcomes; checkmate, for instance, may be achieved only by adhering to pre-existing stipulations, yet the Ideal Game is explicitly open-ended in terms of outcome. Construed in terms of physical causality or expression, in the site of the Ideal Game, the cosmos, events are not totalisable, the world is 'open', though this is in another sense than the one typically adopted in the register of thermodynamics, where an 'open' system is one through which external sources of energy are free to flow.[47] We might also interpret 'each move invents its own rules; it bears upon its own rule' as foregrounding one aspect of *stochastic* probability. Stochastic probability, applied to series, is often characterised as 'non-repeating'; this form of chance is assignable in the case that the series involved is sensitive from one ordinal place n to the next, $n + 1$, to the content of what has gone before (e.g., the previous choice of ball from a lottery draw will remove that value from subsequent selection, though this is a particularly straightforward example); each selection 'bears upon' the previous history of the series. Nevertheless, Deleuze's phrasing suggests a singular form of stochastic chance for this singular game: each move *invents* its own rules; it *bears upon* its own rule, rather than merely the content of the series. In this sense, the Ideal Game represents a kind of chance that is definitively non-repeating, positively in constant variation. Far from undermining the second principle in Deleuze's philosophy of difference, repetition, we are presented here with a model of that which conforms neatly to and illuminates his insistence that that which repeats, repeats *as* difference.

The third and fourth rules are lengthy, but of most interest here is the presence in both of the idea of a minimum division of time; rule 3 asserts: 'Each throw is itself a series, but in a time much smaller than the minimum of continuous, thinkable time; and to this serial minimum, a distribution of singularities corresponds' (LS, 59). While rule 4 elucidates the relation of 'thought' to this minimum division: 'Each thought forms a series in a time which is smaller than the minimum of consciously thinkable continuous time' (LS, 60). In the context of this argument, then, the contrast of the Ideal Game to more familiar versions serves to contrast the linear time of Chronos, associated with those more familiar games, to the non-linear form of Aion, in which all remains constantly yet to be or just having occurred by dint of the infinite divisibility of time: 'let us understand that each event in the Aion is smaller than the smallest subdivision of Chronos' (LS, 63–4).

It is this relation between the time of thought and the time of the event, and the relation of these time-signatures to chance, which is also in play in the appendix with respect to the Lucretian text. The task announced in this appendix is (once again) the 'overturning of Platonism', for which the Lucretian simulacrum is recruited as a figure of absolute contingency, with respect to specific features of the *clinamen*. For Lucretius, the swerve of the *clinamen* occurs in an 'unassignable' time, more swiftly than the speed of thought (*intervallo minimo*). The chance occurrence of the *clinamen*, then, is unassignable (Deleuze insists on 'unassignable' for the Latin *incertus*, rather than 'undetermined') due to its speed relative to the cognitive and perceptual faculties; the event is transcendental, the contingencies of the physical world noumenal in this sense. This in its turn accounts at this level for both the non-totalisable nature of the Ideal Game and the distinction between 'domestic' chance (Bayesian) and the radical contingency belonging to the *clinamen*: 'the clinamen manifests neither contingency nor indetermination. It manifests something entirely different, the *lex atomi*, that is, the irreducible plurality of causes or of causal series, and the impossibility of bringing causes together in a whole' (LS, 270). And here we may join the strands bearing on the Ideal Game together, serving to clarify the implicit role of the transcendental in the above: 'The atom is that which must be thought, and that which can only be thought' (LS, 268). The formulation here, that which must and can only be thought, is fashioned to refer to the transcendental condition; Deleuze adopts it as a kind of shorthand for the orientation of thought to the transcendental, and it is especially prevalent in his book on Bacon, *Francis Bacon: The Logic of Sensation*.[48] If the Ideal Game exists only in thought, far from consigning its status to the realms of the imagination or 'mere' cognition, it is a matter of the relative speed of thought and atomic-scale action; a transcendental barrier to thought which, nevertheless, claims Deleuze, places the physical action and the thought on the same continuum, due to the infinite divisibility of thought (time) and percept (space):

> The Epicurean method is a method of passage or transition: guided by an analogy, and, as the sensible is composed and decomposed, we go from the sensible to the thought and from the thought to the sensible by means of transitions. We go from the noetic to the sensible analogue, and conversely, through a series of steps conceived and established according to a process of exhaustion. (LS, 268)

Here, 'exhaustion' is a reference to that Greek geometric precursor to the 'sum toward a limit' of calculus, entailing infinite divisibility. Given the above, Deleuze's line of reasoning represents a dense act of synthesis between the thought of the Stoics, Kant and Lucretius, and moreover allows us to see that this reading of *De rerum natura*, far from distancing his position from Bergson, re-inscribes an essentially Bergsonian insight, acknowledged in Deleuze's Bergson monograph: 'What, in fact, is a sensation? It is the operation of contracting trillions of vibrations onto a receptive surface. Quality emerges from this, quality that is nothing other than contracted quantity' (B, 74). The language is a direct echo of Bergson's phrasing in *Creative Evolution*.[49] At this point we can return with fresh perspective to the nature of the Game as 'thought' and 'work of art', to recognise that what is essentially at stake is the multiple time-signatures of the world which for Bergson serve to disabuse the philosopher of a simple notion of simultaneous co-existence; to recognise that all the immediate givens are in fact always already synthetic contractions of the relative speeds of the material world, apprehensible not so much through percept but through intuition. Deleuze glosses as follows: 'Intuition is not duration itself. Intuition is rather the movement by which we make use of our own duration to affirm and immediately recognize the existence of other durations, above or below us' (B, 33). It is precisely the mismatch between the minimum interval of thought and the minimum interval of physical action which serves to place Lucretius in contact with Deleuze's Bergson. Consequently for both there is no sense in which our action in the world may be adequate to the present circumstances, no sense that our purpose, intention or goal may have any bite in the temporal regimes of the subatomic; for this we would have to be Maxwell's demon. Nor is the point any less salient on the scale of geological tectonic movement. Yet if there is any true co-existence, it is the co-existence of these time-scales as such. The contingencies of the world are 'above and below' us at once, just about to happen and having already happened. It is for this reason that Deleuze is motivated to describe the domestic versions of games as 'partial', in that 'they retain chance only at certain points, leaving the remainder to the mechanical development of consequences or to skill, understood as the art of causality' (LS, 59). In contrast, the Ideal Game lacks any such external punctuation to the expression of chance; how could our own action be anything other than a game or result in anything other than a work of art, when the conditions to which we are responding are both behind us and yet to happen in the time of the event? Just as the player in the middle of a game of chess, just as the artist intuitively divining the direction of the work in progress, we are obliged to intuit the long-term tendencies beneath each particular stochastic branching, and in the Ideal Game this obligation remains without distribution into punctuated occasions (our 'turn'), without a juncture at which the operation of chance freezes before the next cast of the dice, the next taking up of the brush; it remains an absolute condition of process itself, unslowed down, unretarded. In our relation to the physical action of the world, we are in the position of Calder's musicians, able only to intervene in chance, to respond to those intuited (and transcendentally empirical) convergences of the contingent conditions with the schema before us, to wait until the mobile configures in a way that offers correspondence to our own unfolding; finally, rather, it is only in being stretched in tension, folded between these multiple durations, that our own subjectivity, our own opportunity for intervention, emerges. The pre-eminent character of the event for Deleuze is a reciprocal determination, a resonance between co-existent time-signatures. From this perspective, we can see more clearly the problems in identifying the Deleuzian event with the bifurcations of chaos theory; it cannot help but be continuous, since the tension between time-signatures never once ceases. A full account of the reciprocal influence of past, present and future would require a fulsome treatment of the three syntheses of time in *Difference and Repetition*, but this would occupy more space than we have.[50] In the next chapter, we shall rather pursue further the implications of the principles of retardation and delay with respect to the idea of complexity, but it remains first to revisit the opening problematic of this chapter.

The contrastive strategy of the argument presented here brings into perspective some interrelated conclusions. Deleuze's Ideal Game, his assertion of a certain radical contingency, can be differentiated from the (for Kant) dizzying prospect of a world of singular instances, of rules or laws for which each slightest event is the sole instantiation; the game board of Deleuze's world rather consists in constant variation, each move bears upon its own rule. Just as with Serres' networks, the novelty of the world as a whole consists in the immediate recasting, redistribution, of its singularities attendant on each move; the network is a new network, the game a new game, but with a consistency borrowed from the passage of nature. In short it is variation which lends consistency. This is one way to understand the seemingly paradoxical assertion that each throw of the dice bears both on its own outcome and the whole of chance at once. And it is only through acknowledging the operations of reciprocal determination that we can appreciate this character of physical action.

Bearing in mind that Kant presented his singular instance/singular rule scenario in the end to refute it (and that Deleuze explicitly embraces Kant's reasoning on this point, if not with respect to 'affinity of the manifold' as such, at least we could say in the name of 'consistency in the chaosmos'), it is worth reflecting how the strategies played out here bear upon speculative discourse in the field of cosmology. It is not uncommon for physicists considering frameworks of physical law to conjecture on counterfactual universes – those in which the observed regularities of this universe are 'run' with slightly altered values, say altered atomic weights (e.g., the proton-electron mass ratio) or relative strengths of forces. The object of the exercise is of course to explore the potential for such universes to evolve, and to consider in what way these salient differences may affect that evolution, thereby hopefully illuminating the character of our own physical law. In this respect, Kant's singular instance/singular rule scenario may be seen as a kind of limit case of this speculative thinking, for not all scenarios turn out to promise the longevity and robustness of this our observed cosmos. Quite the reverse: the apparent fragility under change of the set of physical values pertaining to this universe is a feature routinely commented upon; the given specific values of the constitutive elements of our world are often demonstrated to serve as a precondition for any possibility of evolution toward order; speculative variation of the relative strength of gravity offers upper and lower thresholds beyond which nucleosynthesis (the formation of elements in energetic solar processes) proves impossible, since either gases remain too dissolute to coalesce into stars at weaker assigned values for gravity, or for stronger values, the Big Bang fails to impart sufficient momentum to prevent a kind of stillborn recollapse into a Big Crunch. This is a well-established narrative in cosmology, which is referred to formally as the 'fine-tuning' or 'Goldilocks' problem ('not too hot and not too cold').[51] From this perspective, there are intriguing parallels between Kant's singular event/ singular law scenario and the welter of minimally viable worlds countenanced by the cosmologists' counterfactual worlds scenarios; among them, in principle, there must be an overwhelming number whose overall calibrations allow for no more than a singular event. Nor is this 'in principle' a wholly unwarranted imputation; one quantum rationale for the Big Bang countenances a pre-Bang scenario in which the energy inherent in vacuum gives rise, at uncertain times, in uncertain places, to random, fleeting conversions of the energy to mass and instantaneous reconversion to energy; this is the so-called 'quantum foam'. It is only, so the argument goes, under certain precipitating conditions that this conversion assumes, by a kind of massive chain reaction, the overwhelming creative power of the Big Bang; for the most part, the emergence of matter would remain vanishingly fleeting, a singular event, a proto-universe. Equally, string theory has become notorious for the sheer profligacy of its mathematically 'allowable' worlds, running in some estimates to the astonishingly large number of 10^{500}, with a corresponding range of 'viability'. Finally, for the terms of this argument, it may plausibly make no substantive difference that Kant's scenario is intended to represent a manifold, a kind of all-at-onceness of the disparate singular events, in apparent contrast to the stillborn speculative proto-universes of physics; in the absence of 'affinity', there is definitive causal disconnect among the events of this world. In a sense which conjoins both with the Leibnizian relational understanding of space and time pursued here, and with its relativistic, even quantum descendants, Kant's chaotic manifold would strictly speaking represent as many disparate universes, lacking even any topologically derivable metric furnished by Riemannian mathematics. In this sense, there could be no real meaning to the 'all-at-onceness' of such an entity, the manifold, nor indeed any meaningful way in which the singular events could be said to occupy the same location or space. Many physicists are willing to countenance 'causal disconnect' as a sufficient condition for separate universes, including in some cases those regions of our own cosmos which are merely beyond the light cone of our own region (these will be causally disconnected in a relativistic framework by the constant of the speed of light, c, which rules out in principle any physical influence between regions further away from each other in distance than could be traversed by light in the time since the beginning of the universe; as such it is considered plausible that their evolution may have proceeded in a way that need not resemble ours). Martin Rees, an advocate of the 'multiverse', is one such: 'From a reluctance to deny that galaxies with redshift 10 are proper objects of scientific enquiry, you are led towards taking quite seriously quite separate spacetimes, perhaps governed by quite different laws.'[52] These considerations hopefully serve to throw into stark relief the ramifications of the different orientations of Kant and Deleuze with respect to chaos. For Kant, chaos is there at the end of a road of subtraction, of increasingly pulverised necessity, there where no repetition is possible in principle, for there are no laws to govern it. The way out is deduced from within our own finitude; to the extent that our own cognition is coherent enough to detect pattern, we must be the product of conditions that allow for such coherence, there must be affinity among phenomena. For Deleuze, it is not law which serves to explain repetition, but repetition which serves to constitute law. Each move bears upon its own rule.

We can now return to shed light on the problematic raised at the start of this chapter: What status to apply to the Bergsonian/Deleuzian disavowal of disorder, transcendental or empirical? And how, if at all, may this problematic be orientated to any possible scientific project? Consider the epistemological position of a theorist proposing a mechanism for the genesis of the universe. It has never once been lost on the scientific community that any such model cannot in any straightforward sense be tested empirically. Even should our ability to examine the earliest states extend (unexpectedly) beyond certain formidable barriers, allowing us to 'witness', say, a quantum fluctuation followed by a Big Bang, there is no empirical purchase on such a singular event.[53] For that we need to observe the creation of more than one universe. If we proceed on the assumption that everything (even the Big Bang) is subject to law, we are irredeemably in the position of attempting to identify which among the laws we impute to our own universe could serve as the condition for any possible universe. If we think rather in terms of conditions, the transcendental point of view, in the case of both Kant and Deleuze, reminds us that the condition may not resemble in the slightest that which it conditions. The point of contention rests further on, in the formulation arising from the Ideal Game; for Deleuze, we should not seek the laws, the necessities which labour invisibly beneath the phenomena, but the repetitions which serve to constitute the law (and work to undo it). And what is that but to experience, to observe, to follow the traces of the folding and unfolding processes around us? In this sense, the transcendental and the empirical are intertwined for the philosophy of difference. And as much could be said for the cosmologist, who is just as surely conscious that assertions about the state of the universe are accompanied without exception by questions about conditions for the multiverse. Deleuze's chaosmos serves not so much to render these questions perennial, here and now, as to foreground that it was ever thus.

4. *Order as Complexity*

There are a number of points in *Difference and Repetition* which serve to confirm that Deleuze is working with the notion of retardation in its fully Bergsonian sense. It is referenced in allusive fashion, for instance, in a discussion of what he calls 'centres of envelopment' – a term referring to those systems or sets of systems which reach a threshold or a coupling that serves to sustain a relatively enduring meta/stability. He highlights a dual aspect of such processes:

> At the moment when they are explicated in a system (once and for all) the differential, intensive or individuating factors testify to their persistence in implication, and to eternal return as the truth of that implication. Mute witnesses to degradation and death, the centres of envelopment are also the dark precursors of eternal return. (DR, 256)

Set, as it is, closely following a discussion of entropy, this dual aspect of 'degradation' and 'dark precursor' corresponds in detail to Bergson's distinction between entropic, mechanistic order and the open, vital order, entwined as tendencies within or between any given system(s). Death (equilibrium) as mechanistic condition is always immediate, a collapse, 'once and for all', yet forever deferred, retarded by the persistence of 'implication', the continuous intertwining of series.

Paradoxically, it is precisely this most Bergsonian duality which provides Deleuze once again with the impetus by which he departs from Bergson's text, folding, as it were, Bergson back against himself. In the insistence on the ontological priority of 'intensive' over 'qualitative' relations, Deleuze pronounces the Bergsonian critique of intensity 'unconvincing'.

Deleuze's departure from the Bergsonian schema is part and parcel of his motivation to provide a genetic account of becoming which evades any residue of hylomorphism, of form or essence imposed on an inert material substrate. As Deleuze makes clear, for him it is not enough that Bergson's 'differences in kind', or 'qualitative differences' are contrasted to 'quantitative differences', in the terms through which Bergson presents this contrast. For Bergson, qualitative differences cannot augment or develop without changing in nature, while quantitative differences remain in static relation to each other. Bergsonian 'quality' nevertheless retains too much of the flavour of essentialism to furnish the basis for continuous variation which Deleuze would locate as the root of all change.

> Let us take seriously the famous question: is there a difference in kind, or of degree, between differences of degree and differences in kind? Neither. Difference is a matter of degree only within the extensity in which it is explicated; it is a matter of kind only with regard to the quality which covers it within that extensity. Between the two are all the degrees of difference – beneath the two lies the entire nature of difference – in other words, the intensive. (DR, 239)

It is only in the process of *explication*, then, that quality is expressed. For Deleuze, it is this very expression which cancels out the operation of the intensive, masking under its own movement the more profound movement of intensity. Thus qualities may be perceived in extension, but intensities remain transcendental. And Deleuze is fully aware that these paired terms, difference of degree and difference in kind, are synonymous for Bergson respectively with mechanism and the vital, and quantity and quality. All these correspondences are at stake; Deleuze is effectively claiming that these differences, so important for Bergson, are epiphenomenal on the underlying intensity which produces them all, but only on condition of cancelling itself out in explication. There are two striking aspects of this departure from Bergson which should be noted, however.

The first is that the terms in which Deleuze performs this breach bear the very same rationale set out by Bergson himself, serving to relocate the analysis as a whole at a level of differential process below that of quality, rather than to disturb the philosophical machinery as such:

> in the passage from one quality to another, even where there is a maximum of resemblance or continuity, there are phenomena of delay ['*décalage*', 'time-lag'] and plateau, shocks of difference, distances, a whole play of conjunctions and disjunctions, a whole depth which forms a graduated scale rather than a properly qualitative duration. Finally, if intensity were not there to attend to, support and relay quality, what would the duration attributed to quality be but a race to the grave, what time would it have other than the time necessary for the annihilation of difference in the corresponding extensity, or the time necessary for the uniformisation of qualities themselves? (DR, 238)

This passage in effect re-allocates the function of retardation to intensity rather than to quality, or difference in kind. It is *intensity* which resists the entropic 'race to the grave' of Bergsonian mechanistic order, intensity which retards, rather than, as Bergson would have it, the vital. This shift is significant; indeed, for our present line of reasoning, decisive. As we shall see, it goes hand in hand with questions of 'locality' and 'non-locality' in post-relativistic physics.

The second striking aspect of this departure from Bergson – especially from this, the most astute of his commentators – is that it may plausibly be said to carry force only by dint of a blind spot in Deleuze's reading here. A blind spot the more notable since lacking elsewhere. Deleuze's stated object of attack is Bergson's critique of intensity. This is almost certainly a reference to the first chapter of *Time and Free Will*, with its reflection on the work of what Bergson calls the 'psychophysicists', among whom the chief target is Fechner. Bergson takes issue with intensity in the sense that Fechner's work entails the idea of *magnitudes of intensity* as the basis for analysing changes in affect and percept. Bergson counterposes his notion of quality as free of this quantitative approach. As Christian Kerslake points out in *Immanence and the Vertigo of Philosophy*, it can be argued that the root of Bergson's argument here is entirely a resistance to the use of the term 'magnitude' understood by analogy to extensive/quantitative relations. The oxymoron 'intensive quantity' conveys precisely the mistake in misrecognising one form of order (the qualitative/vital) for another (the quantitative/mechanistic) which Bergson will lay at the feet of scientific method in *Creative Evolution*. It is a contradiction in terms, and hence, as Kerslake has it, Bergson 'is in effect using the notion of an intensive relation to argue against what he calls "intensity"'.[1]

Deleuze's blind spot here has something of a wilful character, then, when we recognise that elsewhere he fully appreciates Bergson's allusions to intensive processes, and indeed their underwriting of qualitative phenomena; he cites Bergson on the dependence of the perception of qualities on 'trillions of vibrations', for instance, in *Bergsonism*.[2]

This marking of the hermeneutic scorecard points beyond simple scholarly monomania, however, since it serves to foreground the real site of contention for Deleuze's departure from Bergson. It is not, as professed, the relative priority of 'intensity' over 'quality'; the real schism lies elsewhere, and moreover marks a significant future line of travel for Deleuze. There is indeed a deep subterranean shift taking place, which we might now see rather as a Deleuzian commitment to implications from within the Bergsonian schema which Bergson himself did not fully countenance. If, as Deleuze insists, differences in kind (quality) and differences in extensity, or degree (quantity), are both produced by the movement and explication of intensity, what place does this leave for the mechanistic order *tout court*? We have seen that Deleuze displaces the retardative function to the level of intensity ('phenomena of delay and plateau'). This is certainly the first import of the assertion here, but a closer reading reveals more. Where Bergson held *mechanism* culpable for entropic degradation, this charge is broadened out by Deleuze's twist, in a kind of reciprocal default, to include Bergson's 'quality'. And in effect, this renders the mechanistic and vital orders equivalent in this explanatory framework. Both are harbingers of the grave. And, according to the dual correspondence we have been upholding between the vital as complexity and the mechanistic as entropy, we must expect any subsequent development in Deleuze's thought to reflect this foreshortening. We should be alert to the recalibrations in the relations between complexity and entropy. To follow this thread first entails a discussion of the second term at stake here: delay. Some care must be taken to distinguish between the concept of 'retardation', with its Bergsonian particularities, and the concept of 'delay'. Both of these concepts recur in Deleuze's writing, though he does not go so far as to topicalise either term as such, or confer on either the weight of a technical term within his own philosophy of difference.

Jay Lampert, whose work has astutely foregrounded the concept of 'delay' in philosophy, tracing the thematic issue from the Greeks through Husserl, not least highlighting its importance in understanding the Deleuzian event, draws our attention to a passage in Hume's *A Treatise of Human Nature*. It so closely resembles the Bergsonian analysis of mechanism as to offer the neatest possible parsing between retardation and delay:

> Now if any cause may be perfectly co-temporary with its effect, 'tis certain ... that they must all of them be so ... The consequence of this wou'd be no less than the destruction of that succession of causes, which we observe in the world; and indeed, the utter annihilation of time. For if one cause were co-temporary with its effect, and this effect with its effect, and so on, 'tis plain there wou'd be no such thing as succession, and all objects must be co-existent.[3]

Lampert glosses the implications on Hume's behalf: 'One might almost say that a delay is one of the causes in the causal series.'[4] And so much is true too for Bergsonian retardation, we would conclude. Yet, in the absence of the counter-principles of 'life' and 'complexity', we may choose to reserve the term 'retardation' to account for the causal character of physical action. This serves as an initial distinction. Therefore, although the two concepts 'retardation' and 'delay' seem to be motivated by the same intuition, yet the explanatory corollaries may be very different indeed, allowing us to parse the two moments of this thought as it develops in Deleuze's work.

Lampert's treatment characterises the term delay far more thoroughly than this initial default distinction. He develops the concept in counterpoint to the (often fraught in both science and philosophy) concept of simultaneity:

> In its simplest form, simultaneity consists of two or more events at one time, and delay consists of one event at two or more times. By varying the formal relations between the unity and multiplicity of events, and the unity and multiplicity of time, we might deduce forms of simultaneity and delay.[5]

In the concluding chapter of *Simultaneity and Delay*, Lampert systematically parses the possible formal relations, furnishing eight possible combinations in all, from 'one event in one time' to the disjunctive relation 'one *or* two events in one *or* two times'. With respect to what is most germane to the philosophy of Deleuze, Lampert emphasises the simultaneous co-existence of his three syntheses of present, past and future. This simultaneity is of course more than the common-sense conception of states-of-affairs occurring at a punctum – Lampert treats in detail the numerous sources in philosophy and contemporary science which problematise this picture; the co-existence of the three syntheses, he claims, serves to make explicit what is already implicit in Bergson, that simultaneity does not serve to halt the flow of time: 'it is precisely', he says, 'simultaneity that constitutes flow'. In other words, simultaneity is best conceived as a syncopated oscillation between multiple time-signatures, which may operate over significant, potentially infinite distances of Chronic, linear time. Lampert emphasises that this is due, for Deleuze, to a 'model of delayed reaction', so to speak, a theory of delay. He is referring here to the nature of the Deleuzian event, which is never exhausted in any here and now, but retains the potential to re-emerge in combination with continuously varying series in the passage of nature:

> it is not that there exist two events separated in time, the potentials in the earlier event getting resolved in the later, or the later reacting to the earlier. Instead, there is one event occurring at two distant moments in time at once.[6]

We are dealing not with succession as such when we talk of the Deleuzian temporality of the event; indeed, in all that we are offered in the three syntheses of *Difference and Repetition* and with respect to the nature of Aionic time in *The Logic of Sense*, events are to be seen as intimately imbricated in connected series both forward and back in linear time. It is Lampert's nuanced construal of the three syntheses in terms of simultaneity and delay which is of most interest here, helping to open up the distinction between 'delay' and 'retardation':

> in its multiplicity, simultaneity is delayed. If we live our lives at different temporal levels at the same time in different ways, each moment of life has its lived time at many times later than the time it is formed. The very structure of simultaneity is delay.[7]

Let us articulate the contrast. Firstly, for both Bergson and Deleuze after him, *retardation* is identified with those factors in the passage of nature which resist the onward, downward encroachment of entropy. And for both, the attainment of equilibrium achieved on a cosmic scale would produce not merely a moribund state of inactivity, but the cessation of existence as such. What retardation retards, so to speak, is the 'degradation' of available free energy for systems, in the direction of equilibrium or disorder. It is 'life' or complexity which performs this retarding function; the tendency of nature to envelop material processes in higher order, stable or metastable structures.

This resistance in the circuits of the world is not nearly so evident with respect to the concept of delay. Rather, delay as such serves to characterise the identity-as-difference of events through their own internal rhythms, the syncopation of multiple time-signatures. This is every bit as much a form of complexity, no doubt, but one which is directly predicated on a temporal rather than a material enfolding. Retardation of necessity endures the weight, the friction and the braking effect (as Serres would have it) of explication; it belongs to locality, it furnishes the world with location. Delay belongs to non-locality.

The idea of retardation, clearly identifiable within Deleuze's own philosophy of difference up to the time of *Difference and Repetition*, undergoes a subtle, implicit, rather than openly topicalised, transformation in later work. This *implicit* character of the change is a result of this concept's subordinate role in relation to the more *explicitly* thematised developments Deleuze performs on Time (which will come increasingly to be viewed as a multiplicity of relative speeds) and 'Life' (which comes increasingly to be viewed as transcending the organism, and indeed the organic as such). In the shifting triangulation between these major developing features of the Deleuzian landscape, 'retardation' undergoes its own silent translations, which bear on the interrelations between entropy and complexity. By the time of *A Thousand Plateaus*, retardation has been obscured by delay. With respect to the first theme, Time, references to relative speeds abound in this work, governing the means by which such concepts as 'stratification' are characterised – a tendency which persists in *What Is Philosophy?*, where 'relative speed' becomes the question of the various orientations of the arts, science and philosophy to the infinite speeds of chaos.

With respect to the second theme, Life, there is an unmistakeable expansion of its role in the later work, a direction marked by the foregrounding of the concept of in- or an- organic life in *A Thousand Plateaus*. Indeed, if the final known short piece by Deleuze, 'Immanence: A Life' can be considered summative, life ultimately comes to characterise the entire domain of the virtual and the immanent as such.[8] If the assertions of *A Thousand Plateaus* leave room in their phrasing for a domain outside of life, a something beyond inorganic life, that corner is painted over by this last work.

This brings us to the key set of questions for this line of enquiry: What room is there left in Deleuze's line of travel for Bergson's 'inert matter' and 'mechanism', even as a never-fully realised ideal? If all nature is increasingly marshalled under one emblem of order alone, 'Life', the complex, then it appears there is nothing (in Bergsonian terms) for this order to push against, no entropy to retard. Equally, if the vectors of time are without direction, as we are led to conclude by the end of the third synthesis in *Difference and Repetition*, if 'the very structure of simultaneity is delay', if the dimensions of present, past and future are governed more by the logic of their own defining forms of synthesis than succession as such, then in what direction could 'degradation' be said to occur? These questions are of course different viewpoints on the same paradox: the arrow of time is commonly understood to be synonymous with the increase in entropy ostensibly displayed by the universe as a whole. And the reader of Deleuze is left in no doubt as to his standpoint on both aspects: entropy is a transcendental illusion, applicable in principle only on the level of the actual, never to the virtual. The arrow of time is merely the stamped imposition of 'good sense' in search of ordered causality in the labyrinth of a paradoxical, recursive nature, a need for the general (indifferentiation) to emerge out of the particular (differentiation), for equilibrium to replace disparity. As such, all these correspondences contribute to Deleuze's *critique* of representation, not to his positive position.

A first step on the way to working these questions through is to note that, in the dramatisations of *A Thousand Plateaus*, by far the most prevalent characterisation of time is not with reference to the three syntheses as such, but to relative speed and slowness. It is by no means the case that the kind of resistance in the circuits of nature to the death represented by equilibrium has disappeared from the discussion; on the contrary, *A Thousand Plateaus* is bristling with figures of sedimentation, of stratification, along with the counter-principles of de-stratification, lines of flight, epistrata. Striated space is counterposed against smooth. It is merely that these structurations and destructurations are subordinate to the interrelations of relative speeds. 'Speed and slowness, movement and rest, tardiness and rapidity subordinate not only the forms of structure, but also the types of development' (ATP, 255). There is a notable shift of emphasis, more of an insistence that it is *only* relative speeds which constitute the underlying condition of the world.

> In any case, there is a pure plane of immanence, univocality, composition, upon which everything is given, upon which unformed elements and materials dance that are distinguished from one another only by their speed and that enter into this or that individuated assemblage depending on their connections, their relations of movement. A fixed plane of life upon which everything stirs, slows down or accelerates. (ATP, 255)

What motivates this change of emphasis with respect to time? And to what extent does it parallel the shift from 'retardation' to 'delay'? I would argue that the intuitions and formulations of *Difference and Repetition* have paid forward, so to speak; the language, the imagery, of entropy, of the 'race to the grave', was already explicitly problematised in the text of *Difference and Repetition*. Entropy as such (as opposed to thermodynamic concepts) was consigned to the status of a transcendental illusion. At the end of the working through of the three syntheses, however, we have definitively arrived at a new scenario; if 'the very structure of simultaneity is delay', if the three syntheses co-exist, then there is no obvious direction of time in which 'degradation' may be said to occur. Strictly speaking, series can be spoken of in terms of relative speeds, but not relative direction; Alice may get bigger 'at the same time' as she becomes smaller; there is no sense in saying that forward orientating series may interact with backward orientating series; all are both at the same time. Which is as much as to say that there is no direction to the arrow of time. In this light, the phrasing which reflects this is the language of relative speed.[9]

This is another way to say that the scientist looking to derive the arrow of time as a function of entropic processes can at most labour under an illusion. In addition, any customary attempt to characterise the vector of time in the direction of the descent from order to disorder is effectively ruled out of court; again, this is highlighted in interesting ways in terms of the mutation from the regime of 'retardation' to the regime of 'delay', but this time best unpacked with respect to the development of the second major theme, that of 'Life'. It can serve only as a surface reading to equate Bergson's 'vital' with Deleuze's conception of Life. The difference is again decisive.

As is well known, the centres of envelopment of most interest in *A Thousand Plateaus* are organisms; as in a sense they are in *Difference and Repetition*, but more provisionally now, still 'mute witnesses to degradation and death' while remaining now more, now less, open to the plane of immanence, to the body without organs. But let us follow the thread once again; for the regime of retardation, it is life, the vital, the complex, which serves to slow the fiat of mechanism, the race to the grave. It is not that order in the Bergsonian schema is under the threat of being devoured by disorder; on the contrary, the mechanistic and the vital are two antagonistic forms of order; there is no such thing as disorder; order is opposed to, intertwined with, complexity. But the order that is opposed to complexity is the order of entropy, of inert matter, of equilibrium; so to speak, too much order all at once.

And so too, we find this sense of 'too much order all at once' in the dramatisations of *A Thousand Plateaus*. The will to the body without organs is the will to maintain the maximum number of open connections to the plane of immanence, to productive difference; this is one definition of complexity, not dissimilar to the notion of 'self-organisation' in chaos and complexity theory. Yet Deleuze and Guattari also acknowledge that for an organism (indeed, a centre of envelopment more generally) to become more complex is for it to 'interiorise', enfold, increasing numbers of productive differences. The tension between the organism and the body without organs arises when this interiorisation goes too far, when there is too much order all at once: 'The BwO howls: "They've made me an organism! They've wrongfully folded me! They've stolen my body!"' (ATP, 159). Yet now this thanatic howl of the enfolded organism, the enclosed system, is tempered by the existence of anorganic life:

> What movement, what impulse, sweeps us outside the strata (metastrata)? Of course, there is no reason to think that all matter is confined to the physicochemical strata. There exists a submolecular, unformed Matter. Similarly, not all Life is confined to the organic strata; rather, the organism is *that which life sets against itself in order to limit itself*, and there is a life all the more intense, all the more powerful, for being anorganic. (ATP, 503, emphasis added)

Finally, it is *this* formulation which comes to seem inevitable retrospectively: 'that which life sets against itself in order to limit itself'.

In the departure from the Bergsonian schema, what perhaps comes to constitute its real meaning is not so much the shift from 'quality' to 'intensity' as the elision of inert matter, the equilibrial, the entropic mechanism. And if we read 'complexity' there where Deleuze writes 'life', then these triangulations of life and temporality, retardation and delay, seem inevitably to lead us to this substitution of one formula for another; no longer the antagonism of order versus complexity, of the mechanistic versus the vital, but life, the vital, versus *itself*, which is as much as to say, the complex versus the complex.

The foregoing reading of the philosophy of difference has served to foreground features of Deleuze's philosophy which are largely unaddressed in the literature and which deserve both attention and consolidation. Most significantly, there are three interrelated conclusions which bear at once on the remit of natural philosophy and of science: the first is that the line of development of Deleuze's thought increasingly rules out any, even ideal, role for inert matter; life (or complexity) is what limits itself, not inert, mechanistic matter; the second, potentially much more contentious, conclusion is that the philosophy of difference appears on this reading to entail a truncation of distinctions which have served natural philosophy and science indispensably; the demarcations between states of disorder, order and complexity are abolished in favour of one sole term, the complex. It should be said that this diagnosis, while drawn from central threads of the Deleuzian corpus, is subject to certain caveats; the argument runs only if we track the development of Deleuze's thoughts with respect to order and complexity against the genesis and development of more explicit and developed themes. Indeed, there are points in the Deleuzian text where he implicitly acknowledges such a useful formal distinction; he speaks of complexity remaining evident within the operation of (simplifying) differen*ci*ation; elsewhere he defines the complexity of an organism in terms of the number of connections it maintains with the body without organs.[10] In this sense, the question of order and complexity pursued in this thesis is one which dwells in the folds and pleats of the Deleuzian fabric, not on the surface. Nevertheless, the implication that complexity is the sole *modus operandi* of nature, if taken in any strong sense, is in danger of removing considerable conceptual traction on the passage of nature; the perhaps almost ubiquitous understanding of the development of the world is predicated on an evolution from simple to more complex forms of being; this tendency has been dubbed 'the arrow of complexity', in that it is taken to confer a direction of time, an index that is most often, though not uniquely, understood to be correlated with the thermodynamic arrow of entropy. Given these (and other) entailments, it may well be that to forego these distinctions of form would be at best unpalatable and at worst nonsensical for those who wish to conceptualise natural processes.

Finally, the third foregrounded aspect: Deleuze's orientation toward the notions of limit and constant. Once again, this is an aspect which enjoys its own subtleties and displays apparent contradictions at different junctures of the Deleuzian corpus. We have touched upon one side of this question with respect to Deleuze's resistance to the reliance of scientific method on constants as such; this is certainly so in *Difference and Repetition*, and is revisited in *What Is Philosophy?* We are left in little doubt that the constants and limits in question refer to those purporting to determine the scope of nature's possible unfolding: absolute zero, the speed of light, etc. And once again, this may represent a stumbling block for many wishing to explore the productive application of Deleuzian philosophy to scientific frameworks. Yet it would be mistaken to interpret Deleuze's resistance to limits and constants as a simple denial of their existence. Indeed, we encounter passages which assign them a productive place, as in *What Is Philosophy?* 'Every limit is illusory and every determination is negation, if determination is not in an immediate relation with the undetermined' (WP, 120). Indeed, 'limiting' may be seen to have a necessary role in the multivalent processes of different/ciation for Deleuze; to claim that 'life is what limits itself' is to offer an answer to the question of how series get caught up in centres of envelopment in the first place. The phrasing of the quotation above from *What Is Philosophy?*, however, indicates a resolution to the apparent contradiction here; it is *negation* which is rejected, rather than limitation as such; the phrasing marks an enduring commitment to Bergson: 'We see, therefore, how all the critical aspects of Bergsonian philosophy are part of a single theme: a critique of the negative of limitation, of the negative of opposition, of general ideas' (B, 47). But what is the positive form of limitation which seems to be implied here?

There are ways in which these potential objections may be addressed, to align them with respect to conceptual developments in modern physics, and to outline the productive role the philosophy of difference may occupy with respect to that ongoing development. Certain figures in the philosophy of science whose work bears a notable affinity to Deleuze's own will be invaluable in this respect: Alfred North Whitehead, David Bohm and Lee Smolin.

In terms of aligning the philosophy of difference with physics after the quantum revolution, the first implication we have voiced through Deleuze is surely the most easily supported: the claim that inert matter does not exist. Indeed, there is no place for it; the very notion is problematised in any number of ways. Young's famous wave/particle duality effectively forces explanation in terms of interference patterns, even in those cases where the experimental set up imposes a 'particle-like' scrutiny, and this even in cases where it is a single particle under consideration. This is a paradox routinely noted in most introductions to quantum physics – that the wave-like nature of particles dictates that their wave-fronts are capable of producing interference *with themselves*. Since the beginning of the quantum age, it has been implausible to represent the action of particles in the manner of statistical mechanics, which deals effectively with the atomic scale as though it were essentially composed of tiny objects, each with its own momentum and speed which remain unchanged until some physical collision with another particle. As Young's slit experiment demonstrates, even single particles are in complex, resonating relations to their associated field. Richard Feynman's formulation of quantum electrodynamics problematises the notion of a 'bare charge' for the particles associated with electromagnetic phenomena, the photon, electron and positron. The bare charge is to be understood as a basic or least energy state. However, due to the continual fleeting production of 'virtual particles' around an electron – a kind of cloud of positively and negatively charged particles of vanishingly fleeting existence associated with the ambient field, pushing and pulling the central particle according to charge – this bare charge is understood to be definitively cloaked. The value is nevertheless derived through a calculation referred to as 'renormalisation', which amounts to a cancellation of infinities. Roger Penrose comments: 'Another point of view is to regard the *bare* charge as being no more than a conceptual convenience, and to take the standpoint that the notion of "bare charge" is actually "meaningless", because it is "unobservable".'[11] However interpreted, the bare charge, understood as the value in effect in absence of interaction with other charges, is far from thereby unproblematically inert. More generally, the energy state of any particle is theoretically derivable only in reference to its 'ground state', its state of least possible activity. This in turn, however, can only be derived by subtracting the energy inherent in its ambient field, entailing another cancellation of infinities. In a Deleuzian register, the construal of quantum particles as enduring patterns of associated fields serves to write disparity into the account at the most fundamental level; all particles are in constant energetic tension with their fields. There is no such thing as inert matter.

A more challenging question is the one relating to the 'arrow of complexity' mentioned above. Taken at root, Deleuze's resistance to the idea of the heat death of the universe goes hand in hand with the associated idea that the universe as a whole must be capable of maintaining a steady measure of order, some distance from the disorder of equilibrium. This seems at first to be supported by the scientific account; complexity seems to be increasing as time goes on, from undifferentiated plasma states shortly following the Big Bang, to structured galaxies, clusters of galaxies and even 'megastructures' occupying significant proportions of the observable cosmos. Biological evolution has evolved from proto-cellular systems to sophisticated trillion-celled organisms. Given this history it seems the arrow of complexity should be able to constitute a kind of arrow of time; we could judge without knowing in advance whether such and such a cosmological state of affairs were earlier or later by some agreed measure of complexity (however hard-won that agreement might be). Most accounts, however, recognise that the development of increasingly complex conditions up to this point in the history of the world is no necessary indicator to the projected overall arc over the lifetime of the universe. The received view is that such accounts should be compatible with acceptance of the second law. For most, the arrow of complexity is expected to describe an arc, peaking somewhere around the midpoint of the cosmic lifetime and declining steadily toward the end, as free energy is depleted.[12] There are dissenting accounts, however, notable among them being that of the complexity theorist Stuart Kauffman. He argues that the arrow of complexity could potentially rise indefinitely, as a function of the 'adjacent possible'. The 'adjacent possible' is that set of chemical products which are attainable given present conditions, but never yet actualised. The potential range and diversity of the universe might, he conjectures, rise indefinitely as a kind of force multiplier:

> As the diversity of molecular species increases, there are always proportionally more novel reactions into the adjacent possible. If we take the formation of a chemical species which has never existed in the biosphere, or perhaps the universe, as a breaking symmetry, then the more such symmetries are broken, the more ways come into existence by which yet further symmetries may be broken.[13]

In other words, complexity begets complexity. Kauffman recognises that this proposition contradicts the second law, but points to the dependence of that law on the essentially ergodic character of nature, and seeks to demonstrate that this does not apply to our universe. This is a significant standpoint in the context of the present argument, since we have identified a certain incongruence inherent in Deleuze's adoption of the argument from eternal return with respect to the ergodic hypothesis and its attendant principle of indifference. Having noted that chaos theory essentially renders untenable the principle of indifferentiation as utilised in classical thermodynamics (due to the tendency of particles to resonate in tandem under certain conditions, rather than indifferently to bounce off one another), we encounter here the stronger proposition that ergodicity itself is implausible. Kauffman's argument is predicated on two observations. The first is that the level of complexity of organic molecular species within our biosphere has 'exploded' over the course of the earth's history, from the modest tens or hundreds of varieties, including methane, cyanide, etc., to some hundreds of trillions if we include the diversity of genetic expression. The biosphere has expanded exponentially (far from indifferently) into its adjacent possible. The second observation is that the realm of the adjacent possible into which increasingly more complex molecular species could expand is vastly greater than those already realised. According to Kauffman's calculations: 'It would take the known universe, chunking along on the Planck timescale, 10^{39} times its current lifetime to make all proteins of length 200.'[14] Nor are proteins of length 200 the upper bound of known forms of protein; the exponent rises accordingly for greater lengths. The conclusion is twofold: The universe is 'vastly nonergodic, vastly nonequilibrium at the level of complex organic molecules'. And 'the total system "wants" to flow into the adjacent possible'. The two are interrelated. For Kauffman, the relationship between the actual and the adjacent possible is one of substrate to product; it is merely that the molecular species of the product has never yet occurred. As such, there is a displacement from the equilibrium conditions all systems seek (an overabundance of substrate components in proportion to product): 'The simple conclusion is that there is a real chemical potential from the actual to the adjacent possible.'[15] The picture we arrive at is that of a 'sink', akin to the thermodynamic sense of a body which draws heat from the neighbouring body. The adjacent possible in effect provides a gradient down which the actual is inclined to flow. The substrate components will always outnumber the product, if not actually then adjacently; a situation which places the world out of equilibrium. The gradient will not resolve unless the 'total system' flows into the adjacent possible, yet that very expansion will in itself open up a new adjacent possible, deferring equilibrium to one remove in an ever-expanding 'workspace'. Complexity begets complexity.[16] It seems in light of the foregoing that to subscribe to the philosophy of difference inclines us to those paradigms which do not rest on or presume the ergodic hypothesis.

COMPLEXITY AS PRINCIPLE

The overall question remains whether the implication we have drawn – that order has no name but complexity – serves to place Deleuze's philosophy beyond any productive orientation to physics.

The quantum theorist and philosopher of science David Bohm resists the notion of disorder in the twin works *Science, Order and Creativity* and *Wholeness and the Implicate Order*. As we shall see, this resistance entails a novel conception of order and complexity bearing striking similarities to Deleuze's own. Bohm calls this form of order 'generative'. It is best understood in contrast to another conception of order commonly found in scientific theory, which I shall collectively refer to as 'indexical'. Though Bohm (and by extension Deleuze) favours the former, his work offers examples of both, and will serve to establish the contrast:

> The question of the meaning of chance, randomness and disorder has been a particular headache, not only in science, but also in mathematics and philosophy. But here it is proposed that whatever happens must take place in some order so that the notion of a 'total lack of order' has no real meaning. Indeed, even what are called random events do happen to take place in a definable and describable sequence and can be easily distinguished from other random events. In this elementary sense they obviously have an order.[17]

The particularities of the route serve to date and place the journey, to index the phenomenon; a fact which in itself, in an 'elementary' sense, rescues nature from disorder. This is precisely the Borgesian character's journey through the library which we have considered and found wanting before; a merely indexical form of order which is nevertheless prevalent in the scientific literature. Not infrequently we find a more formalised definition of this indexical form of order in play in the work of probability theorists. Algorithmic information content is a concept derived from the work of probability theorist Andrei Kolmogorov, in collaboration with Gregory Chaitin and Ray Solomonoff. It is based on the principle that the complexity of a system or set may be indexed by the length of a description required to express it in binary code on a designated operating system. A system or set displaying true randomness will be adequately described only by a bit string containing as many digits as the elements of that phenomenon, while those displaying regularities will require shorter output. DNA sequences may be taken as a case in point, containing a readily identifiable and short set of basic elements, the amino acids, but arranged in repeating combinative patterns capable of expressing the production of proteins. Any repetition in the set of amino acids allows for compression of the descriptive algorithm, and hence reduction of the information content. Thus, the presence of structures periodically occurring along the length of the strand which 'instruct' the DNA how and when to replicate, such as 'introns' and 'outrons', will allow further economy of expression.[18] Algorithmic information content, like all equivalent definitions of order, is not designed to convey any sense of the evolution of a system, the order of its ongoing structuration. In this sense, indexical forms of order are external, while evolutionary or generative forms of order are internal.

A distinct yet related notion was adopted by the physicists Murray Gell-Mann and Seth Lloyd, going by the name 'effective complexity', again predicated on the length of an adequate description of the phenomenon.[19] This latter idea accommodates potentially more subtle structurations (or schemata, as Gell-Mann has it), but significantly for our purposes, Gell-Mann acknowledges a qualitative difference between *internal* and *external* effective complexity; a schema is said to be 'internal' when the schema somehow governs the system under discussion, as when the key to a coded text allows the cryptographer to generate its meaning directly, as opposed to 'externally' indexing potentially significant patterns ('cracking' the code). Indeed, both Gell-Mann and Bohm conclude that any real explanatory power belongs with the internal, rather than the external principle; Gell-Mann ultimately identifies complexity with adaptation in the sphere of life (the 'complex adaptive system' as such, he acknowledges, transcends description purely in terms of schemata) and self-organisation, while Bohm coins and valorises the term which I have adopted here, 'generative order'. Before investigating generative order more fully, it is worthwhile to note that in terms of the ambition of Gell-Mann to describe nature as a whole, this valorising of an internal principle reflects a caution over the notion of laws of nature, considered as immutable, pre-set conditions governing the world. Gell-Mann adheres to a *physis* which is itself in a sense adaptive, conjecturing that what we have traditionally taken for immutable laws may be rather the (relatively durable) results of 'frozen accidents', embracing the idea that structural features such as the left- and right-handedness of molecules may contingently arise in particular parts of the universe for particular intervals only:

> The tree-like structure of branching histories involves a game of chance at every branching. Any individual coarse-grained history consists of a particular outcome of those games. As each history continues through time, it registers increasing numbers of such chance outcomes. But some of those outcomes become frozen as rules for the future, at least for some portion of the universe.[20]

As such, this form of order has much in common with Deleuze's positive sense of limit or constant as 'deployment' rather than negation, as we shall see.

For his part, Bohm's valorisation of the internal, generative form of order, in itself elides any simple distinction between order and disorder, between the simple and the complex. He offers a treatment of order understood as the play between 'different similarities' and 'similar differences'. This is illustrated by the example of the construction of a geometric curve, which may initially be thought of as the repetition of a given line segment augmenting a straight line, the beginning of each segment coterminous with the end of the last added and so forth, each a different similarity. A simple line gets longer by the same amount each time. The difference between one segment and another has only one dimension in this case, that of spatial displacement, which due to its one-dimensionality Bohm names a difference of *first class*. A *second class* difference pertains when the reiterated function or generator contains two separate aspects, as when the line segments are added to each other as before, but this time with a designated angle introduced between the current line segment and the last. Such a procedure, given the invariance of the adopted angle, would ultimately produce a rough circle. For a two-dimensional spiral, orders of third class and above would be required, since both the angle and the length of the line segment would have to be varied by some ratio or other, bearing similarly different relations to each other. Clearly, the generation of lines occupying three dimensions acquires its own further classes of order.

> As the degrees become indefinitely high, we are able to describe what have commonly been called 'random' curves – such as those encountered in Brownian motion ... In this way, we are led to make an important change in the general language of description. We no longer use the term 'disorder', but instead we distinguish between different degrees of order.[21]

This is one fashion, then, in which the distinction between the simple and the complex can be understood as at best secondary and perhaps illusory when viewed through the lens of generative order; from this point of view, complexity is not qualitatively distinct from, does not supervene on, the simple.[22] The distinction between indexical and generative complexity is a significant one, nor is it any less significant that both Gell-Mann and Bohm considered forms of generative order more fruitful. Gell-Mann's example of grammar and Bohm's example of the functions governing the addition of line segments both amount to acknowledging the superior epistemic value of the *instructions* for propagation, the code for self-replication. Indeed we might find an equivalent predilection on the part of most other scientific theorists: Prigogine's valorisation of auto-catalytic reactions in cycles, cycles in which products from the last phase generate the chemical capacity for the next, is one concrete example whereby the flag of order has been planted further into the territory of the non-linear, the chaotic, where the last step in the evolution of a system informs or instructs the next. Nor should this be intrinsically surprising; it is effectively the difference between applying the code for decrypting phenomena and the brute observation of pattern. It may take a decryption programme some time to identify the irrational number in question with only the number-string of its expansion to go on, in comparison to the moments it would take to perform that same expansion given a specified irrational as a starting point. This on the face of it amounts to no more than common sense, yet at the same time it must be said that behind every scientific decision in favour of generative explanations lies a disposition to understand the world in terms of process, of evolution, rather than static structure or pattern. So much is true of the Bergsonian-Deleuzian disposition toward explanation in terms of the temporal rather than the spatial, and equally of Whitehead's emphasis on process and evolution.

Deleuze himself references the idea of evolution as the focus of the investigations of *Difference and Repetition*, not merely in the section devoted to biological evolution, but as a paradigm for the passage of nature as a whole, inorganic processes included. This is in context of his rejection of an account of the world by resemblance, identity, representation, in favour of a repetition which escapes law. He speaks of the need to distinguish two different types of causality with respect to repetition: 'one which concerns only the overall, abstract effect, and the other which concerns the acting cause'. He proceeds to characterise this difference in terms reminiscent of those set out in the discussion of Gell-Mann and Bohm above:

> One is a static repetition, the other is dynamic. One results from the work, but the other is like the 'evolution' of a bodily movement. One refers back to a single concept, which leaves only an external difference between the ordinary instances of a figure; the other is the repetition of an internal difference which it incorporates in each of its moments, and carries from one distinctive point to another. (DR, 20)

We have then, a distinction as above between internal and external difference, couched in terms of evolution, and, tellingly, illustrated by a difference between types of geometrical figure which directly recalls Bohm's own example of the spiral:

> A distinction is drawn between arithmetic symmetry, which refers back to a scale of whole or fractional coefficients, and geometric symmetry, based upon proportions of irrational ratios; a static symmetry which is cubic or hexagonal, and a dynamic symmetry which is pentagonal and appears in a spiral line or in a geometrically progressing pulsation – in short, in a living and mortal 'evolution'. (DR, 20)

LIMITS WITHOUT NEGATION

What is of most interest for the argument developed here is that this concept of evolution is the key to the positive form of 'limitation' for Deleuze; he goes on to develop this connection in the first chapter of *Difference and Repetition*:

> There is a hierarchy which measures beings according to their limits, and according to their degree of proximity or distance from a principle. But there is also a hierarchy which considers things and beings from the point of view of power: it is not a question of considering absolute degrees of power, but only of knowing whether a being eventually 'leaps over' or transcends its limits in going to the limit of what it can do, whatever its degree. 'To the limit', it will be argued, still presupposes a limit. Here limit [*peras*] no longer refers to what maintains the thing under a law, nor to what delimits or separates it from other things. On the contrary, it refers to that on the basis of which it is deployed and deploys all its power. (DR, 37)

'Power' here is something akin to an internal principle of evolution, understood not as the power to arrive at an end state, but a principle which will persevere beyond the provisional constraints pertinent to a given system; a power of mutation. Deleuze is alluding to the positive sense of limitation which the philosophy of difference requires: 'deployment'. It is in this sense we can see something akin to Gell-Mann's 'frozen accidents'. All systems require some constraint or set of constraints, some 'limits' without which no process, no deployment, is possible, but these constraints are themselves subject to evolution. Evolution, repetition, variation, we may summarise, escape the law, the limit and the constant; 'a perseveration is still not a repetition. The constants of one law are in turn variables of a more general law, just as the hardest rocks become soft and fluid matter on the geological scale of millions of years' (DR, 2). These elements in the passage of nature all require limits, but limits which escape the negative, which do not depend on opposition. Laws and constants are not barriers as such, but more like a fulcrum, enabling traction, a precondition for the deployment of power. And once a heavy block is moved, the fulcrum is redeployed to shift it further. These are, as Whitehead would have it, 'decisions'.

Limits are first and foremost a matter of explication, of unfolding. For both Deleuze and Whitehead, explication, the decision, never achieves full determination; what is explicated retains its implication in the ceaseless enfolding of things, each decision carries with it future prehension. Moreover, for both, explication is a precondition for anything at all to occur, for events to actualise, to concresce, into states of affairs, to take (or rather, make) their place among the heres and nows, the local and the global tableau. And for neither can it ever be a simple matter that events simply 'latch' on to the time and the place that invites them, like a seed planted in a waiting field; for each the event is immanently bound up with the manifestation of the very fabric of space and time in which it occurs; there is no pre-existing field, just as for modern physics, the *energetic* field is shaped by the particles associated with it, and particulate matter takes its form and *location* from that field.

We are now in a position to expand on the interconnected and parallel themes of explication and limit, spatial manifestation and cosmological evolution, in the work of Deleuze and Whitehead, with a view to foregrounding productive links with the phenomenon known as non-locality in the physics of the quantum age, and with the increasing prevalence of the evolutionary paradigm in cosmological models.

In both *Science and the Modern World* and *Process and Reality*, Whitehead presents his thought under the rubric of cosmology. It must immediately be conceded that the vocabulary, and indeed the terms of reference, in those works bear scant resemblance to the terminology to be found in reference books on the subject, yet Whitehead's explicit aim is to provide a metaphysics which is adequate to the emerging new quantum physics of the era. His intricate arguments in these works are at once heavily indebted to Leibniz, from whom he derives the important concept of 'prehension' for instance (he acknowledges the debt to Leibniz's 'appetition'), and placed in the service of cosmological speculation.

Whitehead addresses the topic of limits with respect to a deficiency he identifies in Spinoza's metaphysics: the concept of modes of a universal single substance. 'Thus as a further element in the metaphysical situation, there is required a principle of limitation. Some particular *how* is necessary, and some particularisation in the *what* of matter of fact is necessary.'[23] This link between limitation as a *principle* and explication as a matter of actualisation is unmistakeable in the following comment: 'The only alternative to this admission is to deny the reality of actual occasions.'[24] Limitation, actualisation and explication, then, circle round each other in Whitehead's account as they do for Deleuze. As Isabelle Stengers points out, Whitehead's position on this question at once reveals its key importance for his cosmology, and furnishes a final disagreement with Leibniz on the tenet of sufficient reason:

> This is indeed what Whitehead reproaches Leibniz: to have proclaimed that 'there is a reason for everything,' even the choice of God, who has access to the sole genuine reality, to the infinite conspiration of the universe with each state of the monad, or, reversibly, to each state of the monad as a standpoint

implying an entire universe. If Leibniz were right, the true meaning of our experiences would be unlimited, 'behind the scene,' and our choices would be mere appearances, with the divine choice of this world as their hidden reason. Decision must therefore be primordial, and our reasons must be relative to it.[25]

Here, 'decision of God' is synonymous with limitation, for decision is what abstracts, or prehends, both positively and negatively, from the 'envisagement' (might we hazard, for Deleuze, 'complication') of all possible values. Decision is what limits, and without limit there is no substantive actualisation. At the very least, with respect to the alignment of the Whiteheadian register with that of Deleuze, we might note that this limitation-explication shares on both sides a crucial aspect: the expression of disparity, and at a 'primordial' level; Whitehead requires a first disparity which entrains all others. The primordial dissymmetry is closely akin to the swerve of the *clinamen*, at a *non-assignable* time in a *non-assignable* place; there is no reason to it, though all reasons must be relative to it.[26] For all that Whitehead may be said finally to hold back from the principle of sufficient reason, he does so only at this deepest level of his cosmology, and, significantly, for the sake of reinforcing what are essentially the same cosmological intuitions found in Leibniz's work. The primacy of discernibility, the introduction of a limit discriminating 'this' from 'that', is the genetic root of disparity. Limitation works to break the symmetry of 'a general realm of systematic relationships':

> Restriction is the price of value. There cannot be value without antecedent standards of value, to discriminate the acceptance or rejection of what is before the envisaging mode of activity. Thus there is an antecedent limitation among values, introducing contraries, grades and oppositions.[27]

For Deleuze, this 'antecedent limitation' is what forces the move from intensive to extensive relations.[28] In a different register, Whitehead is serving here to embellish the question which troubled Deleuze and Guattari: how do centres of envelopment occur in the first place? Whitehead's answer is that there *is* no reason, due to the fact that primordial limitation is what escapes sufficient reason; it is what bestows reason. And to bestow reason is to introduce 'contraries, grades and oppositions'.

To make these correspondences is to consolidate the essentially Leibnizian shared cosmological intuition established earlier between Serres, Deleuze, Simondon, Lucretius et al.[29] It is also to foreground the connection between limitation and disparity; from the first explication-limitation, the world is dissymmetrical, assembled from fundamentally crooked timber. This is its specific form of sufficient reason. As I hope now to show, this shared intuition is not confined to our grand metaphysicians; it offers further correspondences between contemporary cosmology and theoretical science more generally. Moreover, I will contend that in this transdisciplinary sense, it is *because* the world is dissymmetrical that its central mode is to evolve; disparity and the evolutionary, generative paradigm go hand in hand.

5. Sufficient Reason as Dissymmetry and the Evolutionary Paradigm

Notwithstanding the practical success of reason from symmetry in the formulations of contemporary science, it is not uncommon to find scientific theoretical counterparts of the disposition toward this sufficient-reason-as-dissymmetry. We might go so far as to say that theoreticians are marked by their disposition toward either symmetry or dissymmetry. On the one hand, Einstein, whose theory of relativity might count as an extended argument from symmetry, and Weyl, for whom symmetry serves as the *a priori*; on the other, Dirac, for whom constants may be nothing more than a product of contingent initial conditions, potentially varying throughout the cosmos, and Smolin, for whom constants and laws adapt and evolve. For our purposes, these dispositions in their turn predispose to one of two particular forms of the principle of sufficient reason: as an argument from symmetry or from dissymmetry, as a principle of indifference or difference.

Anaximander's cosmological arguments served us earlier to illustrate the former; if there is complete symmetry in the world, there is insufficient reason for anything to happen. As I hope to have established, the Leibnizian variant of sufficient reason is opposed to this disposition toward symmetry; we might go so far as to say that sufficient-reason-as-dissymmetry rules out of court the use of the principle of insufficient reason in explaining natural processes, for the simple reason that there can be no final symmetry in nature. In the end, for any given scientist, faith in the symmetry of the world is perforce constrained by phenomena; when the practitioner of group theory, for example, divines the mathematical description of physical invariants from among the sophisticated symmetries of an evolving ensemble, this serves first and foremost to distinguish those invariants, those symmetries, from those that have broken. For, as A. Zee points out, nature, if it displayed perfect symmetry, would simply stall:

> Symmetry is beauty, and beauty is desirable. But if the design is perfectly symmetrical, then there would be only one interaction. The fundamental particles would all be identical and hence indistinguishable from one another, such a world is possible, but it would be very dull: there would be no atom, no star, no planet, no flower and no physicist.[1]

This is to say nothing more than that everything is ultimately discernible from everything else. It is also worth noting the striking parallel between Zee's tableau here and that proffered by Bergson. While for Bergson it is a surfeit of mechanism that stalls the world, for the modern philosopher of science, it is a surfeit of symmetry. In a very real sense, this is to some extent merely a shift of register, given the historical convergence of the notions of symmetry with invariance and laws of conservation, which underpin the concept of entropy, and by extension, Bergson's 'mechanism'. In both cases, the diagnosed result is a preclusion of complexity.

In a more distinctly logical vein, we might note an exchange between the astronomer physicist Joe Rosen and Charles Hartshorne. Hartshorne, without doubt the second most influential name belonging to the Process Philosophy movement initiated by Whitehead, devotes a chapter to debunk what he identifies as 'The Prejudice in Favour of Symmetry'.[2] He attacks the tendency of scientific reason to equate simplicity with symmetry, which he equates with the principle of indifference, or of insufficient reason. Hartshorne is in effect critiquing the remote spiritual inheritors of Anaximander. Two assertions in Hartshorne's chapter are closely related and serve further to illuminate our argument: 'Symmetry is in a sense a lack of order', and 'symmetry is a partial or abstract aspect of what, in its concrete wholeness, is an asymmetry'. Commenting on the first assertion, Rosen observes:

> Order is practically synonymous with distinguishability, discriminability, irregularity and heterogeneity. Indeed, symmetry is inversely related to order, distinguishability, discriminability, irregularity and heterogeneity ... Thus we have 'the more symmetry, the more regularity, and the closer to homogeneity'.[3]

For Rosen too, then, a world of perfect symmetry is an inert world. He proceeds to argue, elaborating on Hartshorne's assertions, that 'for change to be possible for a situation, there must be some aspect of the situation that is not immune to the proposed change and can serve as a standard for the change'.[4] Hence invariance or symmetry is necessarily accompanied by some variant or asymmetry. What is more, Rosen notes, asymmetry is prior, a condition in every case pertaining to the total situation; he takes the case of the rotational translation of an equilateral triangle; it is only the existence of spatial surroundings which ensures invariance under rotation through, say, 120°:

But if the equilateral triangle were a universe unto itself, there would be no standard for 120° rotation, so it would not be a possible change ... The existence of the symmetry depends on the existence, somewhere in the world, of a corresponding asymmetry.[5]

In all of this we can see both the operation of a Leibnizian style of reasoning and the motivating impulse behind Whitehead's assertion of the primordiality of a first 'decision' or 'limit' as a precondition for 'reason', and indeed sufficient reason.

The final supporting example for our sense of sufficient reason as dissymmetry is offered by the quantum cosmologist Lee Smolin, who belongs unquestionably and avowedly to the Leibnizian spirit delineated here. Throughout his work, Smolin pursues a critique of recent developments in theoretical physics through the explicit application of Leibnizian ideas. Once again, this critique entails a demurral from the convergence of 'law' with 'symmetry'. The adoption of the principle of sufficient reason, he argues, militates against any presumption of eternal, ubiquitous laws presiding over events in the world; under the presumption of a 'relational' world, on the contrary – by which he means that of Leibniz, Mach and Einstein – it is illegitimate to treat any element in nature as immune to reciprocal determination; laws, for Smolin (as they were for Peirce), are that 'par excellence' which demand an explanation, a reason. Smolin acknowledges the intricate association of the principle of sufficient reason with the principle of the identity of indiscernibles, and teases out its implication for modern science with respect to dependence on arguments from symmetry:

> Another consequence of the PSR [principle of sufficient reason] was stated by Leibniz as The Principle of the Identity of Indiscernibles (PII) ... there cannot be two distinct objects in the world with the same properties. This rules out symmetries in the sense of global symmetries, i.e., transformations which take a system between two physically distinct states which have the same values of all conserved quantities.[6]

And as for symmetries, so for laws:

> Our universe should not be seen as a vast collection of elementary events, each simple and identical to all the others, but the opposite, a vast set of elementary processes, no two of which are alike in all details. At this level fundamental principles may be discerned but there are no general laws in the usual sense.[7]

The critique enables Smolin to identify key components of the framework of physics which are in need of reconceptualisation, in line with our argument here for sufficient-reason-as-dissymmetry:

> For example, in reality, no physical system is translationally invariant because the universe is complex enough that each and every event has a

unique curvature tensor reflecting the influence of distant masses as well as gravitational waves, neither of which can be screened by any physically real material. Another example is the global symmetries of the standard model, which are only approximate when the effects of the fermion masses are ignored. To put it in slightly simpler terms, the proton is slightly lighter than the neutron.[8]

The examples Smolin offers here are somewhat more central to the scientific corpus than those generally acknowledged. The much-noted (for example by Feynman) asymmetry of beta-decay tends to figure in the literature as an interesting anomaly which does not in itself disturb the general faith in arguments from symmetry. In contrast, Smolin acknowledges that his argument serves to undermine the cornerstone work of Emmy Noether in the formalisation of the laws of conservation.[9]

This is a particularly significant standpoint for the present argument, since it was Noether who formalised every known and widely accepted conservation law, in line with the theorem named after her: 'Every symmetry corresponds to a conserved quantity.'[10]

The formulations are each expressed in mathematical notation, but are translatable into statements expressing equivalence or invariance. Spatial Invariance, for instance, equals conservation of momentum, while rotational invariance equals conservation of angular momentum. Dave Goldberg draws out the fundamental importance of Noether's work for the underpinnings of modern physics as a whole:

> Noether's Theorem describes much, much more. It describes and explains the conservation of spin, electrical charge, of 'color' (the equivalent of charge in the strong nuclear force), and on and on, ultimately providing the mathematical foundation for much of the standard model of particle physics.[11]

Noether's formalisations of conserved quantities (or constants) include the conservation of energy. The specific invariant underlying the conservation of energy is 'time'. Time invariance equals conservation of energy. Put slightly differently, this equivalence states that, *given* the invariance of the laws of physics over time, energy will be conserved. This at once serves as the preconditional first law of thermodynamics *and* precisely what is contested in evolutionary cosmological paradigms. Hence Smolin's position comes into contention with the first law of thermodynamics, and by extension the second law which depends on it. In these terms, then, Smolin's position lends some credence to Deleuze's own position with respect to entropic processes.

Another aspect of particular importance follows from Smolin's reasoning. In the absence of any true translational symmetry, he describes the world as 'a vast set of elementary processes, no two of which are alike in all details'. It is this last formulation of what we are calling sufficient-reason-as-dissymmetry with which both Deleuze and Whitehead share the most telling ground; the absolute singularity of the event for Deleuze is everywhere proclaimed as loudly in Whitehead's work. In all of the above, the central point of departure from arguments from symmetry relies on a more or less explicit recognition that Leibniz's principle of the identity of indiscernibles is inseparably dovetailed with the principle of sufficient reason. There is no reason under the sun which can rely on perfect symmetry.

Smolin's Leibnizian heuristic rather satisfyingly speaks to the arguments marshalled here, and hopefully embellishes the association of 'limit' (or constant, or law) with sufficient-reason-as-dissymmetry in closer dialogue with the discourse of science. Nevertheless it would be misrepresentative to claim that such broadside correspondences, much less any general suspicion of the universality of entropic processes, can unproblematically be assigned to all scientific thinkers who are disinclined to accept arguments from symmetry. Such a case in point is Roger Penrose, who expresses caution over the axiomatic use of arguments from symmetry.[12] The argument for his own 'Conformal Cyclic Cosmology', however, goes so far as to insist that the second law of thermodynamics should hold firm not only within the lifetime of one cosmos, but between the expiry of one cycle of the universe and the commencement of the next from its ashes.[13]

LIMITS AND NON-LOCALITY

If the correspondences between limits and dissymmetry allow us to identify a shared ground between the philosophy of difference and certain paradigms in scientific discourse, there is a second aspect to the nature and role of 'limits' as proposed by Whitehead which aligns his cosmology with Deleuze's own. It opens up further correspondences with contemporary physics. This aspect is encapsulated in the following quotation from *Science and the Modern World*:

> By 'limitation' as applied to the spatio-temporal continuum, I mean those matter-of-fact determinations – such as the three dimensions of space, and the four dimensions of the spatio-temporal continuum – which are inherent in the actual course of events, but which present themselves as arbitrary in respect to a more abstract possibility.[14]

It is clear from this assertion that Whitehead has in purview an 'abstract possibility', a virtual, which extends far beyond any simple extrapolation from the actual to the possible; indeed, as Deleuze would have it, this abstract possibility *as condition* is not constrained to resemble that which it conditions. The particular exemplar here – the contingent dimensionality of the spacetime continuum – is for Whitehead as arbitrary in the particulars of its expression (three dimensions of space, one of time) as it is for Deleuze, who speaks of a preconditional Depth whose dimensions remain undetermined prior to differen*c*iation, or explication (DR, 229–31). This is as much as to say that the parameters for expression proper to nature include a topology of n dimensions in the domain of the virtual which enjoys delimitation only through the process of explication, of decision, of limitation.

Deleuze closely echoes Whitehead's assertions with respect to spatio-temporal dimensionality in his discussion of the Idea in *Difference and Repetition*: 'An Idea is an n-dimensional, continuous defined multiplicity ... By dimensions, we mean the variables or coordinates upon which a phenomenon depends; by continuity, we mean the set of relations between changes in those variables' (DR, 128). On the face of it, we might take the word 'dimensions' in this quotation in a sense more related to the 'dimensions' of a state space as accommodated by the Hamiltonian or Lagrangian, with no necessary connection to spatio-temporal coordinates; indeed, the supporting example of colour values suggests as much. Deleuze goes on, however, to make clear that spatio-temporal dimensions *are* to be included as variables in the Idea:

> Such relations are precisely non-localisable ideal connections whether they characterise the multiplicity globally or proceed by the juxtaposition of neighbouring regions. In all cases the multiplicity is intrinsically defined, without external reference or recourse to a uniform space in which it would be submerged. Spatio-temporal relations no doubt retain multiplicity, but lose interiority. (DR, 183)

This elaboration serves to cast phenomena, Ideas, in the (acknowledged) stamp of Riemannian multiplicities, which are explicitly conceptualised as independent of any homogeneous embedding space. A key factor of Riemannian topology is that relationships between points are assumed in advance of any metric which may assign distance between them. Relations are understood independently of any pre-determined dimensional order which frames them, 'a system of multiple, non-localisable connections between differential elements which is incarnated in real relations and actual terms'.

This higher-order topology figures prevalently in the underpinning narratives of post-relativistic and post-quantum physics, whose most flamboyant expression remains string theory and its derivative hypotheses, M-theory or Brane-theory, but is no less in play whenever quantum theorists undertake to conceptualise non-locality.

It may be argued, for instance, that any *realist* interpretation of the wave-function, such as that of de Broglie or Bohm, implies perforce a commitment to spatial higher-order dimensionality.[15]

For Whitehead, some expression of the spatio-temporal continuum *must* be in play as a prerequisite for actualisation:

> Further, the status of all possibility in reference to actuality requires a reference to this spatio-temporal continuum. In any particular consideration of a possibility we may conceive this continuum to be transcendental. But in so far as there is any definite reference to actuality, the definite *how* of the transcendence of that spatio-temporal continuum is required. Thus primarily the spatio-temporal continuum is a locus of relational possibility, selected from the more general realm of systematic relationship.[16]

The implication that things may be (or may have been) otherwise than our three-dimensional spacetime, that other 'decisions' may have arisen, is explicitly embraced by Whitehead in *Modes of Thought*: 'Perhaps in the dim future mankind, if it then exists, will look back to the queer, contracted, three-dimensional universe from which the nobler, wider existence has emerged.'[17] In other words, the particular order of extension we are familiar with is, potentially, a contingent matter-of-fact, a *how*, pertaining to the particular cosmic epoch in which we find ourselves.

Whitehead's thinking on this point reflects an all-encompassing sense of the mutability of any and every element of nature. That the order of dimensions may change, along with the 'natural kinds' we encounter therein, is a consequence of the mutual interaction between those natural kinds and the regimes of organisation in which they are implicated, the constants and laws such as the speed of light and the conservation of angular momentum. Whitehead's coinage for natural kinds, 'societies', is tellingly chosen to reflect this character of mutability, of epochal nature:

> The laws of physics are the laws declaring how the entities mutually react among themselves. For physics these laws are arbitrary, because that science has abstracted from what the entities are in themselves. We have seen that this fact of what the entities are in themselves is liable to modification by their environments. Accordingly, the assumption that no modification of these laws is to be looked for in environments, which have any striking difference from the environments for which the laws have been observed to hold, is very unsafe. The physical entities may be modified in very essential ways, so far as these laws are concerned. It is even possible that they may be developed into individualities of more fundamental types, with wider embodiment of envisagement. Such envisagement might reach to the attainment of the posing of alternative values with exercise of choice lying outside the physical laws.[18]

What is at stake here, then, is a certain conception of 'limitation' and its corollary, 'openness', which is, I would argue, fully consonant with Deleuze's own metaphysics, the counting God and the Ideal Game. Each limit and each constant is susceptible to breach through the incremental modulation of nature itself; each 'problem' to be solved by nature in search of itself, *natura naturans*, is recast anew by the ensuing regime. It is at this point we can recognise the 'structurally schematic' notion of the Problem which Deleuze inherits from Lautman in operation at the cosmological scale; each solution which paradoxical nature proposes, each epoch and each regime, is structurally driven to supersede itself. There is a certain shared view of contingency, chance as the only necessity. These correspondences between the two thinkers, along with Whitehead's more explicit motivation toward a metaphysics adequate to the relativistic and quantum sciences of the day, allow us at once to foreground ways in which contemporary physics may be said to express similar paradigms, and to consolidate our picture of Deleuze's concept of the limit.

With respect to the first question, it is generally understood that the work of contemporary physics is to determine the particularities of the ubiquitous and continuous exchange between matter and energy. On this broadest characterisation, Deleuze's investigation of the relation between the extensive and the intensive stands full square on the same territory, though important caveats bar any simple identification between 'the intensive' and 'energy'. Rather, it is more apt to consider the intensive and the extensive as in effect two regimes of energy; the first characterised by continuous multiplicity, the second by discrete multiplicity. For Whitehead too, intensive relations assume priority over extensive.[19] More generally, it is important to note that, for both thinkers, the energy which is directly amenable to empirical observation necessarily displays an inherently adumbrated set of behaviours in comparison to the intensive, virtual realm. This represents for Deleuze the essential block to any direct empirical access to intensive phenomena as such:

> Nevertheless, we encounter severe difficulties when we attempt to consider Carnot's or Curie's principles as local manifestations of a transcendental principle. We know only forms of energy which are already localised and distributed in extensity, or extensities already qualified by forms of energy. (DR, 223)

Whitehead expresses essentially the same problematic in *Science and the Modern World*:

> But energy is merely the name for the quantitative aspect of a structure of happenings; in short, it depends on the notion of the functioning of an

organism. The question is, can we define an organism without reference to the concept of matter in simple location?[20]

Whitehead is using the term 'organism' in a rather specific sense here, one which does not refer solely to an organic living entity. In his terminology, an organism is simply any system or set of systems which embodies a somewhat stable, more or less coherent range of pattern or rhythm; chemical cycles would count as an example.[21] What is shared between the quotations from both thinkers is a conception of energy inclusive of, but distinct from, its instantiation in specific locations. Whitehead's critical term 'simple location' here makes reference to a line of argument he offers against classical physics in light of the revolution of relativity; to conceive of phenomena uniquely in terms of action between contiguous elements in the way we find in classical dynamics is to prolong the illusion that both micro- and macro-physics deal with forces exerted between spatially well-defined bodies, 'simply' located, an illusion he dubs 'the fallacy of misplaced concreteness'. This thread of argument in *Science and the Modern World* is orientated first and foremost to the problematisation of the notion of simultaneity in relativistic theory. The import behind the critical term 'simple location' may thus leave ambiguous whether Whitehead believes in a kind of 'distributed' event which acts without contiguous connection, but the phrasing in the shortly subsequent *Process and Reality* is both unequivocal and serves as a remarkably prescient intuition of issues in quantum physics that would arise as the source of a major controversy that is yet to be resolved:

> Provided that physical science maintains its denial of 'action at a distance,' the safer guess is that direct objectification is practically negligible except for contiguous occasions; but that this practical negligibility is a characteristic of the present epoch, without any metaphysical generality. (PR, 308)

For 'direct objectification', we may read 'contiguous causal influence' here, but only with respect to macroscopic phenomena in our own epoch; there may be others, Whitehead infers, in which direct objectification, causal influence, does not rely on contiguity. In terms of the history of modern physics, we might observe that Whitehead was writing at a time shortly after the Copenhagen Interpretation was being consolidated at the Solvay Conference in 1927; arguably, this could be said to be the point at which 'action at a distance' was instantiated as an implication of quantum theory, yet this was not foregrounded as problematic as such until almost a decade later, in 1935, in a series of papers Einstein was to write, precisely against 'action at a distance'. What is more prescient in retrospect is the key idea that such phenomena may be more or less prevalent in given epochs – an aspect that is echoed in certain recent theories, as we will see.

In terms of the history of philosophy, we should recognise that the fallacy to which Whitehead refers is in direct contention with David Hume's picture of causality, which placed spatial contiguity at the centre of what it was to be considered a cause.[22] The critical term 'misplaced concreteness' finds its counterpart in the positively employed term in quantum physics, 'non-locality' – a concept which contradicts Humean causality equally unambiguously. The term refers in the first instance to a phenomenon conjectured as an unavoidable inference from the tenets of quantum theory as it was being consolidated in the 1930s. The phenomenon in question is 'entanglement', understood to describe that circumstance where two (or more) particles are attuned to each other's states through interaction. Quantum principles entail that the wave collapse of one entangled particle, prompted by measurement thereof, will dictate a corresponding immediate collapse of its partner's wave (technically, they are the same thing), resulting in a directly correlated value with respect to the property investigated, say spin or polarisation. The paradox is that such a phenomenon must apply even in those circumstances where the particles in question are separated by distances which rule out communication within the constraint imposed by the speed of light; in other words, this implication of quantum theory is found to entail a contradiction of the fundamental principle of relativity theory that nothing (no causal influence) can travel faster than light.[23] The paper which raised this undesirable consequence was in fact published by Einstein, Podolsky and Rosen in 1935, with the intention of debunking those aspects of quantum theory which entailed such sacrilege, or at least to demonstrate that quantum physics must be incomplete. In fact, the undesirable consequence in question, which Einstein was famously to label 'spooky action at a distance', has been well verified in subsequent experiments, and was given conceptual credence independently of any given quantum framework by John Stewart Bell in 1964.[24] Bell's reasoning was based on the specific characteristics of the phenomenon referred to as 'spin' in the quantum formalisation, and the niceties of measurement of that 'property'. The word 'property' is in quotation marks here, since precisely what is at stake in Bell's proposed resolution of the disagreement between Einstein, Podolsky and Rosen (EPR) contra the quantum mechanical account is whether or not the phenomenon under investigation – spin – can be considered a property of the particles in question in the normal sense of that word. The argument we can draw from the EPR side was that if the measuring instrument came to show a reading for spin value (or any given measured aspect) for a particular particle – its rotation with respect to a particular chosen axis, along with an attendant direction, clockwise or counter-clockwise – then the particle in question must already have had that characteristic, that property. The quantum mechanical account, whose chief protagonist in this struggle over interpretation was Niels Bohr (he and Einstein had crossed swords many times over the issue before the EPR formulation), proposed rather that any given particle contains the potential for both measurable outcomes (spin-up and spin-down in this case), despite the fact that they are contradictory, right up until the moment when the measurement occurs. In this sense, it could not be said to possess determinate properties at all in the classical sense. This is equally true for all other aspects that physics tends to treat: location, speed and so on. In short, by the quantum mechanical model, what a particle is 'composed' of at the most fundamental level is a bundle of undetermined probabilities. It is the act of measurement itself which forces this wave of probabilities to collapse, thereby determining determined values for the aspect under investigation: spin, speed, direction, etc.

John Bell recognised that these competing interpretations could be investigated empirically and that it would be possible to distinguish between the two by dint of statistical disparities over many reiterations of an experimental run. Brian Greene specifies: 'Bell showed that if EPR were correct, the results found by two widely separated detectors measuring certain particle properties (spin about various randomly chosen axes ...) would have to agree more than fifty per cent of the time.'[25] By contrast, Bell reasoned, the quantum mechanical interpretation would produce 'agreement' (specific correlation) exactly fifty per cent of the time. That statistical inequality would be the hallmark of one interpretation or another.

In order to achieve the capacity for distinguishing between one framework and another, two devices for measuring spin around a chosen axis would have to be located at a significant enough distance to rule out communication between the particles – that is, at a great enough distance to exclude the possibility that one particle's interaction with its measuring device could be conveyed to the other as some means to effect the observed correlation between them. This for the purpose of being able to adjudicate over a fundamental principle at stake between the two camps. EPR were arguing that all interaction can take place only locally, in the sense that physically separate entities can affect each other only through intervening media (forces, fields), at a speed of propagation whose upper bound is that of light. Dual measurements conducted close enough to each other to allow for any such propagation would fail to establish the distinguishing criterion; the essential charge from the EPR side was that the interpretation of entanglement in terms of instantaneous collapse of the probability wave for each entangled particle entailed an absurdity which we could not countenance: non-local communication between distant entities. By rights of quantum principles, there was no such boundary to the distance over which particles may sustain entanglement. Therefore, in light of the observed correlation between entangled particles, EPR strongly disposes to the explanation that such a correlation is forged at the moment when the particles in question become entangled; the correlation is the result of a shared property which each particle now carries.

Unfortunately for the EPR argument, the experiments subsequently carried out by Alain Aspect in the early 1980s, observing the conditions for Bell's distinguishing criteria, served solidly to disconfirm the EPR interpretation and to back up the quantum theoretical framework: Aspect's work gave a firm return of fifty per cent correlation. Nevertheless, the correct interpretation of non-local action and its demonstration (or not) in the case of entanglement cannot be said to be finally settled. Reservations remain over whether the set-up itself of experiments may predispose outcomes (Aspect himself recognised this possibility, introducing rapidly switching orientations in the measuring devices so that the choice of axis for measurement was somewhat randomised). Novel interpretations include retro-causality, whereby it is proposed that the collapse of the wave for a partner of an entangled pair is understood to reset the correlation in the past, at point of entanglement. There remains the question of whether investigations of entanglement can be finally squared with relativity. And of course, as with all theories, the quantum mechanical account remains vulnerable to the discovery of some as-yet unrecognised or undemonstrated hidden variable. For now, however, it is an established mainstream view that any complete description of causality must be able to account for non-local action:

> Einstein, Podolsky and Rosen set out to show that quantum mechanics provides an incomplete description of the universe. Half a century later, theoretical insights and experimental results inspired by their work require us to turn their analysis on its head and conclude that the most basic, intuitively reasonable, classically sensible part of their reasoning is wrong: the universe is not local. The outcome of what you do at one place can be linked with what happens at another place, even if nothing travels between the two locations – even if there isn't time enough for anything to complete the journey between the two locations.[26]

Equally, for Deleuze, 'location' as such, the particular topological structuration of our observed spacetime, is contingent, a result of the particularities of the unfolding of intensive processes. This is the thread behind his concept of 'depth' in *Difference and Repetition*:

> Extensity can emerge from the depths only if depth is definable independently of extensity. The extensity whose genesis we are attempting to establish is extensive magnitude, the *extensum* or term of reference of all the *extensio*. The original depth, by contrast, is indeed space as a whole, but space as an intensive quantity: the pure *spatium*. (DR, 230)

As Deleuze goes on to make clear, it is only with the explication of extensity that it can make sense to talk in terms of direction, length, left or right, and most importantly of metric space. 'Location' does not have any simple meaning in the non-metric space of the virtual. Moreover, the differentiation between the concepts of 'the intensive' and 'energy', to all intents and purposes, rests on the distinction between location and non-locality:

> Only a particular form of empirical energy, qualified in extensity, can be at rest; one in which the difference in intensity is already cancelled because it is drawn outside itself and distributed among the elements of the system. However, energy in general or intensive quantity is the *spatium*, the theatre of all metamorphosis or difference in itself which envelops all its degrees in the production of each ... there is no more an extensity in general than there is an energy in general within extensity. (DR, 240–1)

In the case of the *spatium*, there are certain characteristics which we should note. Firstly, the term is not to be taken to refer to the explicate, to the spatial or the extensive as such. It is nevertheless the condition of all explication; it is what produces space (as we shall see, this formulation serves to align Deleuze with certain strands of thought in quantum physics; specifically the holographic paradigm and loop quantum gravity). The conditions themselves are intensive. But again we should be sensitive to the particularities of the distinction here; while it is tempting to visualise 'the intensive' as 'energy' and 'the extensive' as matter or material space, this does not do justice to the thought. Rather, the passage above first and foremost makes the distinction between two forms of energetic phenomena: the intensive and the 'empirical' (or explicated). What is it that distinguishes them? In Deleuze's word, distribution. The illusion pertaining to entropy, he claims, stems from the fact that we have access only to the already distributed, located forms of energy in the explicate world. In the present context, it is unmissably clear that this claim does *not* depend on energy coming to express itself at a particular point and place, having previously been unlocatable. 'Distribution' is not akin to distribution on a map. Distribution, rather, is what produces space as such, left and right, its metric and its dimensionality. When Deleuze uses phrases such as 'qualified in extensity', this is what he means. The terms of his claim about the illusory nature of entropy are not fully visible until they are understood in this sense: 'Only a particular form of empirical energy, qualified in extensity, can be at rest.' Equilibrium, in other words, is unavailable to the intensive realm since it lacks the site, we may say literally the ground, in which it may take place. The demarcation between the philosophy of difference and modern physics on the question of 'regimes' of energy may not be as clear cut as it at first seems, however. On the face of it, it is relatively uncontroversial to observe that physics encompasses more than one regime of energy. The energy inherent in the vacuum, the so-called 'quantum foam', is so named because it operates under a different regime than the distributed energy which macroscopic or even atomic physics treats. Firstly, it is understood to apply at the Planck scale, many orders smaller than the atomic. Secondly, it is understood not to impinge on the balance of energetic phenomena at higher scales due to the principle of the conservation of energy. The 'quantum fluctuations' of the vacuum take place at distances so short and time-scales so brief that nature proceeds unaffected. Exceptions to this rule are countenanced, however, and spectacular ones at that. One such exception is the central proposition of a theory we have alluded to previously: Edward Tryon's short paper published in *Nature* in 1973 posits the creation of the material universe as a quantum fluctuation of the vacuum which led to the Big Bang.[27] If the 'routine' quantum fluctuation can be considered as a tiny wave arising from a sea of energy, the fluctuation leading to the Big Bang might be called a tsunami; like the tsunami, this super fluctuation would be composed of many coinciding waves acting in tandem, prompting a cascade of symmetry-breaking, breaching the sea-walls of the quantum regime and propagating a new, conjoined material-energetic structure in the form of our observable universe. Clearly, the simple structural similarity between dual regimes of energy in modern physics and the philosophy of difference can only serve as an initial marker. We are bound to ask to what extent the existence of vacuum energy may serve to advance or rebut Deleuze's position on entropy as a transcendental illusion, applicable only in one regime but not the other. This line of questioning is further complicated by the recognition in modern physics of a 'dark energy' which permeates the cosmos and accounts for a staggering proportion of its total estimated mass (due to the equivalence of mass and energy established by Einstein). The nature of this dark energy is thus far a matter of some dispute, and the question as to whether it might constitute a further separate regime must remain a moot one for now. Nevertheless, we will have the opportunity later to examine the implications of vacuum energy for the philosophy of difference in context of the work of Charles Lineweaver and David Bohm.

The distinction in kind between the two regimes of energy is equally reflected, and equally in terms of topological theory, in Whitehead's work, where he assigns 'coordinate' or 'extensive' division only to extensity, or as he terms it, the 'physical pole'.[28] There is for both thinkers, then, an account of causality or expression which makes no fundamental use of the concept of location, and in both cases this is reflected in their conception of the topological structure of nature. Locality is produced through intensive exchange.

In all of these correspondences, we find an emerging shared picture between the two thinkers with respect to extension and its relation to the intensive which at once serves to calibrate their at first apparently tangential attitude to the concept of 'limit' (Whitehead's insistence on the need for a 'principle of limitation' and Deleuze's rejection of the substantive existence of limits and constants) and to orient both toward a metaphysics adequate to the modern era. Firstly, the intensive is primary, topologically multivalent and thereby capable of action at a distance; indeed, this may serve as the major distinction between the intensive and extensive regimes. Nevertheless, for each, the supervenience of the extensive on the intensive is necessary for empirical phenomena to occur. The priority of the intensive in no way mitigates the essential exchange between the two regimes; without the extensive, limitation may not occur. We should not miss the corollary here, however, since it marries together the notions of 'limitation' and 'retardation'. If, by the lights of quantum theory, action at a distance, non-locality, entails superluminal influence, then all production of localised phenomena, all contiguity, is at the same time a retardation. Without the circumscription of intensive topology through explication, there is no 'hesitation', no 'retardation' and thus no creativity.

To establish the correspondences with modern physics, it is instructive to consider the recent 'completion' of the Standard Model in physics represented by the discovery of the Higgs boson in 2012. Prior to this discovery, the existence of the Higgs boson was conjectured as a consequence of the so-called 'electroweak theory': 'But one of the consequences of the electroweak symmetry is that, if nothing new is added to the theory, all elementary particles including electrons and quarks would be massless, which of course they are not.'[29] The mismatch between the observed mass of the elementary particles and their predicted masslessness within the theory was acute, since according to relativity, massless particles are free, indeed bound, to move at the speed of light. In a universe in which all particles move at the speed of light, no material structure is possible. The initial version of the electroweak theory was in other words fundamentally at odds with the observed order of the world. The boson and its associated Higgs field were proposed as the mechanism by which mass is conferred upon elementary particles. Some slowing down, some retardation, was required to square the circle. Rodolphe Gasché recognises the correspondences here, in a discussion of Deleuze and Guattari's chaos in *What Is Philosophy?* The plane of immanence, which serves to slow down the infinite speeds of chaos, is, he says:

> Not unlike the field of forces manifested by the Higgs Boson, which, according to the Standard Model, is comparable to a kind of molasses that permeates space, and prevents the elementary forms of matter from just zooming around at the speed of light by providing them with the mass necessary for there to be atoms, and hence matter, the planes that cut through chaos actualize it in the different shapes of the concepts, functives and percepts/affects through which the particles of chaos become imbued with reality.[30]

Where Gasché adopts the Higgs metaphorically as a figure to characterise the operation of the plane of immanence, the plane which governs the chaoids, philosophy, science and the arts, we might more particularly focus on the correspondences regarding the genesis of matter as such. In the history of physics, the Higgs was posited as a required element of supersymmetry, of which the electroweak theory constitutes a milestone. The central idea behind supersymmetry is that the various disparate forces, fields and natural kinds, with their diverse associated laws, are a remnant in our cooled-down universe of what once was a unified cosmos, governed by one single 'super' force. This being so, the reasoning is that all forces will be found to converge into fewer and fewer manifestations the more proximately we can map conditions pertaining in the high-energy conditions of the early universe. Ultimately all will be subsumed into one at or near the Big Bang. The electroweak force represents just such a step along the way; it displays the unity of electromagnetic force and the 'weak' atomic force (the one governing interactions between atoms and attractions or repulsions within, excluding those in operation in the nucleus) under high-energy conditions. A third force, the 'strong' atomic force, was subsequently reconciled theoretically at yet higher energy levels, leaving only one force currently outside the purview of supersymmetry: gravity. The Higgs boson and Higgs field are understood to be responsible for the cleaving apart of the other forces: 'Although the universe began in a perfectly symmetrical state, the Higgs broke this symmetry and enabled the matter that formed within the universe to evolve into complex and diverse structures.'[31] From the point of view of *material* existence, we might consider this first breaking of symmetry the primordial *limitation* of which Whitehead speaks, introducing 'contraries, grades and oppositions'. Prior to this, the cosmos was an entirely energetic phenomenon, whose only speed was the speed of light. It represents a *retardation*, then. Moreover, the retardation is a precondition for the 'diverse structures' we observe; it is a principle of *complexity*. Lastly, in a quite literal way, we can view the operation of the Higgs field on massless energetic phenomena as an *explication* in our sense, involving an unfolding of dimensionality. The Higgs mechanism is explicitly conceived as such.

As Jim Baggott recounts, the world before the Higgs field takes effect is massless and two-dimensional:

> The mechanism works like this, a massless field particle with spin 1 (a boson) moves at the speed of light and has two 'degrees of freedom', meaning that its wave amplitude can oscillate in two dimensions that are perpendicular (that is, transverse) to the direction in which it is travelling. If the particle is moving in the z-direction, say, then its wave amplitude can oscillate only in the x- and y- directions (left/right and up/down).[32]

The reason for this two-dimensional restriction may be understood simply as a function of the speed of light as an absolute upper speed limit. Any entity moving at the speed of light could oscillate 'forward' only by exceeding that speed limit. Equally, any oscillation 'backward' would by definition fall below the speed of light. But the lesson of the Higgs is in effect a corollary to the principle that massless particles travel only at the speed of light; to fall below the speed of light is to *acquire* mass. The transition from masslessness to finite mass is intimately linked to the transition from two-dimensionality to three-dimensionality, a spatial symmetry-breaking. In effect, it is the presence of the Higgs background quantum field which serves to allow this symmetry-breaking. The field displaces the vacuum energy from zero, forcing phenomena to 'make choices' in seeking their lowest energy state, just as the balanced pencil falls over in one direction:

> Breaking the symmetry creates a massless Nambu-Goldstone boson. This may now be 'absorbed' by the massless spin 1 field boson to create a third degree of freedom (forward/back) ... In the Higgs mechanism the act of gaining three-dimensionality is like applying a brake. The particle slows down to an extent which depends on the strength of its interaction with the Higgs field.[33]

Again, there is an inseparable connection between the explication described here and the retardation or braking effect. The Higgs field introduces inertial mass into the world, but in the process redefines the way inertial mass itself is to be understood:

> The inertial mass of an object is a measure of its resistance to acceleration. Our instinct is to equate inertial mass with the amount of substance the object possesses. The more 'stuff' it contains, the harder it is to accelerate. The Higgs mechanism turns this logic on its head. *We now interpret the extent to which the particle's acceleration is resisted by the Higgs field as the particle's (inertial) mass.*[34]

In the Deleuzian register, the intensive regime, the *spatium*, provides the conditions for the extensive, including its dimensionality, through a process of explication. Energy becomes 'distributed'. It is not the limited thing which defines the limit, but the limit which produces the limited thing. It is not the retarded thing which defines retardation, but retardation which produces the retarded thing. Let us not forget that when Deleuze speaks of the 'freeze-frame' which science imposes on the plane of immanence (the scientific 'frame of reference'), this is no mere cognitive framing; it refers to physical processes too: 'It is a fantastic *slowing down*, and it is by slowing down that matter, as well as the scientific thought able to penetrate it with propositions, is actualised' (WP, 118). As such, the Higgs field might be taken to foreground the role of mass in this account of material genesis. For our purposes, we are now in a position to submit that the philosophy of difference carries traction not only in the classical and chaotic paradigms, but in quantum theory too.

While all these suggestive correspondences fall out of the supersymmetry account quite naturally, there is nevertheless (at least) one circle still to square. The speed of light, albeit staggeringly fast, is not the infinite speed which Deleuze attributes to chaos, nor the plane of immanence. The slowing down in question is of another order we might say. With this observation, it is doubtless tempting to allow the philosopher the metaphorical (perhaps even hyperbolic) latitude which the intrinsically anexact disciplines are due. 'Infinite speed' can be taken to mean nothing more, after all, than 'the fastest possible'. Yet it is too early to allow this distinction to collapse for the sake of alignment with a particular strand of physics. Without embarking on a discussion of whether we can countenance (even from Deleuze) a really existing infinity, let us only earmark the word 'infinity' as a signifier of the mutability of constants-limits and a refusal to arbitrarily curtail this mutability; a reminder that 'the fastest speed possible' is only nominally attached to any given value and indeed any given phenomenon for a world in which the only necessity is chance. This is what Deleuze means when he claims that 'every limit is illusory and every determination is negation, if determination is not in an immediate relation with the undetermined' (WP, 120). An infinity in the service of evolution.

'Limit', 'locality' and 'retardation' are at root different aspects of the self-same phenomenon. But the key thing to recognise is that for both Whitehead and Deleuze, any given limitation is as contingent as limitation *per se* is itself necessary. No limit, no constant, is eternal. No law is forever. Deleuze explicitly connects this non-local characteristic of nature to the contingency of laws: 'Moreover, while the laws of nature govern the surface of the world, the eternal return ceaselessly rumbles in this other dimension of the transcendental or the volcanic *spatium*' (DR, 241). Perhaps the most telling illustration of this is again with respect to the speed of light: it must and does serve as a constant for the special and general theories of relativity, yet as we have seen, this constant, understood as a maximum limit to speed in the propagation of phenomena, is not without its experimentally verified exceptions.[35] Nevertheless, there is little denying that the broad generality of observed phenomena does conform to such a speed limit (Whitehead would add cautiously, in this epoch; Deleuze refers us to the capacity for evolution in the 'volcanic *spatium*'). Indeed, we need only ask what would happen if the speed of light were infinite to recognise the role such a limit must play in the order of nature. Michael Epperson comments:

> it should be emphasized that for Whitehead (and likely as well for Einstein), the critical importance of the constant c had little to do with the phenomenon of light per se; its significance, rather, lay in the derivative invariance of spacetime intervals and the associated possibility of (I) the asymmetrical, logical and causal ordering of events within spacetime reference frames, and (II) the provision of a congruence relation that allows for the comparison of spatial and temporal extensive coordinations across diverse spacetime reference frames.[36]

Here the fact of the speed of light's potential variability (it may have been faster or slower) is not so much the point as that *any* selection of this limit through the calibrations of the cosmos will represent a 'slowing down' from the superluminal speeds of 'abstract possibility', of superluminal 'non-locality', of infinitely fast communication. The limit is necessary, while its value is contingent and potentially mutable. This limit, then, is a prerequisite for any definitive arrow of time, for a 'logical and causal ordering of events'.[37] The 'principle of limitation', as Whitehead has it, is thus equally a principle of retardation, in its outermost scope, and is so in the sense that it bestows order.[38] We are palpably close to Deleuze's assertion that chaos is a matter not so much of disorder, but of the infinite speed with which every form vanishes in an 'infinite speed of birth and disappearance ... without consistency or reference' (WP, 118).

The metaphysics of both Deleuze and Whitehead, then, afford a framework for non-locality, and both insist that locality is a product of the intensive domain, an explication of the implicate order. For the most part, the scientific literature acknowledges that non-locality must be addressed, but this acknowledgement tends to be limited to a rehearsal of the problems and paradoxes attached to EPR-type experiments, pertaining to the entanglement of a pair of or at most several particles. While it can be and has been put to practical use in quantum computing, for instance, non-locality still tends to be seen as an oddity or an exception to the 'routine' operation of quantum events. There are counterpoints to this view, however; two such are the 'network' and 'holographic' paradigms, put forward to address the conditions which must pertain in order to account for non-locality on a cosmological scale, to offer a structure which is faithful to the phenomena.[39]

A NETWORK PARADIGM: LOOP QUANTUM GRAVITY

Loop quantum gravity is an ambitious proposal to reconcile the stubborn persistence of what is perhaps modern physics' most deep-rooted problem: the conceptual mismatch between relativistic and quantum theories. At its most basic, the mismatch consists in the nature of space which each theory depends on; for relativity theorists, space must be a continuum, while for quantum theorists space is essentially discrete. The proposal behind loop quantum gravity is that the basic building block of matter is not particulate, not formed from atoms, nor quarks, nor ultimately from any smaller particle which may remain to be discovered, but from 'loops' of energy at a much smaller scale, which may combine in a multitude of ways to constitute the sub-structure of the particles in the Standard Model. As such, space is understood to be quantised; indeed, there is nothing more to it than the connections afforded by these vanishingly small loops; it is produced by the endlessly imbricated network of such connections. Due to this structuration, however, space has properties which mimic the continuum on which relativity depends.[40] What is discarded in this picture is the criterion of contiguity for nodes of the network to count as neighbours. The key to the network paradigm can be presented in terms of connectivity; any node may be connected to any other at all in the network, regardless of how 'near' or 'far' it may be, not limited to its spatial neighbours; in fact, the relation of neighbouring is better thought of as a function of connectivity than distance. The corollary is that the 'space' of these loops must be conceived as higher-dimensional, allowing for connections not limited to neighbours contiguous in three dimensions, while the relative potential for connection between nodes is a function of available energy. Nodes may connect without regard for distance, even in theory beyond the light cone which represents the limit to the propagation of influence for relativistic theories. The conceptual shift required for this paradigm requires a certain reversal of perspective; the question becomes not 'how do we account for non-local phenomena?', but 'how it is that *locality* arises from such a situation?', 'how does the three-dimensional character of the observable world emerge?' If loop quantum gravity networks rely on non-local connectivity, then localised spatial structures emerge with the loss of those connections. Leonard Susskind expresses this succinctly: 'Things that are separated are not really separated ... There's just a cancellation of the things that are connecting them.'[41] It is useful in the context of this argument to give in full a quotation already alluded to above from Deleuze and Guattari's *What Is Philosophy?*: 'It is difficult to see how the limit immediately cuts into the infinite, the unlimited. Yet it is not the limited thing that sets a limit to the infinite, but the limit that makes possible a limited thing' (WP, 120). It seems that the required reversal of perspective is not lost on Deleuze here; indeed, we have encountered just such an insight with respect to lines of flight – the question 'how do lines of flight escape centres of envelopment' is reversed in favour of the real question, 'how do intensities come to be enveloped in the first place?' – here, however, the same problematic touches much more illuminatingly on the themes of topological limitation-explication and retardation, following as it does after a discussion of the 'constant-limit', such as the speed of light in science. While it is true that not all the phenomena envisaged by Deleuze's term 'constant-limit' are quite so directly associable with speed (he references the quantum of action and absolute zero), we should bear in mind that in Deleuze's framework, *all* phenomena, including constants of nature, are repeatedly referred back to relative speeds:

> Such limits do not apply through the empirical value that they take on solely within systems of coordinates, they act primarily as the condition of primordial slowing down, that, in relation to infinity, extends over the whole scale of corresponding speeds, over their conditioned accelerations or slowing-downs. (WP, 119)

Non-locality is prior, then, pertaining until 'cancelled'. For the network paradigm in loop quantum gravity, it is the number of connections sustained by the network which dictate the topological character of the world, and this in turn is dictated by the energy available; in a maximally energetic system, each node would be connected to every other, in a manifold which includes, but is not limited to, the three dimensions we are familiar with.

Lower-energy patterns offer a different story. They're just what we want. Each grain connects to just a few others, forming a regular grid like a honeycomb or woven fabric. The notion of distance regains meaning: some grains are close together, the rest far apart. The network is nice and roomy. The principle of locality holds: for an influence to go from one place to another, it can't hop straight there, but must work its way through the network. The passage of the signal takes time, which would explain why the speed of objects through space is limited (by the speed of light).[42]

Further, then, the topology of the world dictates the causal character of the world; contiguity may be more or less salient; non-local connections are not an 'all or nothing' condition of nature; the path from full connection to null may drop off cancellation by cancellation. In higher-energy conditions, effects may occur instantaneously at a distance. In lower-energy states, causal influences will have to propagate through the contiguous nodes of the network.

We are now in a position to map the detailed exemplification of this theory in physics onto principles outlined in the metaphysics we have been discussing. We can translate from one register to another.

The quantum network described by loop quantum gravity is not space as such, but that which produces space, a *spatium*. The 'depth' of the connected network is intensive in that the propagation of energy therein is qualitatively different to the propagation of energy within what Deleuze describes as the 'already distributed' systems which alone are susceptible to empirical investigation; any and every connection is available in the loop quantum *spatium*. The intensive character of the network is inextricable from topological structure, just as for Deleuze the intensive is a topological depth. The network (to enlist Serres' insight) is a continuous multiplicity; no connection may be added without rendering the network anew. Causal influence takes place at superluminal speeds, approximating the infinite speed of relations which Deleuze attributes to the plane of consistency. Distance is meaningless for the quantum network; it is produced by cancellation of connectivity. The intensive regime becomes explicated, space appears along with locality, and the name of that explication is 'cancellation'.[43] These processes certainly avoid what Whitehead referred to as 'the fallacy of simple location'. Explication-cancellation is inextricable from a loss of available energy, a degradation. Cancellation is a limitation, not merely in the loose sense that the synonyms imply, but in the topologically symmetry-breaking terms which Deleuze and Whitehead favour. Finally, the production of space from the intensive structuration is to be understood as the transition from one epoch to another: the transition from the epoch of maximal energy to our cooled-down universe, from one typology of numbers to another for Deleuze's calculating God, whose calculation produces the world.

Is everything here? Is nothing lacking? Can a case be made that order for quantum loop gravity answers to all the requisites of a philosophy of difference? Not as such; there are caveats to observe.

Some reflection on the network model itself suggests a natural distinction between regimes of the loop quantum universe with respect to simplicity (simple order) and complexity. The range of levels of connectivity is from maximal to minimal, from a fully connected matrix in n-dimensional space to a state in which no node is connected to any other. For both limit cases, maximal and minimal, we could say the organisation is simple; each node is identical to every other.[44] As such, the overall levels of complexity over the course of the lifetime of the cosmos according to loop quantum gravity describe an arch, peaking at greatest complexity in the middle and falling away toward the end. The theory does not offer the same escape from the second law as promised by Stuart Kauffman's 'adjacent possible'.

It is a matter of inclination, perhaps, whether we prefer to adhere to Bohm's (and Deleuze's) proposition that there are no states which lack complexity (merely greater or lesser orders thereof), or whether we choose to acknowledge the qualitative distinction between simple order and complexity which suggests itself through the terms of loop quantum gravity. Yet in either case, the lack of an explicitly reciprocal determination between the 'virtual' and 'actual' aspects of the theory may defer any closer equivalence between the nature of complexity we find in it and the philosophy of difference. Perhaps the principle of reciprocal determination itself belongs so resolutely to metaphysics that it can only be 'put in by hand', rather than 'falling out of the equations'. Yet in an important way, outwith the terms of loop quantum theory, Smolin does adhere to reciprocal determination, as we shall see.

With respect to retardation, the devil is in the detail. Undoubtedly the genesis of spatial phenomena is part and parcel of a 'slowing down' of the cosmic network; to lose superluminal connection incrementally as available energy recedes is analogous to an incrementally enforced speed-limit gradually rolled out through a city. Certain districts remain frenetically active, like a scene from *Koyaanisqatsi*, while others adopt the sedentary pace (Smolin says, 'When space emerges in such a model, so does locality. So, also, does the existence of a speed limit for the transmission of signals').[45] The overall potential for speed decreases. Gradually the regime switches from relative domination by the superluminal speed to relative domination by the subluminal. More accurately, everything happens as though the speed-limit roll-out were implemented by reckless, criminally negligent town planners; the superfast districts remain enfolded within the speed-restricted, non-locality nestles inextricably within locality. Nevertheless, the ultimate direction of travel is unmistakeable; the retardation in question is tied to the loss of available energy, to entropy. It is not allotted the same role as Bergson's vital or Deleuze's life. Strictly within the dynamic account of this network paradigm, there is no 'principle of complexity' as such. Yet here again is a juncture at which to parse the concepts. The cancellation of connections, precisely because it entails a localisation of phenomena, can only serve to defer the speed of phenomena. In a universe where available energy is insufficient to sustain maximal connection, as Smolin has it, 'to travel between two widely separated nodes, a particle has to make many hops. It takes time for a particle, or a quantum carrying information, to go a long way.'[46] Yet what is it to 'hop', what is it to be deferred, but to become caught up in the exchanges of the subatomic world? Of photons, of bosons, of the natural kinds of the Standard Model? To join the 'interlacings' described in Serres' account of Lucretius' text? Which is as much to say turbulence and complexity? From this point of view, we are able to identify more parsimoniously just what it is that constitutes the *thalweg* in the loop quantum gravity account of explication/cancellation; it is the production not so much of matter but of space itself, a tract which serves as the incline frustrating the maximal fall which is the fate of all phenomena. This is the real meaning of locality. Yet again, though, there is a circle to square here; it seems intractably that this *geometrogenesis* is a *result* of slowing down, of retardation, not the *cause* thereof. As such, the reciprocality of determination which characterises Deleuze's philosophy of difference so strongly is lacking. The account affords us all the latitude, all the openness, of a Deleuzian-Whiteheadian cosmology, yet seems to stop short of the crucial sense of *expression*. And so it does; for the story it tells is one of the particularities of explication. It says nothing of implication, nor complication. Indeed, it is not in Smolin's network paradigm for quantum gravity as such that we should look for anything corresponding to these ideas, but in the evolutionary account he offers for cosmology writ large, as we shall see.

A HOLOGRAPHIC PARADIGM: DAVID BOHM'S IMPLICATE ORDER

Loop quantum gravity provides no explicit parallel to Deleuze's *implication* as such, the ultimate return of all actualised phenomena to the intensive, virtual regime, ceding place continually to subsequent actualisations. The exchange, rather, as laid out in that theory, is one-sided, from the intensive non-local network to the explicate local.

David Bohm's 'holographic' paradigm offers more direct potential to match the scope of Deleuze's metaphysics, not least in terms of the reciprocal determination of two regimes of energy. Key terms Bohm employs answer quite neatly to those employed by Deleuze himself; he organises discussion of the exchange between the energetic and the physical under the rubric of the 'implicate' and 'explicate' orders respectively.

Bohm adopts the example of the holograph to illustrate a form of causality understood to embrace both the features of 'wholeness' (or 'holism') and non-locality, which he singles out as the essential explananda for physics after the quantum revolution. In his view, the universe is definitively interconnected in all of its parts, or rather, to underline the point, 'sub-wholes', and in ways independent of three-dimensional contiguity. The production of a holograph employs a split-beam laser, one path of which is used to illuminate a body from all sides, then recombined with the other path to create an interference pattern at the surface of a photographic plate. The 3-d image is encoded, or 'enfolded' into all parts (sub-wholes) of the plate by dint of the fact that what is recorded is not the image as such, but the interference pattern itself. The image is not localised, then, in the sense of a one-to-one mapping of visual content, but retains a coherence from multiple viewpoints, with maximum clarity and faithfulness to the original object from one particular angle. 'Locality' in this example corresponds to the 3-d image from a given point of view, the crucial feature being that this apparently autonomous single image viewed from a fixed point is indissociable from the whole of the distributed wave-pattern itself; the single holographic phenomenon may be viewed throughout the bounds of the plate, but will take on different visual aspects (perhaps appearing with a more truncated perspective) depending on the location of the observer. Writ large, this modest example serves to encapsulate the ubiquitous organisation of nature; no localised phenomenon is isolated from the movement of nature as a whole; all relations extend in an interconnected fashion throughout the whole of the universe (Bohm's term for the intertwined forms of order illustrated here is 'holomovement'). Bohm's 'holism' unequivocally frames the question of cosmology in the form 'how is locality produced?', rather than 'how do we account for non-locality?' Our very problem.

For Bohm, the implicate is that same order we have encountered above under the name 'generative'; he uses the terms as close synonyms. It is non-local and transcendental, while the explicate is subject to locality. He attributes the inspiration for this concept to what is known in physics as Green's function. Green's function is a formalisation of what Bohm calls 'the general structure of movement according to quantum mechanics', which 'can be thought of as representing a summation of very many waves'. A Feynman diagram is in essence a visualisation of this process. Both the function and the diagram are designed to account for the way in which a 'particle' may be said to have a 'trajectory'. Both 'particle', understood as subsisting self-same material substance, and 'trajectory', understood as the path taken by such a substance, are definitively relinquished concepts in quantum theory; the eternally enduring, 'uncuttable' atom of the ancient atomists is not that of the particle physicist. Movement at the atomic and subatomic level is rather understood to propagate outwards from a given point in wave-form until some section of the wave encounters another converging from another direction; this encounter in turn determines a fresh point from which radiation propagates outward. It is the point of connection between the wave-fronts which may be considered in terms of particles, though even here, it is better conceived as a locus of energetic exchange between particle types; the original incoming particle is not preserved. A 'trajectory', then, is not the passage of a subsisting entity through space from one point to another, but a successive series of exchanges, a self-renewing pattern of movement. The lack of resemblance to a classical concept of trajectory is all the more stark given that both Green's function and the Feynman diagram allow us to speak of a single trajectory only in abstraction from the 'real' scenario of a vast continuum of other possible pathways along which the movement may take place. Significantly, Bohm locates the twin moments of his explicate/implicate order within these already-established conventions of quantum theory:

> Evidently the Feynman Diagrams give an imaginative picture of a wave motion. In this picture, wavelets can be seen unfolding from each point toward the whole. Yet the very same movement can be thought of as wavelets enfolding toward each point from the whole ... [T]he basic movement of enfoldment and unfoldment is thus a dual one in which there is ultimately no separation between enfoldment and the unfoldment.[47]

There is clearly a great deal of resonance between this framework and the concepts of explication and implication which Deleuze borrows from Renaissance Neoplatonist thought. For Bohm, as for Deleuze, the explicate, or unfolded, order is that amenable to empirical observation. It is the expression in three dimensions dominated by contiguous phenomena of an underlying 'sea' of non-localised, energetic phenomena;

this latter is the implicate order. The terminological confluence centring around the fold, the *pli*, and its etymological affiliates speaks of a broad conceptual convergence. Bohm's 'holism' echoes Leibniz's work in all the ways foregrounded in the above discussion. Nature is understood as the reciprocal determination of the two forms of order and composed of phenomena interconnected throughout:

> This discussion appears, at first sight, to reduce the time order [the explicate] so that it could, in principle, be derived completely from the timeless [the implicate] order. This would indeed be so, if the 'flow' in the implicate, generative stream were only in the 'direction' from the source or origin down to ever more explicate orders of succession. However, because of the two way nature of this flow, there is an inherent dynamism in the theory and such a reduction is not possible.[48]

Each individual is inherently discernible, following Leibniz and Whitehead:

> So the relationship of each moment in the whole to all the others is implied by its total content; the way in which it 'holds' all the others enfolded within it. In certain ways this notion is similar to Leibniz's idea of monads, each of which 'mirrors' the whole in its own way, some in great detail and others rather vaguely. The difference is that Leibniz's monads had a permanent existence, whereas our basic elements are only moments and are thus not permanent. Whitehead's idea of 'actual occasions' is closer to the one proposed here ...[49]

Further than meeting on common Leibnizian ground, however, Bohm's conception of nature offers more specifically Deleuzian parallels. As a result of the holographic, holistic character of the world, we find support lent to Deleuze's insistence that qualities are epiphenomena masking wave after wave of intensive phenomena. Employing the analogously holographic metaphor of a flat-screen TV, George Musser comments on this aspect of Bohm's paradigm:

> Going back to our flat-screen metaphor, you might visualise field entanglement as a nest of wires crisscrossing the screen to link together. For most purposes this isn't a bad image ... [b]ut deep down it fails. Entanglement doesn't mean that the brightness and colour of one pixel can become coordinated with the brightness and colour of other pixels. It means that individual pixels don't actually have brightness or colour values: only groups of entangled pixels do. An entangled field has holistic qualities that do not exist in any one place, but span the entirety of space.[50]

In its own register, then, the holographic paradigm reiterates for us Deleuze's assertion that quality is an epiphenomenon of explication, 'covering over' intensive relations.

As with loop quantum gravity, connections may be drawn between the topology of Bohm's cosmology and Deleuze's own idea of 'depth'.

The process of explication in each case relies on a *spatium* which has its own order of dimensions, independent of locality or contiguity:

> One discovers, instead, both from consideration of the meaning of the mathematical equations and the results of the actual experiments, that the various particles have to be taken literally as projections of a higher-dimensional reality which cannot be accounted for in terms of any force of interaction between them.[51]

The implicate order, first and foremost for Bohm, is a structuration of the prodigious energy inherent in the vacuum, the so-called 'Dirac Sea', which underlies the phenomena we encounter in the explicate order. Its sheer latent power, he recognises, dwarfs the 'already distributed' forms of energy in the explicate world: 'what we call empty space contains an immense background of energy … matter as we know it is a small, "quantized" wavelike excitation on top of this background, rather like a tiny ripple on a vast sea'.[52] We encountered the Dirac equation, treating, initially, the behaviour of electrons, in Chapter 2, as an example of arguments from symmetry. It is worthwhile expanding on Dirac's thought processes at this point, especially with regard to the concept of the 'Dirac Sea', since this will help us to lay out some nuances in the argument to follow, in connection with the concept of 'false vacuum' and Charles Lineweaver's speculations on entropy at a cosmological scale.

Dirac was working in 1928 to reconcile the quantum mechanics of electrons with special relativity. Experiment had advanced to a level of accuracy whereby the predictions established by Heisenberg and Schrödinger concerning the dynamic behaviour of electrons were shown to deviate slightly from observed results, and moreover, the principles underpinning their account were drawn from a Newtonian rather than the more pertinent Einsteinian model. Hence the need for reconciliation.

Dirac introduced factors into the reckoning intended to square the circle. The first was the spin associated with the electron, which had been neglected up to that point. Second, in response to the fact that the algebraic formulae associated with quantum processes were (and today still tend to be) presented in terms squared rather than with simple values, Dirac sought a mathematical solution which would avoid the need to do so. It was not that he was simply searching for something neater; rather he was resistant to the implications behind that formalisation, which paid notional adherence to the concept of negative energy – indeed the only rationale for presenting values squared was to avoid the occurrence of negative values for energy in any given equation (the minus sign disappears from any number multiplied by itself). The third innovation Dirac introduced was a result of his failure to achieve the second (negative values continued inconveniently to feature in the non-commutative matrices he adopted); rather than take this failure as defeat, he switched tack and proposed what he saw as a plausible physical meaning for the concept of negative energy. Thus came about the first recognition of antimatter: the idea that a particle may – in fact must – have a natural partner alike in all respects except for charge, which takes the reverse value. The electron, Dirac realised, would have its anti-electron, which we now refer to as the positron. The model he conceived extends the account governing the capacities and restrictions of electrons to occupy given positions in the energy shells of atoms well beyond its initial application. Pauli's 'Exclusion Principle' states that no two electrons with the same set of properties can occupy the same location within the atom. Frank Close conveys the boldness of this conceptual extension:

> Having realised that his equation implied that electrons could have negative energy, Dirac used this exclusion principle as the basis of a brilliant idea. He suggested that what we call the vacuum is not actually empty, but is like a bottomless pit, descending into which is a ladder each of whose rungs corresponds to a possible quantum state, a resting place for an electron. The top of the ladder corresponds to zero energy, all the rungs below being the possible negative energy states for electrons. Dirac's insight was that if all these negative levels are already filled, no electrons can fall into a negative energy slot and so matter remains stable. What we call the 'vacuum' would be like a deep calm sea that is unnoticeable so long as nothing disturbs it. The filled sea is the base level relative to which all energies are defined; Dirac's 'sea level' defines the zero of energy.[53]

With this scenario, Dirac was able to furnish a physically meaningful version of the phrase 'negative energy'. He conjectured that, given sufficient energetic excitation, particles could be knocked out of their place in the sea, effectively creating a positron, which in accordance with the conservation of energy would of necessity be paired with a given electron; they would serve to 'cancel each other out', meaning literally that the electron and the positron, created simultaneously, would annihilate together almost instantaneously. This was the first account of what would come to be known as virtual particles. In Dirac's account, the positron was nothing more than a gap in the energetic structuration of this Dirac Sea, though contemporary accounts assign a more substantive existence to the particle, now long confirmed by observation. Indeed, the quantum field theory which grew out of Dirac's insights went on to generalise the partnering of material particles with antimatter equivalents to particles of all and any kind.

Though quantum field theory no longer subscribes to the particular structuration Dirac envisaged for the vacuum (substantive existence for antimatter particles obviates the need), it is nevertheless that Dirac Sea to which Bohm is referring when he says that empty space 'contains an immense background of energy'. Indeed it is a moot question whether the more speculative version of the holographic paradigm he promotes – whereby successive and increasingly powerful tracts of energy interacting reciprocally underly the actuality we observe – can maintain traction absent some equivalent structuration to Dirac's Sea. This notwithstanding, contemporary physics certainly attributes vast energetic resources to the vacuum; it is at best only a working assumption that there is some upper bound. In any case, the Dirac/Bohm vacuum will serve as an instructive foil when we come to discuss the role of the false vacuum in the work of Charles Lineweaver.

For Bohm, this underlying energetic order in itself should force us to reappraise the structuration of energy we find in the explicate order, in particular to recognise that true causal efficacy belongs to phenomena of the implicate order rather than the explicate.[54] Bohm's two regimes of energy are equally two regimes of order, with profoundly different properties. It is not that Bohm recognises the importance of the two forms of energy in a way that other physicists do not; the concept of vacuum energy is routinely conveyed in most introductions to modern physics, most often in context of its significance for the cosmological constant. Rather, in Bohm's speculative physical theories, the two regimes of energy serve to prompt an overall conception of nature bearing striking correspondences to Deleuze's philosophy of nature. The inexhaustibility of the implicate order both informs the detail of Bohm's understanding of cosmic evolution, and serves to clarify the implications of Deleuze's resistance to the second law. The reader will also be struck by palpable similarities between Bohm and Deleuze with respect to the Event as an exchange between two regimes of order, and two orders of time:

> science has, up to now, emphasized the sequential order of successive changes. In the larger scale this includes, for example, the theory of evolution. In the generative order, however, time is not put into the first place. Rather, time has to be related in a fundamental way to the generative order. The image of a stream is helpful in this respect. The stream can be studied by following an object that floats along it, in a time process. However, it is also possible to consider the entire stream all at once, to reveal the overall generative order that goes downstream from the source or origin.
>
> But the stream is only an image. The essential flow is not from one place to another but a movement within the implicate and superimplicate (generative) orders. At every moment, the totality of these orders is present and

enfolded throughout all space so ... they all interpenetrate. The flux or flow is therefore between different stages and developments of these orders. However, because of the possibility of loops, this flow may go in a pair of different 'directions' at the same time.[55]

In the relativistic and quantum physics literature, it is not uncommon to encounter claims that linear time, or indeed time of any sort, is birthed concomitantly with space, and the above quotation certainly conforms to that tenet, but what is most striking here is the way Bohm is drawn to envision the consequences of this conclusion in terms of the two domains of order. There is much in common between Deleuze's discussion of the temporal regime of the Aion in *The Logic of Sense*, wherein series may ramify both backward and forward in time, potentially infinitely, and Bohm's 'loops of time' in the generative order.

EVOLUTIONARY EXPANSIVENESS

The general aspect of nature is that of evolutionary expansiveness.
A.N. Whitehead[56]

... and the rules of actualization are not those of resemblance and limitation, but those of difference or divergence and of creation.
Gilles Deleuze (B, 97)

If limitation is a real factor in the passage of nature, it may never be so in the sense of negation or opposition; we are enjoined by Deleuze always to bear in mind the infinite speeds of relata on the plane of consistency, the infinite mutability of both pieces and rules, laws and natural kinds in the Ideal Game.

What serves to consolidate this particular thought of limitation beyond the clutches of negation is the process of evolution; the passage of nature is evolutionary.

The history of science, and indeed of the philosophy of science, is not short of examples of thinkers who adopt 'evolution' as a descriptor for the passage of nature, the unfolding of cosmological history as a whole, rather than restrict the term to the adaptation of life. Nor should this be particularly surprising, given the general acceptance that the universe has altered during the course of its history not merely from configuration to configuration but from one state to another.[57] Evidently there is a necessary looseness of the metaphor: could it ever make sense to speak of 'adaptation' in this context? To what might a cosmos, the entirety of being, adapt? And if we were to allow 'descent with modification' in the case of cyclical cosmologies, it is not clear what mechanism, if any, could serve analogously to genetic recombination, nor even that any such mechanism could survive the annihilating transition from one cycle to another.

The key identifying feature of the evolutionary paradigm which we will adopt for this argument is the reciprocal determination of law, constant and natural kind in the development of nature. From this criterion, we might identify four variants of the paradigm, each of which have gained currency in scientific discourse:

1. Those accounts which posit varying natural conditions in *causally disconnected* regions of the universe. Adherents would include Paul Dirac and Fred Hoyle.[58] Rather surprisingly, it is also possible to include the more speculative Newton in this category.[59]
2. Those which posit the *cyclical renewal* of the universe, with conditions cast anew at each reiteration. Roger Penrose's Cyclical Conformal Cosmology would be an example, as would Lee Smolin's multiversal account, which goes so far as to identify a mechanism of 'natural selection' based on the superior propensity of universes with a relatively high density of black hole production to give rise to subsequent cycles.[60]
3. 'Bubble universe' accounts, which posit the ongoing creation of branching universes from within our own. These are predicated on the phenomenon of 'inflation' proposed by Alan Guth.[61]
4. Those accounts in which laws, constants and natural kinds co-vary within a given region over time. David Bohm's work must be included here, as must that of Murray Gell-Mann, and again Lee Smolin.[62]

At this point, it becomes clear that if we are to pursue Deleuzian/Whiteheadian metaphysics on the landscape of modern cosmology (though the list above is by no means exhaustive), the variant that offers the most productive exchange is the fourth kind: those accounts which favour the concept of *internal* evolution. The cosmos as a chaosmos. For it is this version most directly in which creativity, the Event, may be said to be continuous, never to cease ('*il ne cesse pas*'). Just as the Event does not hold in abeyance for the disjunctions of chaotic bifurcation, nor does it await the branching of bubble universes, or the transition between cycles from one universe to the next. As for causally disconnected regions of the universe, these are difficult to square with a thoroughgoing non-local account. It seems, then, we have a criterion in the metaphysics which is sufficiently salient to favour or disfavour specific variants of the cosmic evolutionary paradigm. If the chaosmos is a 'multiverse' it is so because of the internal multivalency of the conditions which it comprises. Universes are enfolded within it. The volcano rumbles on underneath the explicate order. But it is not the singularity of the cosmos alone which marries the fourth category of cosmology above with the philosophy of difference; it is also the fact that each example adheres to a certain sense of 'openness'. Here again the openness in question is not only, not limited to, the openness of chaotic open systems. It is the triple mutability of constants, natural kinds and laws.

While much argument has been devoted thus far to Deleuze's adherence to the principle of reciprocal determination, it is worthwhile to devote a little time to consolidating the degree to which his text entails the specific application of this principle to the evolutionary triad of law, constant and natural kind. With respect to law, a quotation at greater length from a passage we have already seen:

> The constants of one law are in turn variables of a more general law, just as the hardest rocks become soft and fluid matter on the geological scale of millions of years ... [I]f repetition is possible, it is due to miracle rather than to law. It is against the law: against the similar form and equivalent content of the law. If repetition can be found, even in nature, it is in the name of a power which affirms itself against law, which works underneath laws, perhaps superior to laws. (DR, 2)

This opposition to 'the law' is not so much a lawlessness as a nonindexical, generative principle of order, in the first instance a divergence of series; there is no content to the law which may operate 'from above' upon the phenomena; all events are immanent.

So too with limits and constants; limits are as necessary as they are subject to supersession; they are valid only insofar as we bear in mind the infinite speeds of relata on the plane of consistency. It is the limit that makes possible the limited thing. We have seen with the aid of Whitehead that this thought takes us to a primordial breaking of symmetry, a primordial divergence which constitutes the reasonless root of sufficient reason. Indeed, bearing in mind the close association of the constant or invariant with the notion of symmetry, we have seen how chimerical the notion of symmetry may be in the first place; it can be no final arbiter in a world where each event, no matter how large or small, contributes its own unmeasurable quantum of discernibility, of incommensurability.

If there is much in the Deleuzian text to consolidate our association of the principle of reciprocal determination with these first two terms, law and constant, there is perhaps less explicitly to underwrite such an association with 'natural kinds', even though we might from the outset suspend any essentialist connotations that phrase bears. Nevertheless, there is sufficient material to point this way; the insistence that relative speeds are all that differentiate entities on the thousand plateaus is a case in point. By the same token, is it not one implication of the assertion quoted above with respect to limits, that the very typology of 'limited things', of natural kinds, is a function of the contingent limit supervening on the open-ended plane of consistency? It is of course part and parcel of the radical contingency of the philosophy of difference that these limits may have been other than they are, and hence the 'things' different in kind. It is just this kind of idea that Deleuze and Guattari have in mind with the claim: 'There is no reason to think that all matter is confined to the physico-chemical strata: there exists a submolecular, unformed Matter' (ATP, 503). And again: '[Chaos] is a void that is not a nothingness but a virtual, containing all possible particles and drawing out all possible forms, which spring up only to disappear immediately' (WP, 118). Deleuze and Guattari describe the fate of a science bound to a 'plane of reference' (in contrast to the plane of consistency) forever to 'bifurcate', to produce new axes of reference, in response to the contingent limits it encounters along its journey. Due to its reliance always on pre-set coordinates, science is bound to investigate only the underside, so to speak, of an already-distributed natural landscape, whose limits have already closed over, whose tectonic plates already dovetail:

> The history of the sciences is inseparable from the construction, nature, dimensions and proliferation of axes. Science does not carry out any unification of the Referent but produces all kinds of bifurcations on a plane of reference that does not pre-exist its detours or its layout. It is as if the bifurcation were searching the infinite chaos of the virtual for new forms to actualize by carrying out a sort of potentialization of matter: carbon introduces a bifurcation in Mendeleyev's table, which, through its plastic properties, produces the state of organic matter. The problem of a unity or multiplicity of science, therefore, must not be posed as a function of a system of coordinates that is possibly unique at a given moment. As with the plane of immanence in philosophy, we must ask what status before and after assume, simultaneously, on a plane of reference with temporal dimension and evolution. Is there just one or several planes of reference? (WP, 123–4)

The outline here unmistakeably casts the scientific project as doomed always to traduce the creativity of nature, its genius for the baroque production of novel form. The choice of carbon as an example is a particularly telling one in the history of physical chemistry, since it presented a seemingly insurmountable challenge of explanation. On the principle that all lighter elements are converted into heavier elements, there was a problem encountered by Fred Hoyle, working in the early 1950s, in accounting for the transition from helium to carbon; it requires a qualitatively different process than that which produces helium from hydrogen, yet all heavier elements must subsequently be synthesised from carbon. Hoyle conjectured that what was required was a particular excited state of carbon atom which could conform in its mass to a triangulated combination of various forms of helium; this was quickly confirmed by experiment.[63] In short, unlike the syntheses of lighter elements, which were in large part produced during the Big Bang, carbon requires a bridging form for its nucleosynthesis; a form which requires the energy of stellar formations. The measure of this breakthrough is the success of Hoyle's conviction that nucleosynthesis occurs largely at the heart of stars. Nature changes its tactics in the course of completing the periodic table. May there not be times in the history of the cosmos when it is free once again to adopt new tactics in the production of previously unimagined natural kinds? This is the meaning of the question, are there one or many planes of reference? From a different perspective, given the well-established tendency of modern physics to understand matter as simply the expression of patterns of energy, then any mutation in the way those patterns express is by the same token a mutation of material kinds themselves. Plasma gives way to atomic kinds.

Yet if the evolution of natural kinds falls within the purview of Deleuzian thought, it is once again Whitehead who draws out the theme most fully, and who perhaps establishes the necessity of this phenomenon in a world in which constants and laws co-vary. Firstly, Whitehead commits to an explicitly evolutionary account of nature as a whole from *Science and the Modern World* onward: 'On the materialistic theory, there is material – such as matter or electricity – which endures. On the organic theory, the only endurances are structures of activity, and the structures are evolved.'[64] This is as much as to say that the world is a becoming, comprised of structures of activity, events, inheriting their character from preceding events and in turn bestowing their own modifications to subsequent generations of events.[65] By the evolutionary analogy, the characteristics of family can be shared only through a directly related lineage; the family (Whitehead prefers to talk of 'species' or 'societies') propagates locally, so to speak. Yet for Whitehead, these local events are not divorced from the global environment in which they take place:

> The causal laws which dominate a social environment are the product of the defining characteristics of that society. But the society is only efficient through its individual members. Thus in a society, the members can only exist by reason of the laws which dominate the society, and the laws come

into being by reason of the analogous characters of the members of that society. (PR, 90–1)

If the conception here places us recognisably on that same territory which Murray Gell-Mann captures with the phrase 'frozen accidents' (all the more so, since Whitehead is given to speak of 'protonic' or 'electronic' societies), nevertheless, Whitehead more forcefully identifies a positive momentum in the evolutionary transition from one epoch to the other: 'Thus a system of "laws" determining reproduction of some portion of the universe gradually rises into dominance; it has its stage of endurance, and passes out of existence with the decay of that society from which it emanates' (PR, 91). Whitehead's 'societies' are natural kinds. Just as does Nietzschean-Deleuzian active force, they too 'go beyond the limit' of their power.

This metaphysics goes so far as to dispose toward those theories of cosmology which propose the co-varying permutation of each of these terms together. Indeed, the congruence is explicitly acknowledged in the quotation below, from Roberto Unger:

> Consider three styles of explanation that have wide-ranging use in natural history ... we have no good reason to reject out of hand their application in thinking about the universe and its history ... we can call them the principle of path-dependence, the principle of the mutability of natural kinds, and the principle of the co-evolution of laws and phenomena.[66]

Lee Smolin has made an extended case for a version of cosmological evolution which broadens the analogy with the principles of biological evolution far beyond the sense pursued here, but his collaboration with Roberto Unger focuses more compatibly on our narrower terms. Equally, David Bohm's conception of cosmological evolution provides an example of the kind favoured by Deleuzian-Whiteheadian metaphysics. It is Bohm's version which I will argue jibes most favourably in the final nuances. I intend to conclude the argument by reading off these respective ideas against a particular hypothesis recently put forward by C.H. Lineweaver. In conclusion, this will help to establish more nicely the contention that for Deleuze, 'order' must be heard first and foremost as 'complexity', and complexity in its turn as 'evolution'.

We have already seen the broad use of Leibnizian principles by which Smolin hones his cosmological argument; no less is true of Unger, his co-writer for *The Singular Universe and the Reality of Time*. Unger develops the theme of a causative relation prior to and independent of law. This is for the sake of an open cosmic evolution. It is when he brings this to bear on Leibnizian-Machian principles that the points of intersection with the line of argument we have been pursuing come to the fore. Neither Leibniz nor Mach, he claims, quite succeeded in stating a 'relational position' adequate to the open-endedness of the evolution of nature: Leibniz because his philosophy 'hollows out the meaning of causation', while Mach 'confusingly combines a relational perspective with a very traditional, indeed Newtonian, view of causation'.[67] In short, the potential for evolution of constants and laws is not brought within the purview of either statement of the relational position. The quotations below, given at length to draw out connections to Deleuze, are unequivocal on the matter:

> The chief distinction between cosmic time under a relational and a cosmic view is that, for the relational account, the global character of time resides in the unbroken and inclusive web of connections in the singular universe and its singular history rather than in some independent place: the place of the invariant background or of the eyes of God.[68]

Thus far, we are securely on the territory of the Leibniz–Clarke correspondence, yet Unger goes on to elaborate on the centrality of 'cosmic time' to a relational approach in a way that joins hands with Deleuze through Bergson:

> It may be objected that this statement simply alters the meaning of words, by calling change and causation time. However, something of great consequence is at stake. Nothing is for keeps in nature: no typology of being (as described by particle physics and by the periodic table), no set of laws of nature, no ways by which some things change into others. Only changing change endures.[69]

It is here, where the notion of causation is uncoupled from law, that we can see a recoupling, perhaps axiomatic after Bergson, with a duration synonymous with chance, creation, evolution and complexity. Unger is familiar with Bergson's insistence on the reality of time (indeed, this very phrase is part of the title of the work quoted) independently of deterministic, extensive relations, and his concern here echoes Bergson's: to resist the relativistic conflation of space and time in complementary dimensions. Deleuze is close to marshalling all the arguments of *Creative Evolution* when he expresses the same idea:

> But the fact that real space has only three dimensions, that Time is not a dimension of space, really means this: There is an efficacy, a positivity of time, that is identical to a 'hesitation' of things and, in this way, to creation in the world. (B, 105)

To include time as a fourth dimension is to risk seeing time as a container brimming with all the pre-set possibilities, to enclose micro- and macrocosm within a totality. In this light, we would not be wrong to associate Deleuze's formulation 'chance is the only necessity' with Unger's 'only changing change endures'.

But if Unger dovetails with the metaphysical arguments, this is clearly in the service of a more adequate natural history of the evolution of the universe. He takes issue, for instance, with those models of cosmic natural history which are intended to simulate the early conditions of the universe in keeping with the established laws of our observable epoch: 'The trouble is that the laws and other regularities of nature fail to explain change beyond or before nucleosynthesis.'[70] The point here is precisely that raised by Deleuze and Guattari when they enquire whether there is one plane of reference or many. Since nature is capable of adopting different tactics, seems to have done precisely that in prior epochs, and may switch again, it is illegitimate to extrapolate the plane of reference derived from our present epoch forward or backward to others. Unger's point entails the further claim that phase shifts between one cosmic state of affairs and another are not to be understood as governed by 'meta-laws', but rather evolve from one to another. In a Whiteheadian register, the only endurances are structures of activity, and the structures are evolved. The particulars of the correspondence between the physics and the metaphysics are striking.

C.H. Lineweaver, of the Australian National University's Planetary Science Institute, recently produced an article devoted to nature's potential for sustaining complexity in light of entropic boundary conditions. It touches closely on our highlighted themes – the supersession of limits, changing constants, cosmological evolution – and offers one way to understand just how the second law of thermodynamics may apply to the explicate order, while remaining an illusion, as Deleuze would have it.

Lineweaver first points out that as a necessary but not sufficient condition, nature's potential for complexity is a function not of the total amount of energy, which is understood to remain constant, but of the available free energy, understood to deplete through the operation of entropy. This, he proposes, may be understood in terms of the difference between the level of entropy accrued by any given time in the history of the universe, and its maximum entropic state; to estimate the remaining free energy at any point requires only that we subtract the former from the latter. Between this maximum and minimum, order and complexity are able to flourish. He identifies a number of useful gradients (in terms of making 'work' possible) from which free energy may be extracted: luminosity, redox chemistry, pH, humidity, density, gravity, etc., along with a floor, the energy associated with the vacuum, below which no gradient can extend.

Granted a cosmos in which all constants are retained, this scenario should outline the boundary conditions for the evolution of complex systems, between the maxima and minima of the 'entropy gap'. Yet, as Lineweaver is at pains to point out, both maximum and minimum values are subject to changing conditions over the life-history of the cosmos, which necessitates some scrutiny of accounting. The maximum potential for free nuclear energy – that energy locked into the fusion of lighter elements into heavier – cannot figure on the balance sheet of the early universe, he observes, since it lacked the solar formations necessary to engineer such nucleosynthesis – the principle established by Fred Hoyle. Equally, the expansion of the universe shortly after the Big Bang served to defer potential fusion, and therefore narrow the entropy gap, until such massive structures as stars could emerge.[71]

If the upper bound is no fixed constant, neither, more importantly for our concerns, is the lower. Lineweaver focuses on the phenomenon referred to as inflation, with the related opposition between a 'false' and a 'true' vacuum. The concept of inflation was introduced into the cosmological narrative in 1979 by cosmologist Alan Guth.[72] It is intended to account for the apparent 'flatness' of the observed universe, with its attendant uniform densities of matter and energy.[73] This uniform 'flat' spread is considered unlikely between systems which have never been in contact and thus have had no chance to equilibrate. This it was thought must be true of the wider extremes of the universe, since any realistic extrapolation backwards to earliest times of the then current estimated ranges for the speed of expansion fell short of the required opportunity for communication between disparate regions. Guth's conclusion was that there must have been a period of prodigious expansion, a hyper-inflation, at the very earliest point in the history of the universe, effectively spreading a single, compact, highly energetic system outward uniformly beyond any means of subluminal communication. This brief, dramatic episode was powered by the unstable existence of a 'false' vacuum energy ensuring a floor, a minimum, destined to break through to a lower energy state (the 'true' vacuum), both releasing free energy and allowing new forms of matter to emerge. The stream found a lower *thalweg*.

Lineweaver's speculative innovation is to propose that such phase transitions may repeat, perhaps indefinitely, from one false vacuum to another; at the outer limit, as Serres asserts, there is no 'lowest *thalweg*', no true vacuum. The overall effect of such an evolution would be to maintain and perhaps increase the entropy gap from epoch to epoch; the minimum falls ever away. The accompanying conjecture is that each transition may allow for a further 'collapse' of matter. Just as hydrogen and helium are given scope to fuse into higher elements after the transition from inflation, so, we may conjecture, decaying protons, or other seemingly stable particles, may provide a source of free energy for the next epoch of lower vacuum energy.

From this synopsis, we can identify the importance Lineweaver's speculation carries for Deleuze. The association of order or complexity with the accessibility of energy gradients, free energy, aligns the argument (uncontroversially) with Deleuze. To frame this accessibility in terms of the gap between maxima and minima at once preserves the (productive) sway of the second law and the indefinite potential for novelty from epoch to epoch, as successive collapses unlock ever further potential from the limitless 'Dirac Sea'. Are we not then free to identify on Deleuze's behalf a certain illusory status for the second law as it operates within Lineweaver's scenario? To reserve the logic of this law for the explicate order of each epoch, inapplicable to the underlying aleatory evolution of the implicate? Almost, and this almost is instructive. The quotation below allows us to bring to the fore a substantive element which maintains distance between our metaphysics and this scientific speculation on cosmological evolution:

> If an infinite number of such free energy sources are identified then the universe can keep on evolving ... forever. On the other hand, if we have already identified all the sources of free energy in the universe, then the acceleration of the expansion of the universe and its asymptotic approach to a vacuum state will lead to the heat death of the universe.[74]

In Lineweaver's scenario, successive collapses of the minimum may potentially unlock sources of free energy understood as already inherent in the cosmic body, some recognised, others to emerge subsequently or not, as the case may be. We have, then, a distinguishing criterion, for by the lights of our metaphysics, such collapses should be attended by a *repopulation* of natural kinds, new relations and new relata, not yet within the range of 'envisagement' of the evolving cosmos. Such a repopulation need not be taken as an absolute fiat; just as the 'quark-gluon soup' remains under actually occurring (if rare) conditions in our epoch, so Whitehead countenances the persistence of superseded (or rather, 'other-than-dominant') form from one epoch to another. But the very modes by which the implicate order unfolds into the explicate and vice versa must alter. Coupling constants may change, the relative weight of protons and electrons may alter, any variability in the strength of gravity relative to the other forces will affect the tendency of matter to clump together, the relative diversity of boson and fermion types may shift. For our metaphysics, a change in the regime of energetic exchange must lead to a variation in the taxonomy of natural kinds. Whitehead says as much: the members, the societies and the environment of the world are reciprocally determinative. Deleuze's Ideal Game requires no less. Nor yet Roberto Unger's resistance to 'meta-laws'.

And it is here that the speculative risk of the metaphysics lies: its amenability to discreditation or ultimately disproof, at least in principle.[75] By extension, it is the same risk run by scientific theorists wedded to this specific variant of the evolutionary paradigm. There may ultimately be inherent limits to the permutation-space; the calculating God may reach the final typology of number. Whatever these limits might turn out to be, they will already be expressed in some fashion in the typology of matter-energy Lineweaver (and the Standard Model more generally) refers to; they may not be transparent in the quiddities of any given epochal transition, but ultimately they would 'shake out' as true invariants, symmetries and harbingers of equilibrium.

In turn, this rather sombre conclusion reveals to what extent the radically evolutionary moment of our metaphysics must entail, and may be the only standpoint which truly entails, an illusory status for the second law. To return to Emmy Noether's formulation, 'what is conserved in temporal symmetry is energy', let us recall at the same time that this may be couched in conditional terms: 'given the unchanging endurance of the laws of nature, energy will be conserved'. There is a counterpoint to this reasoning which appears frequently in the literature on thermodynamics. Henri Poincaré reflects on the potentially incommensurable and heterogeneous forms of energy which had been marshalled under the name 'heat' in the time of Carnot: 'As we cannot give a general definition of energy, the principle of the conservation of energy simply signifies that there is a *something* which remains constant.'[76] This *something* may be nothing more than a mirage produced by our adopted measuring practices, by conventional calibrations ensuring parity. Deleuze was sensitive to this reasoning, and indeed quotes this passage in support of the idea of disparity in *Difference and Repetition*. Poincaré continues:

> Whatever fresh notions of the world may be given us by future experiments, we are certain beforehand that there is something which remains constant, and which may be called *energy*. Does this mean that the principle has no meaning and vanishes into a tautology? Not at all. It means that the different things to which we give the name energy are connected by a true relationship; it affirms between them a real relation. But then, if this principle has a meaning, it may be false; it may be that we have no right to extend indefinitely its applications, and yet it is certain beforehand to be verified in the strict sense of the word. How, then, shall we know when it has extended as

far as is legitimate? Simply when it ceases to be useful to us – i.e., when we can no longer use it to predict correctly new phenomena.[77]

In other words, Noether's definition remains unhelpfully circular should we suspend the assumption that all forms of energy we encounter are simply variants of the same underlying energetic phenomenon.

This critique is decided unambiguously from the standpoint of our metaphysics: it is patently implausible to maintain that energy is conserved when the very forms of energy (matter included) and modes of energetic exchange are amenable to permutation from one epoch to another. For if there really is no such thing as 'energy in general', where then is the 'something' conserved? And if there is no such principle of conservation in the cosmic long term for energy (if the first law does not apply), then it cannot serve as a boundary constraint for the production or consumption of free energy (hence neither can the second). Disparity itself is unbounded. Dissymmetry is the deepest principle and sufficient reason of all that appears. At last we can affirm, after this lengthy redirection back through the Leibnizian version of sufficient reason, the necessity of chance which the Nietzschean version required: 'And are not all things bound fast together in such a way that this moment draws after it all future things? *Therefore* – draws itself too?' And we have gone some way to showing how the sense of this affirmation may in fact be triangulated (we do not say resolved) with conceptual strands of modern physics, as Nietzsche had declared it his ambition to achieve.

Nor are we left to extrapolate these conclusions from Deleuze's own suspicions of symmetry and valorisation of disparity. They are explicitly drawn by David Bohm in the work *Causality and Chance in Modern Physics*. In this work, Bohm aims to establish what he calls the 'qualitative infinity of nature', which entails precisely that openendedness of constants, laws and natural kinds on which we have been focusing. His is an evolutionary cosmology in our sense. In a passage considering the question of the irreversibility of processes and its relation to thermodynamics, he succinctly lays out the implications of a qualitatively infinite nature:

> For, as we have seen, the notion of a law that gives a perfect one-to-one mathematical correspondence between well-defined variables in the past and in the future is only an abstraction, good enough to describe limited domains of phenomena for limited periods of time, but, nevertheless, not valid for all possible domains over an infinite time.[78]

This being so, we are obliged to recognise that no process can be considered indefinitely reversible, since the very channel along which it runs is given over to other modes at each end, future and past, of its viable lifetime. We might note that this is an argument for the innate irreversibility of the arrow of time which does not essentially rely on the thermodynamic arrow of entropy as such. Indeed, Bohm signals a suspicion toward the pre-eminence of the second law in numerous references to the inexhaustible energies of the Dirac Sea. He continues:

> the very entities with which physics now works, satisfying the currently studied laws of physics, must have come into being at some point in the past, while changing conditions, brought about in part by chance contingencies, will eventually lead to a stage of the universe in which new kinds of entities, satisfying new kinds of laws will come into being.[79]

The implication of this standpoint follows:

> The importance of considering the impact of these qualitative changes on the basic mode of being of things is also seen when we consider the predictions of the 'heat death' of the universe ... However long before this comes about, it is evidently quite possible and indeed very likely that qualitatively new developments reflecting the inexhaustible and infinite character of the universal process of becoming will have invalidated predictions [of this type]. For example, just as there may have been a time before molecules, atoms, electrons and protons existed, the further evolution of the universe could also lead to a new time in which they cease to exist, and are replaced by something else again. And new sources of energy coming from the infinite process of becoming may be made available even if atoms, molecules, etc., continue to exist ... [T]he infinite substructure of matter very probably contains energies that are as far beyond nuclear energies as nuclear energies are beyond chemical energies.[80]

It is finally in one and the same sense, then, that Deleuze's resistance to limits of opposition and negation and to the 'heat death' implied by the second law, and indeed his insistence on the illusory status of that law, may be understood. It is the very mutability of constants, laws and natural kinds, and perhaps only this, which could maintain an endlessly enduring complexity and underpin the infinite process of becoming. The philosophy of difference is a philosophy of evolution.

Once more, though, having reached this conclusion, a final pause is due. After all, the point of departure which prompted this exercise in reorientation was the observation that the Event for Deleuze is to be understood as ceaseless. Have we not resolved one horn of the dilemma, the conflict over entropy, to arrive at a framework which requires of the Event a punctuation over a time-scale which could not possibly be longer: the transition from one epoch to another? Have we not recast the role of periodisation on a scale many trillion-fold larger than the chaotic bifurcations which were so problematic? But we must bear in mind the connections drawn between the local and the global.

Each micro-event, the formation of every membrane and every crystal, depends on forces which leap beyond their powers; each 'society' works to its own demise. Each epoch is a mobile army in redeployment. Each and everything is evolving at all times and the single throw of dice conjoins with the whole of chance.

Conclusion

The question has been not so much how to reconcile Deleuze's natural philosophy with fundamental tenets of science, as to establish what it might mean in a scientific register to accommodate the direction of travel. With respect to Deleuze's stated arguments against the substantive existence of entropy, the answer appears to be simply: 'nothing'. The arguments Deleuze adopts against entropic processes risk being dismissed as 'not even wrong', ironically not because they contradict scientific common sense, but because they are unable to secure enough distance from that common sense to meaningfully contradict it. Nor is there more than suggestive support from chaos theory. Even the most forthright advocates of chaos theory stop short of pronouncing any other destination but equilibrium in the very long term.[1] To establish the *illegitimacy* of generalising from the ideal (unachievable) experimentally enclosed system to the world in the wild cannot in itself establish that the world will finally, after all deviations and deferments, avoid the same moribund fate as the enclosed system. Chaos theory cannot ultimately underwrite the broader metaphysical import of Deleuze's critical argument. In the end, however, I hope to have shown that it is not in the *critique* of entropy that we can triangulate Deleuze's resistance to the second law, but in the positive aspects of his metaphysics more generally. Disparity and dissymmetry take on their own powers at the cosmological scale. From one epoch to another, evolution outruns entropy.

Ultimately, at this scale too, we can learn the value of Deleuze's insistence that the Event is ceaseless, always diverging but not contingently on chaotic bifurcation – the principle which sets him apart from an overly complete assimilation to chaos theory. If we are to subscribe to this claim, we must conceive the Event as independent of contiguity, both spatially and temporally. That foreign war a decade ago and this memorial ceremony on home soil are not two events but one and the same event at different times and different places. The asteroid being nudged at this moment out of its orbit as a result of collision is part of the event of the city it will destroy on earth many months hence. The two are conjoined now in the same event long before they converge in the same time and place. There is nothing essentially episodic or periodic about the event. Episode and period are epiphenomena, limitations and distributions of the more fundamental intensive continuity. This is so at a deeper level than the endlessly etiolated interconnection of all phenomena. The very structuration of space supports action at a distance. Non-locality is the deepest motif of a ceaseless event. It is also a key part of the dialogue between the philosophy and the physics. Deleuze's philosophy invites a natural dialogue with the network and holographic paradigms.

In the end, a great part of any value this book may have consists in its establishing a specific meaning for 'openness' with respect to Deleuze's cosmology. The lens bringing this definition into view has been the central question of entropy; entropy is not definitively overcome on this account without the co-variability of laws, constants and natural kinds. At its most simple, there is simply nothing to balance out to equilibrium if we accept that there is no 'energy' in general, and that all manifestations of energy are liable to substitution from one epoch to another. Still, a little further reflection and context is due to the question of openness. For all that it has become a commonplace to speak of the universe as 'open' in scientific and philosophical terms, this word, like any other in complex argument, accrues its own meaning from context. For Alexandre Koyré, the history of cosmology traced a path from the 'closed' world of the ancients to the infinite universe of modern science; 'openness' can mean simply 'infinite' in extent and duration.[2] For Hermann Weyl, the natural world displayed an openness which was intuitively accessible as a potentially infinite 'open field of possibilities'; an openness demonstrated first and foremost by mathematical symbolic construction.[3] For Karl Popper, openness connoted 'indeterminism', a status guaranteed in a universe capable of producing consciousness and cultural strata.[4] From a relativistic point of view, the openness of the universe can be judged by its curvature; this openness is a freedom to expand indefinitely on condition of 'flatness'. The inflationary model of the Big Bang encompasses the multiversal conjecture that each created universe contains within it the conditions to create further universes, in an open cascade of 'bubble' universes. For chaos theory, 'openness' connotes the impossibility of definitively isolating even a single system in the universe as a whole; all systems are open. In all cases, perhaps most especially the last, the question of what it is for the universe to be open has spawned attendant questions on the nature of physical law, and drawn out tensions between determinist and indeterminist treatments of nature. 'Openness' has always been a close synonym for indeterminacy, but the nature of the indeterminacy in question can take many forms. It is perhaps always legitimate to ask of any given theory not merely what *degree*, but also what *type* of openness it entails. This has certainly proven to be the end goal for this investigation.

To accommodate the 'evolutionary expansiveness' which Deleuze and Whitehead envision for their philosophy of nature, and to tune this into the scientific register, is to recognise that trio of elements which must be subject to mutability. It is at the same time to single out those strands of thought in the scientific discourse which speak to the same sense of evolution. They are already there. This particular form of openness is requisite if Deleuze's thought as a whole is to maintain coherence and value in conversation with speculative physics. I am conscious, nevertheless, that some sleight of hand may be suspected in all of this. After all, what elements are there other than laws, constants and natural kinds in the constitution of nature? Does this not encompass *everything*? The original question re-emerges: What remains of order if all fixed points are undone? Is this position not tantamount to the claim that anything can happen at any time? A claim incommensurate with any endeavour that could call itself science? No. There is every reason to insist on a more accurate formula for the Deleuzian thought we are presenting here: 'all things are evolving at all times'.

To appreciate this point, we might consider and contrast the work of Quentin Meillassoux, who claims in apparent agreement with Deleuze that radical chance is the primitive root of everything that appears: '*contingency alone is necessary*',[5] he states, in a palpable echo of Deleuze's 'chance is the only necessity'. Moreover, his reasoning, just like Deleuze's own, is bound up with a rejection of Leibniz's principle of sufficient reason. Despite the apparent common ground, however, I would argue that Meillassoux's conception of radical chance is at direct odds with Deleuze's. The points of contention are worthy of a full exposition and would undoubtedly represent one of the directions in which the work of this book could be developed, but the main crux is encapsulated in the following quotation:

> If we look through the aperture which we have opened up onto the absolute, what we see there is a rather menacing power – something insensible, and capable of destroying both things and worlds, of bringing forth monstrous absurdities, yet also of never doing anything, of realizing every dream, but also every nightmare, of engendering random and frenetic transformations,

or conversely, of producing a universe that remains motionless down to its ultimate recesses, like a cloud bearing the fiercest storms, then the eeriest bright spells, if only for an interval of disquieting calm.[6]

What Meillassoux is presenting here is a contingency without reason, without need of sufficient reason. His formula (his only necessity or absolute), he says, is the principle of unreason, an innate capacity in nature for any random suspension, reversal or transformation of laws whatsoever. But we should understand something further, conveyed by the phrase 'random and frenetic transformations'. 'There is no reason for anything to be or to remain the way it is', he says; 'everything must, without reason, be able not to be and/or to be other than it is'.[7] At every point the persistence of states of affairs and structures is subject to a potential reversal. This is not at odds with the enduring structuration we actually observe; there is equally no reason why it may not persist. Meillassoux draws an ontological difference between this principle and what he calls the 'precariousness' of all entities under the sun which ultimately may cease to exist; that inherent possibility is already encompassed by the lawful regularities of a tame universe. The unreason he envisages is rather a 'lawless destruction of every law'.

There is something missing from this account, something which is everywhere declared in Deleuze's philosophy: a sense of propagation, of explication and folding/unfolding. Of evolution. In Meillassoux's universe, laws are considered somewhat like 'settings' which may be switched on or off here, there or ubiquitously, instantly as if by fiat. The openness entailed by Meillassoux's contingency requires an acute adherence to the weightless equivalence of radically incongruent possibilities, without delay or retardation in actualisation, without mechanism, process or propagation. This is precisely what scientists tend to call 'magic thinking', a charge often laid at the door of religious or theological accounts of nature. Deleuze's own critique of this style of reasoning consists in the injunction always to seek virtual conditions over merely 'possible' eventualities. Meillassoux's position is perhaps the most radical possible affirmation of the reverse. His is the thought corresponding to the formula 'anything can happen at any time'. To the extent that Meillassoux's 'absolute' depends on this formula it is at odds with Deleuzian metaphysics. By contrast, the open evolution of Deleuze's universe is founded on the underlying conditions of the virtual, there where the order of nature lies. To embrace evolution is not to abandon order, but to seize it in process.

There are (at the least) three other areas relating to the work undertaken in this book that have been left relatively underdeveloped, and each of them merits further development. The biggest omission without doubt is the thermodynamic 'arrow of time'. The topic is so intrinsically bound up with questions of order and entropy in the scientific literature that each and every line of enquiry pursued here could meaningfully be explored with respect to its implications for the arrow of time. In line with his position on entropy, Deleuze is quite consistent in assigning an arrow of time to the explicate order but not the implicate, yet this does not by any means automatically determine a ready response to the question as a whole. In physics, the basic problematic is commonly accepted: every law of dynamics or mechanics, at both the macroscopic and microscopic level, is neutral as to the direction of temporal evolution of the system they describe. This is often explained in terms of video or film footage: any recording of very large-scale natural processes over a relatively short term would not reveal in itself whether the film were running forward or backward; planets orbit, stars expand or contract and so on. The laws of macro-scale dynamics work equally well forward and backward. It is only when the film depicts a spontaneous increase of order that we detect something amiss: the demolished building reassembles, the drained water conspires to organise itself to radiate back upward and out of the plughole. None of this contradicts the laws of dynamics, we are assured; it is merely vastly improbable that any great spontaneous decrease in entropy, or jump from disorder to greater organisation, should occur rather than the reverse. Discussions of the topic have accrued their own routine paradoxes and thought experiments, from typing monkeys to Boltzmann Brains. Particular variants of the arrow of time are attendant on different definitions of order and complexity.

Beyond these variables in the debate are more bracing theoretical differences. Huw Price argues that the question of the arrow of time has in fact been misframed and is circular.[8] With respect to radiative phenomena, for instance, such as ripples in water, he claims that it is logically no more improbable that wave fronts converge on one point and disappear than that they radiate outwards from an initial disturbance. The assignment of improbability to such 'reverse' phenomena is entirely attendant on a prior assumption that radiation proceeds naturally outwards. If the arrow of time were in the opposite direction, such convergent phenomena would be unexceptional. This being so, derivations of the arrow of time from probabilistic arguments have routinely been guilty of assuming that which they are intended to prove. In one respect, Deleuze's philosophy contains the resources to make the same critique; it is a will to impose a good sense and a common sense on phenomena which illegitimately presupposes a specific direction to time, from the particular to the general, from the differentiated to the undifferentiated and hence from the improbable to the more probable. Yet the details diverge. For Price, there is *de facto* only one direction for the arrow of time (it is merely that one direction cannot be distinguished on grounds of 'natural' probability from the other), while for Deleuze series reach both forward and backward in the living present. It is worthy of investigation whether Deleuze's distinction between Aion and Chronos (a linear conception of time) can coherently be upheld in light of such a critique. Julian Barbour proposes a cosmological model which in effect suspends the question of the arrow of time, arguing that its apparent linear progression is the effect of an inherent dissymmetry at the heart of all phenomena.[9] His model entails an account of the event which is completely independent of contiguity in space and time. Yet once again the similarities to the metaphysics we have laid out here are potentially more than outweighed by the differences, not least in that Barbour's account reduces all duration to autonomous instants. These examples are minimally suggestive of a rich variety of problematic variants on the theme in contemporary physics. A thoroughgoing evaluation of the arrow of time with respect to Deleuze's philosophy is in itself a major project.

A second line of development lies in a deeper examination of the moments of Deleuzian complexity: explication, implication and complication. These moments taken all together represent a truly nuanced concept of complexity as such. We have seen in what sense the notion of explication serves to orientate our metaphysics with contemporary physics, and indeed the recognisable hallmark of implication in holographic paradigms. But what of complication? This concept represents the highest order of folding; complication embraces all series and series of series, all elements regardless of contradiction, the entirety of the virtual and the actual, all difference in itself. It is at once the univocity and the immanence of becoming. In what sense can this final component of the triad be said to speak to natural science? It would seem approachable only transcendentally. Which forces a decision: are we finally to say that there will always be some transcendental sense to the project of science?

These questions underly the final potential line of development: what is 'transcendental empiricism'? Of all Deleuze's scandalous and iconoclastic innovations, this phrase is perhaps the most resolutely oxymoronic. As Marc Rölli puts it: 'Let's face it, almost everyone, both historically and philosophically, is convinced that the systematic positions taken respectively by empiricist and transcendental philosophers are incommensurable.'[10] I would certainly agree; empirical principles, the insistence on observation, would seem to rule out in advance any recourse to that which must remain in principle unobservable for scientific explanation. The initial question becomes for Rölli, 'Can empiricism have a transcendental aspect?' The response necessarily engages a long and fraught negotiation between two grand philosophical traditions, alongside an interrogation of Deleuze's Hume and his Kant. Our initial framing question, from a cosmological point of view, might focus on a more specifically contemporary problematic: 'What is the relationship between observed enduring patterns in this universe and others that are in principle unobservable?' It is a question prompted by the readiness of so many fields of contemporary cosmology to speak in terms of a multiverse rather than a universe. It hardens the question; not only must we ask whether there can be a transcendental aspect to empiricism, but, given seemingly insurmountable barriers to empirical enquiry, whether transcendental speculation is ultimately avoidable. The questions fall out: 'Given that other universes are in principle unobservable, do we discount their existence as a factor in scientific explanation?' 'What scope is there for identifying underpinning conditions for any universe whatever?' 'How might we be forced to adapt our own understanding of the patterns of this universe in light of any such adduced underpinning conditions for the multiverse (perhaps analogously to the conceptual reconfigurations cast backward onto plane geometry by the geometry of curved surfaces)?' For a Deleuzian these questions call on some of the core resources in the corpus – the idea of univocity, of immanence and the nature of the plane of immanence (are there one or many?), of expression, and now as I hope to have established, of evolution.

Notes

1. CHAOS

1 DeLanda, *Intensive Science and Virtual Philosophy*; Massumi, *A User's Guide to Capitalism and Schizophrenia*; Bonta and Protevi, *Deleuze and Geophilosophy*.
2 Deleuze seems to borrow from Husserl the notion of the 'anexact' in use here. The term is coined to recognise that certain ideas contain a positive measure of inexactitude, and that any attempt to substitute more accurate terms would deprive a given description of its intended effect. 'The most perfect geometry and its most perfect practical control cannot help the descriptive student of nature to express (in exactly geometrical concepts) that which in so plain, so understanding and so entirely suitable a way he expresses in the words: notched, indented, lens-shaped, umbelliform, and the like – simple concepts which are *essentially and not accidentally inexact*, and which are *therefore* also unmathematical.' Husserl, *Ideas*, p. 142. Such terms guarantee, therefore, a common ground between science, the arts and philosophy and render untenable the attempt to delimit each to its own sphere. Deleuze and Guattari were to broaden this basic insight into a discussion of the interrelation of these disciplines in *What Is Philosophy?* Each is examined for its relation to chaos, and they are referred to collectively as 'the chaoids'.
3 Deleuze, *Negotiations*, pp. 29–30.
4 It is worth reflecting on how the region of bifurcation functions in chaos theory in much the same way as 'zones of indiscernibility' and the 'object = x' work for Deleuze, and hence how far it is plausible to read back and forth the tensions of equilibrium and disequilibrium, symmetry and symmetry-breaking, between the physics and the metaphysics; these topics will be investigated in detail throughout this book, though with less emphasis on the connection to chaos theory.
5 From Deleuze's 1987 Leibniz lectures, my translation.
6 Bonta and Protevi, *Deleuze and Geophilosophy*, p. 26.
7 Ibid., p. 27.

8 Leonard Lawlor, 'Phenomenology and Metaphysics and Chaos: On the Fragility of the Event in Deleuze', in *The Cambridge Companion to Deleuze*, ed. Smith and Somers-Hall, p. 105.
9 Nietzsche, *The Gay Science*, §109, p. 168.
10 Quoted in NP, 44.
11 Babich, *Nietzsche's Philosophy of Science*, p. 154.
12 Nietzsche, *The Will to Power*, §688, p. 366.
13 Klossowski, *Nietzsche and the Vicious Circle*, p. 103.
14 NP, 37, quoting Nietzsche, *The Will to Power*, §635, p. 339.
15 Nietzsche, *The Gay Science*, 'The Greatest Weight', p. 273.
16 'We know that Nietzsche gave no exposition of the eternal return, for reasons which pertain both to the simplest "objective criticism" of the texts and to their most modest dramatic or poetic comprehension' (DR, 297).
17 Nietzsche, *Thus Spoke Zarathustra*, p. 178.
18 Ibid., p. 179.
19 '[P]lay affirms chance and the necessity of chance' (NP, 183).
20 Eddington, *The Nature of the Physical World*, p. 74.
21 Penrose, *Cycles of Time*, see esp. chapter 1.
22 Though see, for instance, Sean Carroll, *From Eternity to Here*, p. 187, on the limitations of this formulation. While the direction toward disorder as a result of entropic processes remains true as a broad generalisation, the simple identification of 'entropy' with 'disorder' is hard to square without exception; a salient example would be the tendency of an oil-in-water suspension to separate out into mutually exclusive layers, thereby furnishing a more ordered state than thorough miscegenation. This state nevertheless represents the least energetic, closest to equilibrium for such systems.
23 It should be acknowledged that not all classical formulations countenance the distinction between microstate and macrostate. J. Willard Gibbs proposed a definition much in the spirit of information theory which hinged purely on the likelihood or unlikelihood of a given observed state, or more accurately, on the probability of that state with respect to the degree of knowledge we possess of the system in question. See Carroll, *From Eternity to Here*, p. 192.
24 Henri Poincaré, 'Le mécanisme et l'expérience', *Revue de metaphysique et de morale* 4 (1893), quoted in Carroll, *From Eternity to Here*, p. 234.
25 See for instance, Gribbin, *13.8: The Quest to Find the True Age of the Universe and the Theory of Everything*.
26 A. Chakravarty, 'On the Prospects of Naturalised Metaphysics', in *Scientific Metaphysics*, ed. Ross, Ladyman and Kincaid, pp. 27–50.
27 See for instance, Gratton, *Speculative Realism*, pp. 85–107.
28 Stengers, *Power and Invention*, p. 69.
29 Ilya Prigogine insists on the importance of the word 'population' in characterising the elements of a system or ensemble; it is only from the perspective of atomic or molecular 'populations' that phase transition becomes a meaningful concept. It is interesting to note the similarity of terminology

to Whitehead (whose work Prigogine was familiar with) on this point. Whitehead coined the term 'societies' to speak of systems or categories of atomic phenomena, to reflect much the same insight that systems and ensembles assume behaviours distinct from individuals at this scale. See Prigogine, *The End of Certainty*, p. 45, and PR, 34.
30 C.H. Lineweaver, 'A Simple Treatment of Complexity: Cosmological Boundary Conditions on Increasing Complexity', in *Complexity and the Arrow of Time*, ed. Lineweaver, Davies and Ruse, p. 59.
31 Smolin, *Time Reborn*, p. 222.
32 Deleuze's call for 'liquid physics' is an acknowledged echo of the same exhortation issued by Michel Serres in his *The Birth of Physics*.
33 See Schrödinger, *What Is Life?*, p. 70. His original term is 'negative entropy', which quickly became 'negentropy' in the literature.
34 Bohm, *Wholeness and the Implicate Order*, p. 233.
35 Čapek, *Bergson and Modern Physics*, p. 383.

2. ENTROPY AND THE COMPLETE CONCEPT IN LEIBNIZ AND DELEUZE

1 Leibniz, *Discourse on Metaphysics*, in *Philosophical Essays*, §8, p. 41.
2 In the history of thermodynamics, Leibniz's principle of least resistance is recognised as a precursor to Maupertuis's more general principle of least action; this latter still informs modern physics. Leibniz argued, against Fermat, that light travels not by the quickest, but by the easiest route, the one that offers least resistance. Maupertuis essentially broadened this principle to encompass all physical action (see Jennifer Coopersmith's *The Lazy Universe*, pp. 24–5). It is a complementary principle to the four laws of thermodynamics, bearing on the tendency of linear systems to avoid spontaneously expending greater energy than is required in a given situation, thereby moving away from rather than toward equilibrium. The principle is not exceptionless, since non-linear and open systems will not in the short term move toward equilibrium.
3 Leibniz, letter to Arnauld, in *Discourse on Metaphysics, Correspondence with Arnauld, Monadology*, p. 129.
4 Leibniz, *Discourse on Metaphysics*, §8.
5 It should be noted that Leibniz is not construing contingent truths as necessary in the mind of God, due to some predestinative foreknowledge here; he is aware of the implications of predestination and is at pains to avoid them in section 13 of the *Discourse on Metaphysics*. More particularly, with respect to free will, he argues that God *inclines*, but does not dictate, the future action of a subject. Rather, he distinguishes the form of necessity in question from the deductive necessity associated with the containment theory of meaning (whereby once we know the meaning of 'circle', we are justified in saying that all points of the circumference are equidistant from the centre). He writes: 'Now it is evident that every

true predication has some basis in the nature of things, and even when a predicate is not identical, that is, when the predicate is not expressly contained in the subject, it is still necessary that it be virtually contained in it, and this is what the philosophers call *in-esse*, saying thereby that the predicate is in the subject.' Leibniz, *Discourse on Metaphysics*, §8.
6 Smith, *Essays on Deleuze*, p. 75.
7 Aristotle, *De caelo*, 295b, 11–16, quoted in Kahn, *Anaximander and the Origins of Greek Cosmology*, p. 76. Brackets in the original.
8 Kahn, *Anaximander and the Origins of Greek Cosmology*, p. 77.
9 Alexander, ed. *The Leibniz–Clarke Correspondence*, p. 16.
10 Cited in Van Fraasen, *Laws and Symmetry*, p. 298.
11 Leibniz, 'On the Ultimate Origination of Things', in *The Shorter Leibniz Texts*, p. 31.
12 Ibid., p. 32.
13 Ibid., p. 33.
14 Ibid.
15 Ibid.
16 Michel Serres, commenting on 'Ultimate Origination', neatly encapsulates the interplay of these Leibnizian ideas: 'Things are drawn into existence along the steepest route. They seek equilibrium, following a determinant or decisive deviation' (BP, 53).
17 'There are a large number of different physical structures which form spontaneously as their components try to meet certain energetic requirements. These components may be constrained, for example, to seek a point of minimal free energy, like a soap bubble, which acquires its spherical form by minimizing surface tension, or a common salt crystal, which adopts the form of a cube by minimizing bonding energy.' DeLanda, *Intensive Science and Virtual Philosophy*, p. 15. 'Where heat diffusion tends to create instability, surface tension creates stability. The pull of surface tension makes a substance prefer smooth boundaries like the wall of a soap bubble. It costs energy to make surfaces that are rough.' Gleick, *Chaos*, p. 311.
18 See Leibniz, 'On Freedom and Spontaneity', in *The Shorter Leibniz Texts*, pp. 94–5.
19 Leibniz, 'On the Reason Why These Things Exist Rather Than Other Things', ibid., pp. 30–1.
20 Leibniz, 'Remarks on Mr Arnauld's Letter Concerning My Proposition: That the Individual Concept of Each Person Contains Once and for All Everything that Will Ever Happen to Him', ibid., pp. 43–7.
21 Leibniz, 'On the Ultimate Origination of Things', pp. 31–8.
22 This insight is developed by Michel Serres in *The Birth of Physics*, first with respect to the minimal differential change of angle of the atom falling through the void described by Lucretius, then by extension to Leibniz's framing of 'metaphysical mechanics' in 'On the Ultimate Origination of Things'.

23 Ariew and Garber reproduce Leibniz's marginal note verbatim: 'When God calculates and exercises his thought, the world is made.' Leibniz, *Philosophical Essays*, fn. p. 270.
24 Nelson, *The Penguin Dictionary of Mathematics*.
25 Daniel W. Smith, 'Axiomatics and Problematics as Two Methods of Formalisation: Deleuze's Epistemology of Mathematics', in Duffy ed., *Virtual Mathematics*, p. 145.
26 Lautman, *Mathematics, Ideas and the Physical Real*, p. 88.
27 Ibid.
28 Quoted in C. Alunni, 'Continental Genealogies: Mathematical Confrontations in Albert Lautman and Gaston Bachelard', in Duffy ed., *Virtual Mathematics*, p. 69.
29 Ibid.
30 Quoted in ibid.
31 Lautman, *Mathematics, Ideas and the Physical Real*, p. 190.
32 Deleuze and Guattari, *Anti-Oedipus*, p. 77.
33 Zourabichvili, *Deleuze*, p. 170.
34 'Our reasoning is based upon two great principles: first, that of Contradiction, by means of which we decide that to be false which involves contradiction and that to be true which contradicts or is opposed to the false. And the second, the principle of Sufficient Reason, in virtue of which we believe that no fact can be real or existing and no statement true unless it has a sufficient reason why it should be thus and not otherwise.' Leibniz, *Discourse on Metaphysics, Correspondence with Arnauld, Monadology*, §31–2, p. 258.
35 Zourabichvili, *Deleuze*, p. 168.
36 Leibniz writes: 'Now, this interconnection, relationship, or this adaptation of all things to each particular one, and of each one to all the rest, brings it about that every simple substance has relations which express all the others and that it is consequently a perpetual living mirror of the universe.' *Monadology*, §56. Whitehead echoes: 'the notion of "complete abstraction" is self-contradictory. For you cannot abstract the universe from any entity, actual or non-actual, so as to consider that entity in complete isolation. Whenever we think of some entity, we are asking, What is it fit for here? In a sense, every entity pervades the whole world' (PR, 28).
37 Leibniz, *Monadology*, §22.
38 '[T]he meaning of the phrase "the actual world" is relative to the becoming of a definite actual entity which is both novel and actual, relatively to that meaning, and to no other meaning of that phrase. Thus, conversely, each actual entity corresponds to a meaning of "the actual world" peculiar to itself ... An actual world is a nexus; and the actual world of one entity sinks to the level of a subordinate nexus in actual worlds beyond that actual entity' (PR, 28).
39 A caveat should be observed here. While Whitehead's terms 'mental pole' and 'physical pole' do function in isolation much as do Deleuze's

'implicate' and 'explicate' – most importantly for our purposes with respect to the topological relations characterising each regime – Whitehead's metaphysics nevertheless proposes a fundamental species which has no direct parallel in Deleuze's own: the 'Eternal Object'. He employs the term for a similar purpose to that we find motivating Plato's concept of Form or *eidos*, to account for the observed repetition of pattern or forms in nature. This echo of Platonic thought would be directly at odds with the immanent, genetic character of natural structuration on which Deleuze insists, and indeed definitively undermine the correlations between the two respective sets of terms here, were it not for certain specificities of Whitehead's concept. The concept seems a paradoxical one, in that Whitehead asserts of eternal objects apparently irreconcilable features. He says of them: 'The things which are temporal arise by their participation in the things which are eternal' (PR, 40), which would seem to align with the Platonic idea of the Forms as ideal types which token phenomena more or less closely resemble; given objects 'participate' more or less fully in their associated Form. Yet Whitehead also makes the (Aristotelian) claim that 'apart from things that are actual, there is nothing – nothing either in fact nor in efficacy' (PR, 40), which seems to deny independent existence, metaphysical or otherwise, to the eternal objects. Moreover, as a 'category of existence', the nature of eternal objects is glossed as 'Pure Potentials for the Specific Determination of Fact, *or* Forms of Definiteness'. The aspect of the eternal object which reconciles these incompatibilities (timeless form, immanence to actualities), and places some distance between Whitehead's metaphysics and that of Plato, is that no single eternal object can be understood as informing any actual occasion on its own; all eternal objects participate negatively or positively in all actual occasions to a greater or lesser degree, in a permutation which is always a novelty. It is in this sense that individual eternal objects have no independent existence (Whitehead writes: 'The general relationships of eternal objects to each other, relationships of diversity and pattern, are their relationships in God's conceptual realization. Apart from this realization, there is mere isolation indistinguishable from nonentity' (PR, 257)). It is also in this sense that Whitehead's schema affords connections with Deleuze's own; when Whitehead speaks of the 'ingression' of eternal objects into the world, we should understand the relation described less in terms of the eminent (or emanative) causal relation of the Platonic Forms, than as a version of *expression* in nature. Deleuze devotes much time to establishing the superiority of expressive models over causal, and indeed the very terms 'explicate' and 'implicate' are drawn from that Neoplatonic tradition.
40 Prigogine and Stengers, *Order Out of Chaos*, p. 176.
41 Sean Bowden, 'Gilles Deleuze: A Reader of Gilbert Simondon', in *Gilbert Simondon: Being and Technology*, ed. De Boever et al. p. 137.

42 Brian Massumi, '"Technical Mentality" Revisited: Brian Massumi on Gilbert Simondon', in *Gilbert Simondon: Being and Technology*, ed. De Boever et al., p. 33.
43 'The living, at whatever level it is conceived, can be considered as a "centre" that structures the milieu with which it enters into a debate.' Georges Canguilhem, *Connaissance de la Vie*, p. 96, cited in Dominique Lecourt, 'The Question of the Individual in Georges Canguilhem and Gilbert Simondon', in *Gilbert Simondon: Being and Technology*, ed. De Boever et al., p. 177.
44 Anne Sauvagnargues, 'Crystals and Membranes: Individuation and Temporality', in *Gilbert Simondon: Being and Technology*, ed. De Boever et al., pp. 57–70.
45 Massumi, '"Technical Mentality" Revisited', p. 28.
46 Deleuze adopts the term *Eventum Tantum* in association with the Stoic concept of the Aion; it is the Event which embraces all events throughout the course of time, regardless of compatibility or contradiction, the whole of chance at work in the single throw of the dice. Deleuze writes: 'Nothing other than the Event subsists, the Event alone, *Eventum tantum* for all contraries, which communicates with itself through its own distance and resonates across all of its disjuncts' (LS, 176).
47 'Einstein's papers on special relativity ... mark the reversal of a trend: until then the principles of invariance were derived from the laws of motion ... It is natural for us now to derive the laws of nature and to test their validity by means of the laws of invariance, rather than to derive the laws of invariance from what we believe to be the laws of nature. The general theory of relativity is the next milestone in the history of invariance ... It is the first attempt to derive a law of nature by selecting the simplest invariant equation.' Eugene P. Wigner, 'Invariance in Physical Theory', cited in DeLanda, *Intensive Science and Virtual Philosophy*, p. 151.
48 Mee, *Higgs Force*, pp. 160–1.
49 Weinberg, *Dreams of a Final Theory*, p. 158.
50 Woit, *Not Even Wrong*, p. 45.
51 Weyl, *Symmetry*, p. 126.
52 D'Espagnat, *On Physics and Philosophy*, p. 142.
53 Feynman, *The Character of Physical Law*, p. 103.
54 'As Morris Kline writes, "The group of an equation is a key to its solvability because the group expresses the degree of indistinguishability of the [solutions]. It tells us what we do not know about the [solutions]." Or as Deleuze would put it, the group reveals not what we know about the solutions, but *the objectivity of what we do not know about them*, that is, the objectivity of the problem itself.' DeLanda, *Intensive Science and Virtual Philosophy*, p. 151.
55 More accurately, according to Richard Feynman's formulation of quantum electrodynamics, no phenomena may occur which impinge on the energetic balance of nature above the Planck scale, thereby contradicting

the principle of the conservation of energy; all phenomena below this scale are understood to appear and disappear with a rapidity too acute to register in nature's book; the effects of these 'virtual particles' cancel themselves out (see, for instance, Roger Penrose's *The Road to Reality*, pp. 676–7).

56 We should not take Deleuze's reference in this passage to connote the Sartrean definition of the 'in-itself' as inert matter, contrasted with the 'for-itself' of life; the 'in-itself' pertains rather to the radical difference expressed by the dark precursor. This is particularly important for the present argument, since I maintain that Deleuze rules out any such thing as inert matter.

57 Rees, *Before the Beginning*, p. 166.

58 The conclusions which Einstein draws from his relativistic picture nevertheless contrast dramatically to those Deleuze defends from the essentially Bergsonian conception of time. In brief, Einstein elides the passage of time as such from his cosmological picture, in favour of what has come to be known as 'the block universe' view of time, wherein, essentially as a consequence of the relative nature of simultaneity, all that will occur in the history of the universe has in fact occurred already; there can be no privileged standpoint from which to view the passage of time as such, including our own; in extremis, even the viewpoint from the 'end of time' is construable as 'simultaneous' with our own. This is examined at length in Palle Yourgrau's *A World Without Time* (p. 113): 'Now, Gödel understood that the advent of relativity theory enabled one for the first time to cast the questions of the reality of time into a theoretical context amenable to formal mathematical methods. His approach to the philosophy of time, then, would take the form of a frontal assault on the ontological implications of relativity theory. Can one consistently maintain both the existence of time, intuitively understood, and the truth of relativity theory?' Dissenting voices against the block universe view of time in speculative physics are increasingly prevalent, however; for an explicit refutation, see Unger and Smolin's *The Singular Universe and the Reality of Time*.

59 Rees, *Before the Beginning*, pp. 208–9.

60 Atkins, *Four Laws that Drive the Universe*, p. 103.

61 It is nevertheless true that certain branches of current cosmological theory do countenance just such a scenario; notably Brane theory proposes that our universe is a three-dimensional island in a much larger multi-dimensional multiverse. This scenario is of most interest for the present argument, since the separate universes occupying the Brane universe may, according to the theory, collide with each other, and in doing so exchange energy. It is proposed that the energetic remnants of such a collision may be readable in the patternisation of the cosmic microwave background energy. As such, the theory calls into question the energetic isolation of our (and perhaps any) universe and is therefore potentially at odds with the principle of the conservation of energy. This at the very least would complicate the third law, allowing for potential extra-universal

sumps for our own reserves of energy (in that instance where the neighbouring Brane universes were colder, and possessed of a lower value for absolute zero), or indeed influxes of energy into our universe.

62 Lambert, *The Non-Philosophy of Gilles Deleuze*, p. 73.
63 Quoted in ibid., p. 76.
64 Ibid.
65 Quoted in ibid.
66 Borges goes on to write: 'In truth, the Library contains all verbal structures, all variations permitted by the 25 orthographical symbols but not a single example of absolute nonsense.' Quoted in ibid., p. 88.

3. ORDER

1 Serres, *Genesis*, p. 109.
2 The similarities between Bergson's thought here and that of Heidegger are worth noting. Heidegger's notion of *technē* describes a world first and foremost of physical objects 'at hand' or 'to hand'; our basic phenomenological being is in relation to the surrounding environment, which is experienced dynamically in terms of its usefulness for us, and which equally serves to shape those uses, ways and means. For both Bergson and Heidegger, this shared insight serves as the basis for a critique. Bergson insists that this characteristic of the species develops into the scientific appropriation of the world under the banner of mechanism, while Heidegger diagnoses an overly manipulative, technicising root to the scientific impulse.
3 Bergson is routinely cited to this effect in a wide range of scientific literature. See for instance, Prigogine and Stengers, *Order Out of Chaos*, p. 214; Unger and Smolin, *The Singular Universe and the Reality of Time*, p. 301.
4 Newton, *The Principia*, p. 15.
5 So much so that even when Deleuze seems to be pursuing a line counter to Bergsonism, as when he valorises the calculus, the argument remains in the service of an essentially Bergsonian duration. The examples Bergson offers in *Creative Evolution* are marked with the signature of the time elapse in the calculus, dt. In utilising this notation Bergson aligns it with all other mathematical abstractions whose usefulness he unequivocally delimits. Simon Duffy argues convincingly, however, that Deleuze's extended engagements with the calculus are motivated by a will to identify those elements which escape the critique offered by Bergson above, and indeed serve as a continuation of Bergson's more considered position with respect to the differential calculus in the later *Introduction to Metaphysics*. See Duffy, *Deleuze and the History of Mathematics*, pp. 89–115.
6 Bergson, the author of *Duration and Simultaneity*, is well aware that 'simultaneity' here is a word that in post-Einsteinian physics may pertain only to a given local system whose elements are moving at the same speed in the same direction, or whose acceleration is uniform. The apprehension of any two events perceived from a distance as simultaneous is precisely

relative. There is every sense, however, in which the Bergsonian critique is levelled quite as much against relativistic frameworks as Newtonian; indeed, *Duration and Simultaneity* was written to that end, though with mixed success. The specific assertion that scientific time elides duration is not only applicable within the scope of wider relativistic frameworks; it is positively reinforced by Einstein's own understanding of spacetime as a 'block', wherein the passage of time is effectively an illusion, having 'already' run its entire course. See Bergson, *Duration and Simultaneity*, and for a discussion of the 'block universe' view, Yourgrau, *A World Without Time*.

7 'Life', the paradigm of the vital for Bergson, is unequivocally soldered to the notion of 'complexity' in the natural sciences with the arrival in the late twentieth century of the scientific movement going under that name; see for instance the work of Stuart Kauffman, Stephen Jay Gould, Brian Goodwin et al.

8 Bergson, *Matter and Memory*, p. 30.

9 Bergson, *Duration and Simultaneity*, p. 44.

10 Bergson, *Key Writings*, p. 224.

11 Levinas, whose work rested centrally on the encounter with 'nothingness', in a manner avowedly akin but not identical to Heidegger's 'anxiety', from *Time and the Other* onward, remained troubled by Bergson's line of argument here – he refers to it both in that work and many years later in a series of interviews with Philippe Nemo spanning his career, collected as *Ethics and Infinity*. See Levinas, *Time and the Other*, p. 46, and *Ethics and Infinity*, p. 25.

12 The topic here, while framed by Leibnizian thought, is Plato's *Timaeus*, and while the denial of chaos seems to contradict the Deleuze of a Nietzschean stamp, who insists that 'chaos must be affirmed', it is nevertheless evident in context that it is precisely unaffirmed chaos which Deleuze denies; the screen is analogous to that crucible in the *Timaeus* which distributes and differentiates both being and form at one and the same time (though for Deleuze, we should substitute 'becoming' and 'series'), just as does Leibniz's God in the dual refusal of the as-yet unactualised indiscernible and selection of the compossible. It is the screen which affirms.

13 Leibniz asserts that it is God's concern at each moment of selection to leave all the indeterminacies pertinent to any given individual or phenomenon intact in their future – in the *Discourse on Metaphysics*, the question of free will versus determinism is articulated in terms of *inclination*. Prior decisions by God do not necessitate the present or future actions of a given individual, but rather *incline* that individual toward a certain path. Leibniz, *Discourse on Metaphysics* §30, in *Philosophical Essays*, pp. 60–2.

14 Kant, *Critique of Pure Reason*, A90–1/B123, p. 124.

15 Ibid., A91/B123, p. 124.

16 Ibid., A121, p. 144.

17 Alistair Welchman, 'Affinity, Judgement and Things in Themselves', in *The Matter of Critique*, ed. Rehberg and Jones, p. 207.
18 Ibid., p. 212.
19 Kant, *Critique of Pure Reason*, A653–4/B681–2, p. 539.
20 Welchman, 'Affinity, Judgement', p. 213.
21 Ibid., p. 212.
22 Shannon and Weaver, *The Mathematical Theory of Communication*, p. 3.
23 Ibid., p. 8.
24 An account of this breakthrough is given in Simon Singh's *Big Bang*, esp. pp. 207–13
25 For detailed presentations of this current speculative account of the Cepheids' periodicity, see for instance, the Harvard cosmology website: https://chandra.harvard.edu/graphics/edu/earth_scientist_stars.pdf (accessed May 2020). Or the Khan Academy: https://www.khanacademy.org/science/cosmology-and-astronomy/stellar-life-topic/cepheid-variables/v/why-cepheids-pulsate (accessed May 2020).
26 Shannon and Weaver, *The Mathematical Theory of Communication*, p. 4.
27 Ibid., p. 6.
28 In context, 'noise' or 'interference' should be understood in the widest sense as *anything* which distorts a message. The phenomenon known as 'lensing' could serve as an example of interference, whereby gravitational effects interfere with electromagnetic signals. This was initially a prediction of relativity theory, which holds that space bends in the presence of a significant gravitational field, thereby giving the impression to the observer of starlight arriving from a distant source by way of a distorting gravitational field, that the location of the source was somewhat displaced from its usual co-ordinates. Gravity, in other words, affects the channel between the source and the receiver. This effect was famously confirmed by Arthur Eddington on a trip to Africa in 1919 to observe the eclipse of that year. See Singh, *Big Bang*, pp. 135–43.
29 Shannon and Weaver, *The Mathematical Theory of Communication*, p. 6.
30 Wiener is acknowledged in a footnote in the first *Hermès* volume, Serres, *Hermès I: La communication*, p. 41, and subsequently in Serres, *Hermès II: l'interférence*, p. 29.
31 '[L]a rigueur de l'organisation leibnizienne princeps: la communication des substances. L'abstraction la plus haute naît d'une exigence aiguë sur la meilleure communication possible.' Serres, *La communication*, p. 9 (my translation).
32 '[D]eux sommets peuvent entretenir, en effet, entre eux des relations de causalité réciproque, d'influence réversible, d'action et de réaction équivalents, ou même d'action en retour (le *feed-back* des cybernéticiens).' Ibid., p. 14 (my translation).
33 'Lorsque nous disons détermination, nous entendons relation ou action en general.' Ibid., fn. p. 11 (my translation).

34 'Considérons un découpage quelconque de notre réseau: on voit tout aussitôt qu'un flux quelconque sur un (ou plusieurs) chemin quelconque peut aller d'un sommet quelconque à un autre (ou de plusieurs à plusieurs) en un temps quelconque: cela dépend des retards qu'il éprouvera.' Ibid., pp. 19–20 (my translation).
35 'Cette notion de retard est une notion capitale qui sera developpée independamment par ailleurs'. Ibid., fn. p. 20 (my translation).
36 'Enfin il existe une reciprocité profonde entre les sommets et les chemins, ou, si l'on veut, une dualité.' Ibid., p. 11 (my translation).
37 'Un sommet peut être regardé comme l'intersection de deux ou plusiers chemins (une thèse peut se constituer comme l'intersection d'une multiplicité de relations où un element de situation naître tout à coup de la confluence de plusieurs déterminations); correlativement, un chemin peut être regardé comme une détermination constituée a partir de la mise en correspondence de deux sommets préconçues.' Ibid., p. 11 (my translation).
38 '[P]ar exemple [quand] un point ou sommet du réseau change brusquement de place (comme un pion de telle importance – roi, dame, cavalier, etc – sur un echiquier) et l'ensemble du réseau se transforme en un nouveau reseau.' Ibid., p. 12 (my translation).
39 Williams, *Gilles Deleuze's Philosophy of Time*, p. 139.
40 Ibid., p. 41.
41 The phrase 'continuous variation' is the one Deleuze adopts most frequently to refer to the ubiquitous process of self-differentiation; it is held distinct from mere 'variety'. This distinction is important in his explication of life and evolution, urging a change of emphasis from 'natural selection' as the mere selection from amongst pre-existing varieties. It is only on the landscape of the virtual, of intensity, that variation may be continuous, and it is for this reason that Deleuze broadens the call for a change of emphasis in a range of scenarios bearing on the practice of science, as expressed in the characterisation of the distinction between (valorised) 'minor' geometry and its 'major' counterpart in *A Thousand Plateaus*: 'Of course, it is always possible to "translate" into a model that which escapes the model ... But this cannot be done without a distortion that consists in uprooting variables from their state of continuous variation, in order to extract from them fixed points and constant relations' (ATP, 408).
42 Stephen Greenblatt's history of the text, *The Swerve*, enumerates a number of those who read in atomism a form of radical contingency: Thomas More's *Utopia* adopted Epicurean, hedonistic principles while maintaining the Christian warning against those subscribing to any form of atomistic chance; the latter-day atomist Giordano Bruno positively adopted the principle of contingency, satirising the idea of Christian Providence in his 1584 work *The Expulsion of the Triumphant Beast*, in which Providence tasks Mercury with a long list of farcically miniscule tasks to channel some implausibly etiolated divine causal chain. See Greenblatt, *The Swerve*, pp. 231–4. The inverse reading may be found in Cicero's suspicions of the

clinamen in *De fato*, and in Pierre Bayle's echo thereof in the Leibniz–Bayle Correspondence; Bayle considers the notion of the clinamen 'gratuitous'. See Leibniz, *Leibniz's 'New System' and Associated Contemporary Texts*, p. 90.

43 'Ainsi, à chaque page du poème et sous mille aspects divers, nous retrouvons la même idée, celle de la fixité des lois de nature. Cette idée, qui obsède la poète, l'attriste; elle explique sa melancolie, melancolie d'un genre tout nouveau, et qui trouve en elle-même, pour ainsi dire, de quoi se consoler. Incapable de voir dans l'univers autre chose que des forces qui s'ajoutent ou se compensent, persuadé que tout ce qui est resulte naturellement, fatalement, de ce qui a été, Lucrèce prend en pitié l'espèce humaine.' Bergson, *Extraits de Lucrèce avec une commentaire*, Introduction (my translation).

44 '[P]artout des forces qui s'ajoutent ou se compensent, des causes et des effets qui s'enchaînent mécaniquement ... les lois de la nature, lois fatales, font que ces elements se combinent et se separent, et ces combinaisons, ces separations sont rigoureusement et une fois pour toutes determinées'. Ibid. (my translation).

45 See the 'Chronology of Life and Works' provided in Bergson, *Key Writings*.

46 Earle Brown's notes for the score read, 'to have elements exist in space ... space as an infinitude of directions from an infinitude of points in space ... to work (compositionally and in performance) to right, left, back, forward, up, down, and all points between ... the score [being] a picture of this space at one instant, which must always be considered as unreal and/or transitory ... a performer must set all this in motion (time), which is to say, realize that it is in motion and step into it ... either sit and let it move or move through it at all speeds'. Borchardt-Hume, ed. *Alexander Calder: Performing Sculpture*, chapter 2.

47 There are formulations of probability theory (other than the Bayesian) which would equally well serve as Deleuze's target here: Bayes' formulation is most often understood as a function of the knowledge of the observer of a system, whose expectations in terms of outcome are expressed in fractions. Kolmogorov probability is expressed rather in terms of relative frequency of a phenomenon within a system. In both cases, the distribution of probability ranges from 0 to 1. So much is true of the majority of approaches to probability. Deleuze is detaching himself from any such attempts to domesticate chance within a range denumerable in advance, in favour of a more radically open-ended form of chance. For a survey of formulations of probability theory, see Childers, *Philosophy and Probability*, esp. pp. 24–6 on Kolmogorov relative frequency and pp. 61–73 on Bayesian subjective probability.

48 In *Francis Bacon: The Logic of Sensation*, the formulation 'that which cannot be sensed but can only be sensed' refers to the transcendental conditions of the sensible; the sensations are unable to sense their own conditions, yet those conditions belong to the sensible. Equally, thought

is unable to think its own conditions, yet they belong to it. Here, the conditions of thought which Deleuze alludes to are the co-existence of disparate time-signatures in nature; the time of the atom differs radically from the time of the thinker, yet both belong to thought, 'can only be thought'.
49 See for instance, CE, 211, 317.
50 The most intricate exposition of the syntheses of time, especially with respect to the paradoxical expression of the future in the past, is to be found in James Williams's *Gilles Deleuze's Philosophy of Time*.
51 These accounts are rehearsed in numerous monographs on the subject, including Martin Rees's *Just Six Numbers* and Paul Davies's *The Goldilocks Enigma*. More broadly, the fine-tuning problem tends to feature in most general works on cosmology, as an explicandum; the fine tuning in question is held to be perplexing granted the exquisite narrowness of the range of interdependent physical values amenable to the evolution of such a universe as ours, in comparison to the assumed breadth of scope for alternative calibrations. The fine-tuning problem is intractable for essentially two reasons: the perceived vanishingly small likelihood of our form of universe is opaque to quantification by probability in the absence of alternative observable universes, and rests on the assumption that constants of nature can be considered, to some greater or lesser extent, as variable (albeit in this case in alternate universes) independently of each other.
52 Martin Rees, 'Cosmology and the Multiverse', in *Universe or Multiverse?*, ed. Carr, pp. 57–76.
53 While it is a generally accepted principle that the further our telescopes penetrate into the distance, the further back in time are the conditions we observe, nevertheless, there are upper limits to this. Firstly, the light from the very furthest reaches, due to the expansion of the universe and the absolute upper limit on the speed of light, can never in principle reach us, since the expansion is too great. Secondly, the posited opaque nature of light from earliest times up until the 'period of last scattering', some 37,000 years after the Big Bang, renders any empirical observation highly problematic.

4. ORDER AS COMPLEXITY

1 Kerslake, *Immanence and the Vertigo of Philosophy*, p. 164, fn. 108.
2 'When we perceive, we contract millions of vibrations or elementary shocks into a felt quality' (B, 87). Deleuze's phrasing echoes Bergson's: 'In the smallest discernible fraction of a second, in the almost instantaneous perception of a sensible quality, there may be trillions of oscillations which repeat themselves. The permanence of a sensible quality consists in this repetition of movements' (CE, 317).
3 Hume, *A Treatise of Human Nature*, p. 54.

4 Lampert, *Simultaneity and Delay*, p. 79.
5 Ibid., p. 227.
6 Ibid., p. 169.
7 Ibid., p. 166.
8 Collected in Deleuze, *Pure Immanence: Essays on A Life*, pp. 25–33.
9 Deleuze is fully aware of the tension between his philosophy of time and the thermodynamic arrow of time: 'Now, good sense is said of one direction only: it is the unique sense and expresses the demand of an order according to which it is necessary to choose one direction and to hold onto it. This direction is easily determined as that which goes from the most differentiated to the least differentiated, from things to the primordial fire. The arrow of time gets its orientation from this direction, since the most differentiated necessarily appears as past, insofar as it determines the origin of an individual system, whereas the least differentiated appears as future and end' (LS, 75). 'Good sense' here is associated with the linear time of Chronos, and contrasted to the non-linear time of Aion, which escapes the need for choice of direction. Consistent with his claim that entropy is a transcendental illusion, this amounts to the claim that the thermodynamic arrow applies to the explicate world, but not the implicate. Elsewhere he links the arrow of time to the work of 'contraction' in passive synthesis: 'Passive synthesis or contraction is essentially asymmetrical: it goes from the past to the future in the present, thus from the particular to the general, thereby imparting direction to the arrow of time' (DR, 71).
10 'What is the formula for this "evolution"? The more complex a system, the more the values peculiar to implication appear within it. The presence of these values is what allows a judgement of the complexity or complication of a system' (DR, 255).
11 Penrose, *The Road to Reality*, p. 678.
12 See for instance, Carroll, *From Here to Eternity*, pp. 225–7, and Gell-Mann, *The Quark and the Jaguar*, pp. 229–31.
13 Kauffman, *Investigations*, p. 244.
14 Ibid., p. 145.
15 Ibid., p. 143.
16 The argument is presented in full in chapter 7 of *Investigations*: 'The Non-Ergodic Universe: The Possibility of New Laws'.
17 Bohm and Peat, *Science, Order and Creativity*, pp. 179–80.
18 There are essentially two notable (and noted) shortcomings of this external measure of complexity. Firstly, the units encoded into the binary language are prone to a certain arbitrariness depending on the level of parsimony or categorisation adopted by the observer; it will not always be obvious in any given phenomenon which are the most basic elements, and indeed we may arrive at two very different values for the complexity of the system under consideration should we identify the units or primitives by different criteria. Secondly, as Max Tegmark points out in *Our*

Mathematical Universe (p. 342), there is a kind of self-defeating paradox attached to the adoption of this kind of index; taking the example of two contrasted number-strings, each say 16,000 bits in length, one generated randomly, the other representing a segment of the expansion of √2, Tegmark observes that the first, random, string would require by far the longer description, while the more complex, ordered matheme would require perhaps no more than a hundred bits or so to specify instructions for the expansion in question. Yet any description of a designated *subset* of this expansion will of necessity be of greater length than the original instruction, since there would also be a need for an 'address', an ordinal point at which to begin and stop the calculation. In terms of the argument being developed here, this is a result of a certain hybrid mismatch between external and internal, indexical and generative, modes of description.

19 Algorithmic Information content is liable to ambiguity in the choice of the primitives or units chosen from the phenomenon under consideration. Gell-Mann proposed rather a 'schema' as a better way to understand levels of complexity; an example he offers is the grammar of a particular language, whose rules allow the speaker the possibility of compression; the existence of relative pronouns, for instance, averts the need to repeat potentially lengthy noun-phrases. See Gell-Mann, *The Quark and the Jaguar*, chapters 3 and 5.
20 Gell-Mann, *The Quark and the Jaguar*, p. 229.
21 Bohm, *Wholeness and the Implicate Order*, p. 149.
22 As a matter of further acknowledging Leibniz as a precursor to this particular line of reasoning, we might refer to *Discourse on Metaphysics*, §6: 'But it is good to consider that God does nothing which is not orderly ... This is true to such an extent that not only does nothing completely irregular occur in the world, but we would not even be able to imagine such a thing. Thus let us assume, for example, that someone jots down a number of points at random on a piece of paper, as do those who practice the ridiculous art of geomancy. I maintain that it is possible to find a geometric line whose notion is constant and uniform, following a certain rule, such that this line passes through all the points in the same order in which the hand jotted them down.' Leibniz, *Discourse on Metaphysics*, in *Philosophical Essays*, p. 39.
23 Whitehead, *Science and the Modern World*, p. 221.
24 Ibid.
25 Stengers, *Thinking with Whitehead*, p. 226.
26 Deleuze, following a reasoning not dissimilar to Serres, insists on the construal from the original Lucretian text of '*incerte*' as 'non-assignable', rather than, say, 'uncertain', for the reason that no direction, no space effectively, pre-exists this inexplicable swerve, rather it serves to 'install' place: 'In this regard, the *clinamen* is by no means a change of direction in the movement of an atom, much less an indetermination testifying to

the existence of a physical freedom. It is the original determination of the direction of movement, the synthesis of movement and its direction which relates one atom to another' (DR, 184).

27 Whitehead, *Science and the Modern World*, p. 221.
28 This alignment of Whitehead's 'limitation' with Deleuze's sense of 'chaosmos' is contested by Tim Clark in an article entitled 'A Whiteheadian Chaosmos?', though he recognises that Deleuze himself appears to endorse this view in *The Fold*. The point of contention is over the nature of the 'decisions' or 'limitations' which Whitehead's God makes in nature. Deleuze says, '[Whitehead's] God desists from being a Being who compares worlds and chooses the richest possible. He becomes Process, a process that at once affirms incompossibilities and passes through them' (FLB, 81). Deleuze attributes to Whitehead, in other words, those very same terms of departure from Leibniz's cosmos as he himself establishes in *Difference and Repetition*. Tim Clark's close reading of Whitehead on limitation and decision exposes a tension in the reasoning on this point: in order for the two thinkers to agree, the process in play in God's decisions would have to amount to inclusive disjunction. For Clark, the particularities of Whitehead's text can only entail *exclusive* disjunction. This finds support in the phrasing from the quotation above: Whitehead's '*contraries*, grades and *oppositions*' seem to stray onto the forbidden Deleuzian territory of simple negation (negation of limits, negation of opposites). And, as Clark points out, Deleuze himself articulates the indispensable precondition of inclusive disjunction for a chaosmos in *The Logic of Sense*; it underlies the form of synthesis within which 'divergence is no longer a principle of exclusion, and disjunction no longer a means of separation. Incompossibility is now a means of communication' (LS, 174). *Pace* Clark, I believe the case for affinity between the two thinkers on this point is substantial. The sense in which incompossibilities are 'held together' for Whitehead in one chaosmos does not turn finally on questions of abstract mereology, but more centrally on the themes to be treated here: his sense of cosmology as 'evolution', the open and radical shifts of 'envisagement' from epoch to epoch, the n-dimensionality of the *spatium*, and the critique of 'simple location' as a fallacy. See Tim Clark, 'A Whiteheadian Chaosmos?', in *Deleuze, Whitehead, Bergson*, ed. Robinson, pp. 181–99.
29 Serres sums this up most articulately: 'Determination and decision introduce, of themselves, a differential asymmetry, which makes, as the saying goes, all the difference. There is something not at rest here, disquiet, as in the pendulum of a clock. It deviates from equilibrium. Leibniz's universe is doubly regulated, by the principle *De aequiponderantibus* and by that of the small difference. By that of identity, by that of indiscernibles. The principle of sufficient reason breaks the stability with a small deviation' (BP, 52).

5. SUFFICIENT REASON AS DISSYMMETRY AND THE EVOLUTIONARY PARADIGM

1. Zee, *Fearful Symmetry*, p. 212.
2. Hartshorne, *Creative Synthesis and Philosophic Method*, pp. 205–26.
3. Joe Rosen, 'Asymmetry over Symmetry in Physics', in *Physics and Whitehead*, ed. Eastman and Keaton, p. 131.
4. Ibid., p. 134.
5. Ibid., pp. 134–5.
6. Unger and Smolin, *The Singular Universe and the Reality of Time*, p. 369. Smolin observes a caveat here with respect to gauge symmetries, which are adopted to correlate different mathematical descriptions of the same system at a time t.
7. Ibid., p. 371.
8. Ibid.
9. 'But the PII insists that the universe as a whole has no non-vanishing conserved quantities, because, by Noether's theorem, the basic conserved quantities, energy, momentum and angular momentum, are consequences of the corresponding symmetries of spacetime.' Ibid., p. 369.
10. Goldberg, *The Universe in the Rearview Mirror*, p. 111.
11. Ibid., p. 128.
12. '[D]oes the role of symmetry, so prevalent in many ideas for probing nature's secrets, really have the fundamental role that it is so often assumed to have? I do not see why this need always be so. It does not necessarily strike me that basing particle physics on some large symmetry group (which is part of the GUT philosophy) is really a 'simple' picture, as far as fundamental physical theory is concerned. To me, large geometrical symmetry groups are complicated rather than simple things. It might well be the case that there are fundamental asymmetries inherent in nature's laws, and that the symmetries that we see are often merely approximate features that do not persist right down to the deepest levels.' Penrose, *The Road to Reality*, p. 746.
13. See Penrose, *Cycles of Time*, esp. §3.1. His approach resolves an acute problem for any theory which aims to account for the posited low-entropy, highly ordered initial conditions of the universe. Theoretically, thermodynamic models are almost obliged to posit an astoundingly unlikely level of order for the initial conditions of the universe, since entropic processes in play from the outset are held to degrade any state of order toward a state of disorder. As a corollary, our own present state must be some orders of magnitude less ordered than the initial conditions. Given that our own state is demonstrably far from the most likely state (universal equilibrium), the question arises, 'how did the universe begin in such an exquisitely unlikely macrostate?' The level of order of the nascent universe, claims Penrose, would be inherited from the prior cycle. This framework is tantamount to elevating the degradation of entropy to a first principle, however,

and we should be wary of taking any reservations over arguments from symmetry as *necessarily* offering support for Deleuze's claim that entropy is an illusion.
14 Whitehead, *Science and the Modern World*, p. 200.
15 Jill North makes the distinction between configuration spaces in general, of which Hilbert space is one privileged example for quantum formalisation, and the space of the wave-function itself. Because of the phenomenon of entanglement, the wave-function cannot legitimately be resolved into separate waves occupying three dimensions. She argues that because there is no mathematical option but to allow higher-dimensional representations of the processes involved, any commitment to a realist ontology for waves must entail a correlative commitment to really existing higher-dimensional space. Jill North, 'The Structure of a Quantum World', in *The Wave Function*, ed. Ney and Albert, pp. 184–202.
16 Whitehead, *Science and the Modern World*, p. 201.
17 Whitehead, *Modes of Thought*, p. 57. It should be noted here that Whitehead departs from a convention of relativistic terminology which he observes consistently elsewhere throughout his writing: to refer to space and time as conjoined, as four-dimensional (at the least, three dimensions of space and one of time). Indeed, the quotation I cite immediately before this one references the 'space-time continuum' faithfully to this convention, introduced by Hermann Minkowski at the outset of the relativistic revolution. Strictly speaking, in terms of relativistic terminology, it is incorrect to refer to a three-dimensional universe.
18 Whitehead, *Science and the Modern World*, pp. 133–4.
19 Indeed, the priority of intensive relations over extensive is a lesson which Whitehead readily adopted from the quantum revolution: 'Later on, we find the relations of mass and energy inverted; so that mass now becomes the name for a quantity of energy considered in relation to some of its dynamical effects. This train of thought leads to the notion of energy being fundamental, thus displacing matter from that position.' Ibid., p. 28.
20 Ibid., p. 128.
21 In fact, this is to render the notion in an overly simplistic way. Commentators on Whitehead tend rather to avoid defining the term 'organism' too narrowly, since it balances many related ideas within it, such as 'actual occasion', 'feeling', etc. Isabelle Stengers recognises its importance as an open idea which allows not so much a unifying point of view between different sciences as 'what should oblige us to think about the divergence of their questions as a reflection of the "living values" that constitute the order of nature'. Stengers, *Thinking with Whitehead*, p. 130. Dorothy Emmet, who devoted a monograph to Whitehead's 'philosophy of organism', nevertheless conveys only a general sense of how it might be differentiated as a concept: 'the Philosophy of Organism is an attempt to describe the way in which each new characterisation of creativity exhibits both the unity

and the plurality of the universe'. Emmet, *Whitehead's Philosophy of Organism*, p. 73.

22 'I find in the first place, that whatever objects are consider'd as causes or effects, are *contiguous*; and that nothing can operate in a time or place, which is ever so little remov'd from those of its existence. Tho' distant objects may sometimes seem productive of each other, they are commonly found upon examination to be link'd by a chain of causes, which are contiguous among themselves, and to the distant objects; and when in any particular instance we cannot discover this connexion, we still presume it to exist. We may therefore consider the relation of CONTIGUITY as essential to that of causation.' Hume, *A Treatise on Human Nature*, p. 54. Although Hume did in fact countenance exceptions to this rule, he confined them to the realms of the moral, the soul and perception.

23 A caveat must be made here: the observed uniformity of the cosmic microwave background radiation seems to contradict this principle. Given the unlikelihood of uniform energetic values between systems not in contact, the even temperature of the background radiation at the most far-flung reaches of the observable universe seems to imply communication at super-luminal speed, for the simple reason that the distance between the most disparate systems exceeds the furthest possible reach of light emitted at the estimated birth of the universe. Nevertheless it is widely acknowledged that the speed of light is a maximum only *within* the fabric of spacetime; this speed-limit does not apply to the expansion of space itself; explanations for the uniformity of the background radiation may thus be offered in terms of an expanding universe, without contradicting the tenets of relativity. In short, at the very inception of the universe, all energetic systems were within communicating distance, allowing correlations later preserved during expansion across distances which are now at superluminal remove.

24 A systematic account of the fate of the idea of non-locality is offered in Timothy Maudlin's *Quantum Non-Locality and Relativity*.

25 Greene, *The Fabric of the Cosmos*, pp. 112–13.

26 Ibid., pp. 114–15.

27 Edward Tryon, 'Is the Universe a Quantum Fluctuation?', *Nature* 246 (1973), pp. 396–7. On the face of it, the appearance *ex nihilo* of an entire universe such as Tryon describes is (to say the least) massively in breach of the principle of the conservation of energy. In this case, the principle is observed not by the fleetingly brief and subatomic-scale nature of the phenomena (as with virtual particles), since the universe endures at the largest of macroscopic scales. Rather, Tryon proposes that the overall positive energy of the initial conditions for all forces except gravity is balanced by the 'negative' energy represented by gravity. The conserved sum of all energy is therefore understood to be zero; a condition which applies both from the first and throughout the history of the universe.

28 Michael Epperson observes that 'quantum nonlocal phenomena are wholly compatible with Whiteheadian metaphysics'; this compatibility is embodied in Whitehead's distinction between 'the physical pole' and the 'mental pole' of events. While the 'mental pole' is not dependent on contiguity, the 'physical pole' is, 'conditioned heavily by extensive coordinate division'. Epperson, *Quantum Mechanics and the Philosophy of Alfred North Whitehead*, p. 206. Of course, this distinction is not to be identified with the everyday distinction between the mental and the physical; the distinction is rather closer to Deleuze's 'intensive' and 'extensive' relations respectively.
29 Steven Weinberg, Foreword to Baggott, *Higgs*, xv.
30 Gasché, *Geophilosophy*, p. 57.
31 Mee, *Higgs Force*, p. 8.
32 Baggott, *Higgs*, p. 85.
33 Ibid., p. 88.
34 Ibid., pp. 88–9.
35 Arguments intended to preserve the success and usefulness of relativistic theories tend to focus on the inability in principle of phenomena of the kind described in EPR-type experiments to transmit *information* as such, understood as separable from superluminal-speed communication of values such as spin. Entangled particles, according to this view, could not serve as the basis for faster-than-light communication. A consequence of this is that relativistic theories are not in essence contradicted by the phenomena in question.
36 Epperson, *Quantum Mechanics and the Philosophy of Alfred North Whitehead*, p. 177.
37 We are bound to add, as Whitehead would have recognised, that this definitive ordering of events is true only for those sharing our own light cone; relativistic theories do assert that observers occupying different light cones may perceive events as occurring in a different order than each other. Nevertheless, there is no claim that effects from one light-cone history may influence events in another 'before they happen' so to speak. Indeed, the upper speed limit of c in fact ensures this to be the case; while simultaneity is relative, no causal influence can supervene 'from the future', and hence we retain a 'logical and causal' order of events.
38 The passage in Whitehead's *The Concept of Nature* to which Epperson refers here is the following: '[the critical velocity of c] simply marks the fact that our congruence determination embraces both times and spaces in one universal system, and therefore if two arbitrary units are chosen, one for all spaces and one for all times, their ratio will be a velocity which is a fundamental property of nature expressing the fact that all times and spaces are really comparable'. Whitehead, *The Concept of Nature*, p. 193.
39 George Musser attributes the origins of the concept of space as a network to a number of prominent theorists, such as John Wheeler, Roger Penrose and David Finkelstein. He includes David Bohm in this list, though the

holographic paradigm by which Bohm conceives non-local interactions has its own distinct characteristics and its own subsequent subscribers, such as Juan Maldacena, who adopts the 'holographic principle' to argue that events in the volume of space may be interpreted from conditions at the boundary thereof. Musser, *Spooky Action at a Distance*, p. 182, pp. 165–6.

40 'In General Relativity, as we have seen, the geometry of space turns out to be dynamical. It evolves in time, in response to matter moving or gravitational waves propagating. But if geometry is really quantum at the Planck scale, the changes in geometry of space must come from changes occurring at that scale. There must, for example, be oscillations in the quantum geometry of space corresponding to the passage of a gravitational wave. A triumph of loop quantum gravity is that the dynamics of spacetime, which is given in general relativity by Einstein's equations, can indeed be coded in simple rules for how the graphs evolve in time.' Smolin, *Time Reborn*, p. 178.

41 Leonard Susskind, quoted in Musser, *Spooky Action at a Distance*, p. 188.
42 Ibid., p. 185.
43 Smolin refers to this process as *geometrogenesis*, and conjectures that the initial hyper-connected structure of the highly energetic early universe may help to explain the uniformity of the cosmic microwave background radiation, a uniformity persisting in afterglow after that maximal connectivity failed.
44 Murray Gell-Mann makes just this observation with respect to connected networks: 'Isn't the property of having all dots connected just as simple as that of having no dots connected?' *The Quark and the Jaguar*, p. 31.
45 Smolin, *Time Reborn*, p. 192.
46 Ibid., p. 181.
47 Bohm and Peat, *Science, Order and Creativity*, pp. 174–5.
48 Ibid., p. 196.
49 Bohm, *Wholeness and the Implicate Order*, p. 263.
50 Musser, *Spooky Action at a Distance*, p. 141.
51 Bohm, *Wholeness and the Implicate Order*, p. 237.
52 Ibid., p. 242.
53 Close, *Antimatter*, p. 43.
54 This point is conveyed by analogy with a goldfish bowl filmed from the side and the front simultaneously; the observer of both screens would recognise congruent but not identical movement on the part of the swimming fish, and perhaps come to the conclusion that a displacement of one kind on the one screen was in some way the cause of an exactly proportional move on the other. Those privy to the overall set-up, fish bowl plus multiple points of view, would recognise the shortcomings of this reasoning; regularities observed are not due to any causal relation between screens, but between the movement of the fish and the resulting multiple viewpoints communicated to each screen. Clearly, the world

of the fish bowl represents the true locus of events, the implicate order. Such is the reasoning required to account for such phenomena as the apparent trajectory of a particle. Green's function formalises this as an iteration of energetic exchanges, rather than the continuous progress of a self-same atomic-scale entity; the regularity lies in the underlying energetic order. See Bohm, 'Quantum Theory as an Indication of a Multidimensional Implicate Order', in *Wholeness and the Implicate Order*, pp. 236–40.

55 Bohm and Peat, *Science, Order and Creativity*, p. 195.
56 Whitehead, *Science and the Modern World*, p. 116.
57 Cosmologist Fred Hoyle's defence of a 'Steady State' universe in the 1940s and '50s could perhaps be seen as the last gasp of a disposition to present the universe as essentially unchanging. Along with his colleagues Hermann Bondi and Tommy Gold, Hoyle theorised that the expansion of the universe observed by Hubble may be caused by the fresh creation of matter in the empty crucible of space between galaxies. It was a counter-proposal to the Big Bang model – indeed, it was Hoyle who christened the 'Big Bang' with ironic intent – though its ironic connotation failed to take any real hold. Even in Hoyle's case, however, there was a readiness to entertain the idea that the laws of nature might differ from region to region. See Singh, *Big Bang*, pp. 337–53.
58 See Kragh, *Higher Speculations*, p. 259.
59 'Since space is divisible ad infinitum and matter is not necessarily in all places, it will also be allowed that God is able to create particles of matter of several different sizes and figures and in several proportions to Space and perhaps of different densities and forces and thereby to vary the laws of nature and make worlds of several sorts in several parts of the universe. At least I see nothing of contradiction with all this.' Newton, 1730, Query 32, quoted in D.R. Finkelstein, 'Physical Process and Physical Law', in *Physics and Whitehead: Quantum, Process and Experience*, ed. Eastman and Keeton, p. 180.
60 See respectively Penrose's *Cycles of Time* and Smolin's *Time Reborn* and *The Life of the Cosmos*.
61 'If a region inflates then it necessarily creates within itself the conditions for further inflation to occur from many sub-regions within. This process can continue into the infinite future with inflated regions producing further sub-regions that inflate ... in each of the inflated bubbles beyond our visible horizon and all over the past and future things will have fallen out differently ... they can end up with different numbers of dimensions of space or different constants and forces of nature.' Barrow, *The Constants of Nature*, pp. 190–1.
62 See respectively: Bohm, *Causality and Chance in Modern Physics*; Gell-Mann, *The Quark and the Jaguar*; Unger and Smolin, *The Singular Universe and the Reality of Time*.
63 See Singh, *Big Bang*, pp. 391–400.

64 Whitehead, *Science and the Modern World*, p. 135.
65 In fact, Whitehead does allow for phenomena which do not contribute directly to the evolutionary direction of the epoch; the ideal order of the epoch, he maintains, will therefore always fall short of 'perfect attainment'. Moreover, this tenet furnishes for him the only sense, provisional and relative to the given epoch, in which 'disorder' is to be understood: 'disorder is a relative term expressing the lack of importance possessed by the defining characteristics of the societies in question beyond their own bounds' (PR, 92). The provisional status of the 'societies' (systems) in question as disorderly does not preclude an epoch in the past or future in which their characteristics would resonate more productively, placing them within the ambit of 'order' for that epoch. Indeed, Whitehead posits that the presence of these untimely societies within a given epoch is precisely what allows for the eventual transition to another.
66 Unger and Smolin, *The Singular Universe and the Reality of Time*, p. 58.
67 Ibid., p. 229.
68 Ibid., p. 230.
69 Ibid., p. 230.
70 Ibid., p. 210.
71 The salient factor in the relatively narrow entropy gap of the early universe is the predominance of what Lineweaver refers to as the 'quark-gluon soup', or the overwhelming predominance of plasma, which represents a high-energy indifferentiation of component elements; macroscopic boundaries are requisite for energy gradients to emerge. Similarly, the almost exactly equal production of matter and antimatter served to proscribe the differentiation required until after mutual annihilation. In this closely parallel sense, the emergence of the macroscopic, the extensive as such, requires a certain extrication, or indeed explication, of the radiation-dominated early form to the matter-dominated later form, without which energy gradients cannot emerge; in the Deleuzian register, the intensive must differentiate and unfold.
72 See Singh, *Big Bang*, pp. 477–9.
73 'Flatness' here pertains to Riemannian rather than Euclidian geometry; according to Einstein, the universe must either be warped or flat, as a Riemannian manifold may be, according to the relative uniformity of the distribution of matter-energy overall. On the very large scale, sophisticated triangulation methods have confirmed the universe to be flat, though of course local variations in density (e.g., black holes) produce the gravitational dips and valleys familiar from so many diagrams.
74 C.H. Lineweaver, 'A Simple Treatment of Complexity: Cosmological Entropic Boundary Conditions on Increasing Complexity', in *Complexity and the Arrow of Time*, ed. Lineweaver, Davies and Ruse, p. 62.
75 Of course, the principle is a highly abstract one, depending on any number of assumptions, not the least being the ability of potential future observers

to survive the transition from one epoch to another to observe the failure of the world to evolve in the relevant ways.
76 Poincaré, *Science and Hypothesis*, collected in *The Value of Science*, p. 126.
77 Ibid.
78 Bohm, *Causality and Chance in Modern Physics*, p. 162.
79 Ibid.
80 Ibid., p. 163.

CONCLUSION

1 It would be untrue to say that nobody has drawn this inference. Karl Popper, writing in 1956, drew on the early results of Ilya Prigogine's work to suggest that heat death could legitimately soon be deposed from the cosmological account (see Popper, *The Open Universe*, pp. 173–4). Prigogine himself has been more circumspect about arguments extrapolating from or to the cosmologically long term, not least because they tend to depend upon the assumption of exquisitely ordered initial conditions for the universe, a surfeit of improbability. 'Whatever the past', he says, 'there exist at present two types of processes: time-reversible processes, where the application of existing dynamics has proved to be successful … and irreversible processes like heat conditions, where the asymmetry between past and future is obvious. Our objective is to devise a new formulation of physics that explains, independently of any cosmological considerations, the difference between these behaviours.' Prigogine, *The End of Certainty*, p. 28.
2 Koyré, *From the Closed World to the Infinite Universe*.
3 Weyl, *The Open World*.
4 Popper, *The Open Universe*.
5 Meillassoux, *After Finitude*, p. 65.
6 Ibid., p. 64.
7 Ibid., p. 60.
8 Price, *Time's Arrow and Archimedes' Point*.
9 Barbour, *The End of Time*.
10 Rölli, *Gilles Deleuze's Transcendental Empiricism*, p. 1.

Bibliography

WORKS BY GILLES DELEUZE

Bergsonism. New York: Zone, 1988.
Desert Islands and Other Texts. Los Angeles: Semiotext(e), 2004.
Difference and Repetition. London: Athlone, 1994.
Empiricism and Subjectivity. New York: Columbia University Press, 1991.
Expressionism in Philosophy: Spinoza. New York: Zone, 1990.
Francis Bacon: The Logic of Sensation. London: Continuum, 2003.
Negotiations. New York: Columbia University Press, 1995.
Nietzsche and Philosophy. London: Bloomsbury, 2006.
Pure Immanence: Essays on A Life. New York: Zone Books, 2012.
The Fold: Leibniz and the Baroque. Minneapolis: University of Minnesota Press, 1993.
The Logic of Sense. London: Athlone, 1990.

WORKS BY GILLES DELEUZE AND FÉLIX GUATTARI

Anti-Oedipus. London: Athlone, 1984.
A Thousand Plateaus: Capitalism and Schizophrenia. London: Athlone, 1988.
What Is Philosophy? London: Verso, 1994.

COMMENTARY ON DELEUZE

Ansell-Pearson, Keith, ed. *Deleuze and Philosophy: The Difference Engineer*. Abingdon: Routledge, 1997.
Ansell-Pearson, Keith. *Germinal Life: The Difference and Repetition of Deleuze*. Abingdon: Routledge, 1999.
Badiou, Alain. *Deleuze: The Clamor of Being*. Minneapolis: University of Minnesota Press, 1999.
Bell, Jeffrey A. *Philosophy at the Edge of Chaos: Gilles Deleuze and the Philosophy of Difference*. Toronto: University of Toronto Press, 2006.

Bonta, Mark and John Protevi. *Deleuze and Geophilosophy: A Guide and Glossary*. Edinburgh: Edinburgh University Press, 2004.

Bowden, Sean. *The Priority of Events: Deleuze's Logic of Sense*. Edinburgh: Edinburgh University Press, 2011.

Bryant, Levi R. *Difference and Givenness: Deleuze's Transcendental Empiricism and the Ontology of Immanence*. Evanston: Northwestern University Press, 2008.

Butler, Rex. *Deleuze and Guattari's* What Is Philosophy? London: Bloomsbury, 2016.

Crockett, Clayton. *Deleuze Beyond Badiou: Ontology, Multiplicity and Event*. New York: Columbia University Press, 2013.

De Beistegui, Miguel. *Immanence: Deleuze and Philosophy*. Edinburgh: Edinburgh University Press, 2012.

DeLanda, Manuel. *Intensive Science and Virtual Philosophy*. London: Continuum, 2002.

Duffy, Simon B. *Deleuze and the History of Mathematics: In Defense of the 'New'*. London: Bloomsbury, 2013.

Gaffney, Peter, ed. *The Force of the Virtual: Deleuze, Science and Philosophy*. Minneapolis: University of Minnesota, 2010.

Gasché, Rodolphe. *Geophilosophy: On Gilles Deleuze and Félix Guattari's* What Is Philosophy? Evanston: Northwestern University Press, 2014.

Herzogenrath, Bernd, ed. *Time and History in Deleuze and Serres*. London: Bloomsbury, 2012.

Hughes, Joe. *Deleuze's* Difference and Repetition. London: Continuum, 2009.

Jones, Graham and Jon Roffe, eds. *Deleuze's Philosophical Lineage*. Edinburgh: Edinburgh University Press, 2009.

Kaufman, Eleanor. *Deleuze, the Dark Precursor*. Baltimore: Johns Hopkins University Press, 2012.

Kerslake, Christian. *Immanence and the Vertigo of Philosophy: From Kant to Deleuze*. Edinburgh: Edinburgh University Press, 2009.

Lambert, Gregg. *In Search of a New Image of Thought: Gilles Deleuze and Philosophical Expressionism*. Minneapolis: University of Minnesota Press, 2012.

Lambert, Gregg. *The Non-Philosophy of Gilles Deleuze*. London: Continuum, 2002.

Lampert, Jay. *Deleuze and Guattari's Philosophy of History*. London: Continuum, 2011.

Lampert, Jay. *Simultaneity and Delay: A Dialectical Theory of Staggered Time*. London: Bloomsbury, 2012.

Lord, Beth. *Kant and Spinozism: Transcendental Idealism from Jacobi to Deleuze*. Basingstoke: Palgrave Macmillan, 2011.

Lundy, Craig and Daniela Voss, eds. *At the Edges of Thought: Deleuze and Post-Kantian Philosophy*. Edinburgh: Edinburgh University Press, 2015.

Marks, John, ed. *Deleuze and Science*. Edinburgh: Edinburgh University Press, 2006.

Massumi, Brian. *A User's Guide to Capitalism and Schizophrenia: Deviations from Deleuze and Guattari*. Cambridge, MA: MIT, 1992.
Robinson, Keith, ed. *Deleuze, Whitehead, Bergson: Rhizomatic Connections*. Basingstoke: Palgrave Macmillan, 2009.
Roffe, Jon. *Badiou's Deleuze*. Durham: Acumen, 2012.
Rölli, Marc. *Gilles Deleuze's Transcendental Empiricism: From Tradition to Difference*. Edinburgh: Edinburgh University Press, 2016.
Smith, Daniel W., *Essays on Deleuze*. Edinburgh: Edinburgh University Press, 2008.
Smith, Daniel W. and Henry Somers-Hall, eds. *The Cambridge Companion to Gilles Deleuze*. Cambridge: Cambridge University Press, 2012.
Somers-Hall, Henry. *Deleuze's* Difference and Repetition. Edinburgh: Edinburgh University Press, 2013.
Timmermans, Benoit, ed. *Perspective: Leibniz, Whitehead, Deleuze*. Paris: VRIN, 2006.
Van Tuinen, Sjoerd and Niamh McDonnell, eds. *Deleuze and* The Fold*: A Critical Reader*. Basingstoke: Palgrave Macmillan, 2010.
Williams, James. *Gilles Deleuze's* Difference and Repetition*: A Critical Introduction and Guide*. Edinburgh: Edinburgh University Press, 2003.
Williams, James. *Gilles Deleuze's* Logic of Sense*: A Critical Introduction and Guide*. Edinburgh: Edinburgh University Press, 2008.
Williams, James. *Gilles Deleuze's Philosophy of Time: A Critical Introduction and Guide*. Edinburgh: Edinburgh University Press, 2011.
Williams, James. *The Transversal Thought of Gilles Deleuze: Encounters and Influences*. Manchester: Clinamen Press, 2005.
Zourabichvili, François. *Deleuze: A Philosophy of the Event / The Vocabulary of Deleuze*. Edinburgh: Edinburgh University Press, 2012.

PHILOSOPHICAL AND SCIENTIFIC WORKS

Alexander, Amir. *Infinitesimal: How a Dangerous Mathematical Theory Shaped the Modern World*. London: Oneworld, 2014.
Alexander, H.G., ed. *The Leibniz-Clarke Correspondence*. Manchester: Manchester University Press, 2005.
Al-Khalili, Jim. *Quantum: A Guide for the Perplexed*. London: Weidenfeld & Nicolson, 2004.
Ansell-Pearson, Keith and John Mullarkey, eds. *Henri Bergson: Key Writings*. London: Continuum, 2002.
Aristotle. *Physics*. Oxford: Oxford University Press, 1999.
Aristotle. *The Metaphysics*. Harmondsworth: Penguin, 1998.
Arntzenius, Frank. *Space, Time and Stuff*. Oxford: Oxford University Press, 2012.
Atkins, Peter. *Four Laws That Drive the Universe*. Oxford: Oxford University Press, 2007.
Babich, Babette. *Nietzsche's Philosophy of Science: Reflecting Science on the Ground of Art and Life*. New York: SUNY, 1994.

Bachelard, Gaston. *The Dialectic of Duration*. Manchester: Clinamen Press, 2000.
Badiou, Alain. *Being and Event*. London: Continuum, 2005.
Badiou, Alain. *Logics of Worlds*. London: Bloomsbury, 2009.
Baggott, Jim. *Higgs: The Invention and Discovery of the 'God Particle'*. Oxford: Oxford University Press, 2012.
Baggott, Jim. *The Quantum Story: A History in 40 Moments*. Oxford: Oxford University Press, 2011.
Ball, Philip. *Branches*. Oxford: Oxford University Press, 2009.
Barbour, Julian. *The End of Time: The Next Revolution in Our Understanding of the Universe*. London: Weidenfeld & Nicolson, 1999.
Barrow, John D. *The Constants of Nature: From Alpha to Omega*. New York: Vintage, 2003.
Bergson, Henri. *Creative Evolution*. London: Macmillan, 1911.
Bergson, Henri. *Duration and Simultaneity: Bergson and the Einsteinian Universe*, ed. Robin Durie. Manchester: Clinamen Press, 1999.
Bergson, Henri. *Extraits de Lucrèce avec une commentaire, des notes et une étude sur la poésie, la texte et la langue de Lucrèce*. Paris: Librairie Ch. Delagrave, 1884.
Bergson, Henri. *Key Writings*. London: Continuum, 2002.
Bergson, Henri. *Matter and Memory*. New York: Zone, 1988.
Bergson, Henri. *Time and Free Will: An Essay on the Immediate Data of Consciousness*. London: Allen & Unwin, 1910.
Bohm, David. *Causality and Chance in Modern Physics*. Abingdon: Routledge, 2004.
Bohm, David. *Wholeness and the Implicate Order*. Abingdon: Routledge, 2002.
Bohm, David and B.J. Hiley. *The Undivided Universe*. Abingdon: Routledge, 1995.
Bohm, David and F.D. Peat. *Science, Order and Creativity*. Abingdon: Routledge Classics, 2011.
Borchardt-Hume, Achim, ed. *Alexander Calder: Performing Sculpture*. London: Tate Publishing, 2015.
Boyer, Carl B. *The History of the Calculus and its Conceptual Development*. Mineola: Dover, 1959.
Čapek, Milič. *Bergson and the Modern Physics*. Netherlands: D. Reidel, 1971.
Čapek, Milič. *The Philosophical Impact of Contemporary Physics*. Princeton: D. Van Nostrand Company, 1961.
Carr, Bernard. *Universe or Multiverse?* Cambridge: Cambridge University Press, 2007.
Carroll, Sean. *From Eternity to Here: The Quest for the Ultimate Theory of Time*. London: Oneworld, 2011.
Childers, Timothy. *Philosophy and Probability*. Oxford: Oxford University Press, 2013.

Chown, Marcus. *The Magic Furnace: The Search for the Origin of Atoms.* New York: Vintage, 2000.
Chown, Marcus. *We Need to Talk About Kelvin: What Everyday Things Tell Us About the Universe.* London: Faber and Faber, 2010.
Close, Frank. *Antimatter.* Oxford: Oxford University Press, 2010.
Close, Frank. *The Void.* Oxford: Oxford University Press, 2007.
Coopersmith, Jennifer. *Energy, the Subtle Concept: The Discovery of Feynman's Blocks from Leibniz to Einstein.* Oxford: Oxford University Press, 2015.
Coopersmith, Jennifer. *The Lazy Universe: An Introduction to the Principle of Least Action.* Oxford: Oxford University Press, 2017.
Coveney, Peter and Roger Highfield. *The Arrow of Time.* London: Flamingo, 1991.
Curley, Edwin, ed. *A Spinoza Reader: The Ethics and Other Works.* Princeton: Princeton University Press, 1994.
D'Espagnat, Bernard. *On Physics and Philosophy.* Princeton: Princeton University Press, 2013.
Dainton, Barry. *Time and Space.* Durham: Acumen, 2001.
Davies, Paul. *The Goldilocks Enigma: Why Is the Universe Just Right for Life?* Harmondsworth: Penguin, 2007.
Davies, Paul, *The Last Three Minutes.* New York: Basic Books, 1995.
Davies, Paul and Niels Henrik Gregerson, eds. *Information and the Nature of Reality.* Cambridge: Cambridge University Press, 2014.
De Boever, Arne, Alex Murray, Jon Roffe and Ashley Woodward, eds. *Gilbert Simondon: Being and Technology.* Edinburgh: Edinburgh University Press, 2012.
Deutsch, David. *The Beginning of Infinity: Explanations That Transform the World.* Harmondsworth: Penguin, 2012.
Deutsch, David. *The Fabric of Reality.* Harmondsworth: Penguin, 1997.
Duffy, Simon, ed. *Virtual Mathematics: The Logic of Difference.* Manchester: Clinamen Press, 2006.
Eastman, Timothy E. and Hank Keaton, eds. *Physics and Whitehead: Quantum, Process and Experience.* New York: SUNY, 2003.
Eddington, Arthur. *The Nature of the Physical World.* Cambridge: Cambridge University Press, 1928.
Emmet, Dorothy. *Whitehead's Philosophy of Organism.* London: Macmillan, 1966.
Epperson, Michael. *Quantum Mechanics and the Philosophy of Alfred North Whitehead.* New York: Fordham University Press, 2004.
Farmelo, Graham. *The Strangest Man: The Hidden Life of Paul Dirac, Quantum Genius.* London: Faber and Faber, 2009.
Ferguson, Kitty. *Pythagoras: His Lives and the Legacy of a Rational Universe.* London: Icon, 2011.
Feynman, Richard. *QED: The Strange Theory of Light and Matter.* Harmondsworth: Penguin, 1990.

Feynman, Richard. *The Character of Physical Law*. Harmondsworth: Penguin, 1992.
Floridi, Luciano. *The Philosophy of Information*. Oxford: Oxford University Press, 2013.
Galfard, Christophe, *The Universe in Your Hand: A Journey Through Space, Time and Beyond*. London: Macmillan, 2015.
Garber, Daniel. *Leibniz: Body, Substance, Monad*. Oxford: Oxford University Press, 2009.
Gell-Mann, Murray. *The Quark and the Jaguar: Adventures in the Simple and the Complex*. London: Little, Brown and Company, 1994.
Gleick, James. *Chaos*. London: Heinemann, 1988.
Goldberg, Dave. *The Universe in the Rearview Mirror: How Hidden Symmetries Shape Reality*. New York: Penguin, 2013.
Gratton, Peter. *Speculative Realism: Problems and Prospects*. London: Bloomsbury, 2014.
Greenblatt, Steven. *The Swerve: How the Renaissance Began*. New York: Vintage, 2012.
Greene, Brian. *The Fabric of the Cosmos*. Harmondsworth: Penguin, 2004.
Gribbin, John. *13.8: The Quest to Find the True Age of the Universe and the Theory of Everything*. London: Icon, 2015.
Griffin, David R., ed. *Physics and the Ultimate Significance of Time*. New York: SUNY, 1986.
Hallward, Peter. *Badiou: A Subject to Truth*. Minneapolis: University of Minnesota Press, 2003.
Hartshorne, Charles. *Creative Synthesis and Philosophic Method*. London: SCM, 1970.
Hiley, B.J. and F.D. Peat, eds. *Quantum Implications: Essays in Honour of David Bohm*. Abingdon: Routledge, 1991.
Hume, David. *A Treatise of Human Nature*. Oxford: Oxford University Press, 2000.
Husserl, Edmund. *Ideas*. Abingdon: Routledge, 2012.
Kahn, Charles H. *Anaximander and the Origins of Greek Cosmology*. New York: Columbia University Press, 1985.
Kaku, Michio. *Hyperspace*. Oxford: Oxford University Press, 1994.
Kant, Immanuel. *Critique of Judgement*. Oxford: Oxford University Press, 1953.
Kant, Immanuel. *Critique of Pure Reason*. London: Macmillan, 1929.
Kauffman, Stuart. *Investigations*. Oxford: Oxford University Press, 2000.
Kirk, G.S., J.E. Raven and M. Schofield. *The Presocratic Philosophers*. Cambridge: Cambridge University Press, 1983.
Klossowski, Pierre. *Nietzsche and the Vicious Circle*. London: Athlone, 2000.
Koyré, Alexander. *From the Closed World to the Infinite Universe*. London: Forgotten Books, 2008.
Kragh, Helge. *Higher Speculations: Grand Theories and Failed Revolutions in Physics and Cosmology*. Oxford: Oxford University Press, 2015.

Krauss, Lawrence M. *A Universe from Nothing: Why There Is Something Rather Than Nothing*. New York: Simon & Schuster, 2012.
Lautman, Albert. *Mathematics, Ideas and the Physical Real*. London: Continuum, 2011.
Lawlor, Leonard. *The Challenge of Bergsonism*. London: Continuum, 2003.
Leibniz, G.W. *Discourse on Metaphysics, Correspondence with Arnauld, Monadology*. Chicago: Open Court, 1902.
Leibniz, G.W. *Leibniz's 'New System' and Associated Contemporary Texts*. Oxford: Oxford University Press, 2006.
Leibniz, G.W. *New Essays on Human Understanding*. Cambridge: Cambridge University Press, 2009.
Leibniz, G.W. *Philosophical Essays*. Indianapolis: Hackett, 1989.
Leibniz, G.W. *The Shorter Leibniz Texts*. London: Continuum, 2006.
Levinas, Emmanuel. *Ethics and Infinity: Conversations with Philippe Nemo*. Pittsburgh: Duquesne University Press, 1985.
Levinas, Emmanuel. *Time and the Other*. Pittsburgh: Duquesne University Press, 1987.
Lewin, Roger. *Complexity: Life at the Edge of Chaos*. New York: Macmillan, 1992.
Lewis, Peter J. *Quantum Ontology: A Guide to the Metaphysics of Quantum Mechanics*. Oxford: Oxford University Press, 2016.
Lineweaver, C.H., P.C.W. Davies and M. Ruse, eds. *Complexity and the Arrow of Time*. Cambridge: Cambridge University Press, 2013.
Lloyd, Seth. *Programming the Universe: A Quantum Computer Scientist Takes on the Universe*. New York: Vintage, 2007.
Maudlin, Tim. *Philosophy of Physics: Space and Time*. Princeton: Princeton University Press, 2012.
Maudlin, Tim. *Quantum Non-Locality and Relativity: Metaphysical Intimations of Modern Physics*. Oxford: Blackwell, 2011.
Mee, Nicholas. *Higgs Force: Cosmic Symmetry Shattered*. Stockport: Quantum Wave, 2012.
Meillassoux, Quentin. *After Finitude: An Essay on the Necessity of Contingency*. London: Bloomsbury, 2009.
Musser, George. *Spooky Action at a Distance*. New York: Scientific American, 2016.
Nelson, David, ed. *The Penguin Dictionary of Mathematics*. Harmondsworth: Penguin, 2008.
Newton, Isaac. *The Principia*. Amherst: Prometheus Books, 1995.
Ney, A. and D.A. Albert, eds. *The Wave Function: Essays on the Metaphysics of Quantum Mechanics*. Oxford: Oxford University Press, 2013.
Nietzsche, Friedrich. *The Gay Science*. New York: Vintage, 1974.
Nietzsche, Friedrich. *Thus Spoke Zarathustra*. Harmondsworth: Penguin, 1969.
Nietzsche, Friedrich. *The Will To Power*. New York: Vintage, 1968.

Ostriker, Jeremiah P. and Simon Mitton. *Heart of Darkness: Unravelling the Mysteries of the Invisible Universe*. Princeton: Princeton University Press, 2013.
Panek, Richard. *The 4% Universe: Dark Matter, Dark Energy and the Race to Discover the Rest of Reality*. London: Oneworld, 2011.
Penrose, Roger. *Cycles of Time: An Extraordinary New View of the Universe*. London: Bodley Head, 2010.
Penrose, Roger. *Fashion, Faith and Fantasy in the New Physics of the Universe*. Princeton: Princeton University Press, 2016.
Penrose, Roger. *The Road to Reality: A Complete Guide to the Laws of the Universe*. New York: Vintage, 2005.
Poincaré, Henri. *The Value of Science: Essential Writings of Henri Poincaré*. New York: Random House, 2001.
Popper, Karl. *The Open Universe: An Argument for Indeterminism*. Abingdon: Routledge, 2000.
Price, Huw. *Time's Arrow and Archimedes' Point: New Directions for the Physics of Time*. Oxford: Oxford University Press, 1996.
Prigogine, Ilya. *From Being to Becoming: Time and Complexity in the Physical Sciences*. New York: W.H. Freeman and Company, 1980.
Prigogine, Ilya. *The End of Certainty: Time, Chaos and the New Laws of Nature*. New York: The Free Press, 1996.
Prigogine, Ilya and Isabelle Stengers. *Order Out of Chaos: Man's New Dialogue with Nature*. London: Flamingo, 1985.
Rees, Martin. *Before the Beginning: Our Universe and Others*. New York: The Free Press, 2002.
Rees, Martin. *Just Six Numbers: The Deep Forces that Shape the Universe*. London: Weidenfeld & Nicolson, 1999.
Rees, Martin. *Our Cosmic Habitat*. London: Weidenfeld & Nicolson, 2002.
Rehberg, Andrea and Rachel Jones, eds. *The Matter of Critique: Readings in Kant's Philosophy*. Manchester: Clinamen Press, 2000.
Reichenbach, Hans. *The Direction of Time*. Mineola: Dover, 1999.
Ridley, Matt. *The Evolution of Everything*. London: HarperCollins, 2015.
Ross, Don, James Ladyman and Harold Kincaid, eds. *Scientific Metaphysics*. Oxford: Oxford University Press, 2015.
Rovelli, Carlo. *Reality Is Not What It Seems: The Journey to Quantum Gravity*. New York: Random House, 2016.
Rovelli, Carlo. *Seven Brief Lessons on Physics*. London: Allen Lane, 2014.
Savile, Anthony. *Leibniz and the Monadology*. Abingdon: Routledge, 2000.
Savitt, Steven F., ed. *Time's Arrows Today: Recent Physical and Philosophical Work on the Direction of Time*. Cambridge: Cambridge University Press, 1995.
Scharf, Caleb. *Gravity's Engines: The Other Side of Black Holes*. London: Allen Lane, 2012.
Schrödinger, Erwin. *What is Life?* Cambridge: Cambridge University Press, 1992.

Serres, Michel. *Hermès I: La Communication*. Paris: Éditions de Minuit, 1969.
Serres, Michel. *Hermès II: L'interférence*. Paris: Éditions de Minuit, 1972.
Serres, Michel. *Genesis*. Ann Arbor: University of Michigan Press, 1995.
Serres, Michel. *The Birth of Physics*, Lanham: Rowman and Littlefield, 2018.
Shannon, Claude E. and Warren Weaver. *The Mathematical Theory of Communication*. Champaign: University of Illinois Press, 1963.
Singh, Simon. *Big Bang*. London: Harper Perennial, 2005.
Smolin, Lee. *The Life of the Cosmos*. Oxford: Oxford University Press, 1998.
Smolin, Lee. *The Trouble With Physics: The Rise of String Theory, the Fall of a Science and What Comes Next*. London: Allen Lane, 2006.
Smolin, Lee. *Three Roads to Quantum Gravity*. London: Weidenfeld & Nicolson, 2000.
Smolin, Lee. *Time Reborn: From the Crisis of Physics to the Future of the Universe*. London: Allen Lane, 2013.
Stengers, Isabelle. *Cosmopolitics I*. Minneapolis: University of Minnesota Press, 2010.
Stengers, Isabelle. *Cosmopolitics II*. Minneapolis: University of Minnesota Press, 2011.
Stengers, Isabelle. *Power and Invention*. Minneapolis: University of Minnesota Press, 1997.
Stengers, Isabelle. *The Invention of Modern Science*. Minneapolis: University of Minnesota Press, 2000.
Stengers, Isabelle. *Thinking with Whitehead: A Free and Wild Creation of Concepts*. Cambridge, MA: Harvard University Press, 2011.
Talbot, Michael. *The Holographic Universe*. New York: HarperCollins, 1996.
Tegmark, Max. *Our Mathematical Universe: My Quest for the Ultimate Nature of Reality*. London: Allen Lane, 2014.
Unger, Roberto M. and Lee Smolin. *The Singular Universe and the Reality of Time*. Cambridge: Cambridge University Press, 2015.
Van Fraasen, Bas C. *Laws and Symmetry*. Oxford: Clarendon, 2003.
Vattimo, Gianni. *Nietzsche: An Introduction*. London: Athlone, 2002.
Vedral, Vlatko. *Decoding Reality: The Universe as Quantum Information*. Oxford: Oxford University Press, 2012.
Von Bayer, Hans Christian. *Qbism: The Future of Quantum Physics*. Cambridge, MA: Harvard University Press, 2016.
Weinberg, Steven. *Dreams of a Final Theory*. New York: Vintage, 1993.
Weyl, Hermann. *Philosophy of Mathematics and Natural Science*. Princeton: Princeton University Press, 2009.
Weyl, Hermann. *Symmetry*. Princeton: Princeton University Press, 1989.
Weyl, Hermann. *The Open World*. New Haven: Yale University Press, 1960.
Wheeler, John Archibald. *Geons, Black Holes and Quantum Foam: A Life in Physics*. New York: W.W. Norton, 2000.
Whitehead, Alfred North. *Modes of Thought*. New York: The Free Press, 1968.

Whitehead, Alfred North. *Process and Reality: An Essay in Cosmology*. New York: The Free Press, 1985.

Whitehead, Alfred North. *Science and the Modern World*. Cambridge: Cambridge University Press, 2011.

Whitehead, Alfred North. *The Concept of Nature. The Tarner Lectures Delivered in Trinity College November 1919*. Cambridge: Cambridge University Press, 1920.

Wilczek, Frank. *A Beautiful Question: Finding Nature's Deep Design*. London: Allen Lane, 2015.

Wilson, Catherine. *Leibniz's Metaphysics*. Princeton: Princeton University Press, 1989.

Woit, Peter. *Not Even Wrong: The Failure of String Theory and the Continuing Challenge to Unify the Laws of Physics*. London: Jonathan Cape, 2006.

Yourgrau, Palle. *A World Without Time: The Forgotten Legacy of Gödel and Einstein*. Harmondsworth: Penguin, 2005.

Zabell, S.L. *Symmetry and its Discontents*. Cambridge: Cambridge University Press, 2005.

Zee, A. *Fearful Symmetry: The Search for Beauty in Modern Physics*. Princeton: Princeton University Press, 2016.

Index

Note: 'n' indicates chapter note number.

absolute zero, 60–8
action at a distance, 139–40, 176
affinity, 83–4, 106, 107
affirmation, 53
Aion, 100–2, 161, 180, 188n46
algorithmic information content, 123–4
Anaximander, 29–30, 131, 132
anexact, 148, 182n2
appetition, 46–7
Archimedes, *De aequilibro*, 30
Aristotle, 24, 27, 28, 29–30, 50, 84
Arnauld, Antoine, 25–6
art, 99–100, 104
Aspect, Alain, 142
Atkins, Peter, 66
atomism, 20, 94, 156, 193n42
ATP *see* Deleuze, Gilles: and Félix Guattari, *A Thousand Plateaus*
axiomatic mode, 39–41

B *see* Deleuze, Gilles: *Bergsonism*
Babich, Babette, 6
Baggott, Jim, 147
Barbour, Julian, 180
bare charge, 120
Bekenstein-Hawking conjecture, 22
Bell, John Stewart, 140, 141–2
Bergson, Henri, ix, 5, 109–11, 115–17, 132, 190n2
    Creative Evolution (CE), 71–7, 79, 85, 96, 98–9, 103, 111, 167, 190n5
    Duration and Simultaneity, 77, 190n6
    Matter and Memory, 77
    'The Possible and the Real', 77–8
    Time and Free Will, 111
Big Bang, 13, 106, 144, 146, 169, 176, 204n57
Big Freeze, 64–6
black holes, 22, 162
Bohm, David, 21, 70, 119, 122–6, 145, 153, 154–61, 162, 202n39
    Causality and Chance in Modern Physics, 172–3
Bohr, Niels, 141
Boltzmann, Ludwig, 16
Borges, Jorge Luis, 'The Library of Babel', 68–70
Bowden, Sean, 50
BP *see* Serres, Michel: *The Birth of Physics*
Brane theory, 189n61
bubble universes, 162, 176

Calder, Alexander, and Earle Brown, *Chef d'orchestre*, 100, 104
Canguilhem, Georges, 52
Cantorian set theory, 42–3
Čapek, Milič, 21
carbon, 164–5

causal disconnect, 106–7, 162
causality, 140–2, 167
CE *see* Bergson, Henri: *Creative Evolution*
centres of envelopment, 20, 48, 109, 117, 119, 129, 151
Cepheid stars, 87–8
Chaitin, Gregory, 123
Chakravarty, Anjan, 15
chance, 13, 22–4, 55–6, 98, 101–5, 167–8, 172, 174, 177–8
chaos, ix, 1–23, 35, 50, 92, 96, 104, 107, 121, 175, 176, 182n2, 191n12
  bifurcation, 1–4, 40, 42, 49, 96, 104, 162, 175, 182n4
  and complexity theory, 1–5, 17–19
chaosmos, 3–4, 7, 24, 28, 34–6, 44–8, 51, 55–60, 108, 162–3, 198n28
Clark, Tim, 198n28
clinamen, x–xi, 2, 95–7, 102–3, 129
Close, Frank, 159
complete concept principle, 25–8, 29, 33, 44–9, 56, 62–4, 66
complexity, ix, 32, 73–81, 95, 96–7, 98, 147, 153–4, 180, 191n7
  arrow of complexity, 118, 120–1
  and chaos theory, 1–5, 17–19
  effective, 124
  indexical, 123–5
  order as, 109–30, 166–8
  as principle, 122–6
complication, 45, 180
consciousness, 76–7
conservation laws, 59–68, 134
constants, 38, 44, 61–2, 118–19, 124, 131, 162–3, 172, 173, 176, 177
continuous variation, 5, 93–4, 110, 193n41
continuum, 36, 38, 56–7
contradiction, 45, 48–9, 82
convergence, 2, 34–5, 38, 55–6
creativity, 67, 70, 145, 162, 164, 167

Curie, Pierre, 59
cyclical renewal, 162

dark energy, 144
DeLanda, Manuel, 60
delay, 92, 94, 105, 112–14, 116, 118; *see also* retardation
Deleuze, Gilles
  Bergsonism (B), 72–3, 78, 103–4, 111, 119, 161, 167, 190n5
  Difference and Repetition (DR), x, 4, 5–10, 28, 29, 36–8, 39, 43, 44, 50–1, 53, 55, 56–7, 59, 63, 69, 104–5, 109, 110–11, 113, 114, 115, 116, 117, 119, 126, 127, 136, 143, 149, 163, 171, 198n28
  and Félix Guattari, *A Thousand Plateaus* (ATP), 1, 19, 114–17, 164, 193n41
  and Félix Guattari, *What is Philosophy?* (WP), 17, 50, 61, 78, 80, 115, 119, 146, 148, 149, 151, 164, 182n2
  The Fold: Leibniz and the Baroque (FLB), 4, 29, 55, 69, 73, 80, 198n28
  Francis Bacon: The Logic of Sensation, 194n48
  'Immanence: A Life', 115
  The Logic of Sense (LS), 4, 39, 42, 43, 44, 48, 50, 53, 81, 99–104, 113, 161
  Nietzsche and Philosophy, 5–6, 53
differential calculus, 34–5, 92
Dirac, Paul, 57, 131, 158–9, 162
Dirac equation, 57–8
Dirac Sea, 158–60, 170, 173
disequilibrium, 7–8, 36, 56–7, 59, 182n4
disjunctive synthesis, 35–6, 44–56
disorder, 71–3, 78–80, 84–5, 96, 98, 107–8, 117, 122–3, 183n22
disparity, 7, 24, 50–6, 59–60, 68, 120, 129–30, 171, 172, 175

dissymmetry, 24, 26, 29–30, 37, 56–7, 59–60, 62, 129–35, 172, 175, 180
distribution, 143–4
divergence, 2–4, 24, 34–6, 38, 54–6, 163
DR *see* Deleuze, Gilles: *Difference and Repetition*
duration, 10–15, 74, 75, 78

Eddington, Arthur, 10
Einstein, Albert, 57, 61, 131, 139, 140, 189n58
Einstein-Podolsky-Rosen (EPR) paradox, 140–2, 150, 202n35
Emmet, Dorothy, 200n21
energy, 138–9, 144–8, 155
 dark, 144
 free, 10, 18, 60–1, 64–5, 114, 121, 168–70, 172
 gradients, 29–30, 32–3, 50, 52, 55, 60, 66
 negative, 158–9
 vacuum, 49, 106, 144–5, 147, 158, 160, 169–70
 see also general relativity; thermodynamics
entanglement, 140, 142, 150, 200n15
entropy, 10–13, 15–23, 31, 34, 35, 37, 44, 67, 71, 73, 77, 87–8, 95, 96, 109, 112–16, 143–4, 168–9, 173, 175, 176, 179, 183n22, 205n71
Epperson, Michael, 149, 202n28
equilibrium, 6–8, 10–12, 14, 18, 19, 33, 51, 59, 60–8, 95–8, 109, 114, 144, 171, 175; *see also* disequilibrium
ergodicity/Ergodic Principle, 10–15, 121–2
Espagnat, Bernard d', 58
eternal object, 186n39
eternal return, 8–9, 11–14, 22, 28, 36, 55, 57, 62, 66
Euclid, *Elements*, 39

Event, 2–5, 7, 27–8, 30, 41, 43–5, 55, 66, 97–8, 101, 104, 160, 162, 173, 175–6, 188n46
Eventum Tantum, 45, 56, 67, 188n46
evolution, ix, 70, 76, 126–30, 161–74, 175, 177, 178, 181, 193n41
excluded middle, 45–6, 49, 82
explication, 110, 114, 127–8, 147–8, 154–8, 180

Fechner, Gustav Theodor, 111
Feynman, Richard, 59, 120, 188n55
FLB *see* Deleuze, Gilles: *The Fold: Leibniz and the Baroque*
free energy, 10, 18, 60–1, 64–5, 114, 121, 168–70, 172

Galois, Évariste, 57
Gasché, Rodolphe, 146
Gell-Mann, Murray, 124–6, 127, 162, 166
general relativity, ix, 2, 5, 57–8, 64, 131, 139, 140, 149, 150–1, 192n28, 202n35, 202n37
generative order, 70, 124–6, 130
geometry, 39–41, 53–4, 73, 125, 126, 205n73
Glashow-Weinberg-Salam model, 58
God, calculating, 36–8, 44, 56–7, 69–70, 138, 153, 171
Goldberg, Dave, 134
Goldilocks problem, 106
Greenblatt, Stephen, *The Swerve*, 193n42
Greene, Brian, 141
Green's function, 156
group theory, 57, 58, 60, 131
Guattari, Félix *see* Deleuze, Gilles: and Félix Guattari
Guth, Alan, 162, 169

Hacking, Ian, 30
Harman, Graham, 15

Hartshorne, Charles, 132
heat death, 6, 11–13, 22, 33, 56, 60, 62, 120, 173, 206n1
Heidegger, Martin, 190n2
hesitation, 77–8
Higgs boson, 145–8
holographic paradigms, 154–61, 176, 202n39
Hoyle, Fred, 13, 162, 164–5, 169, 204n57
Hume, David, 140
  A Treatise of Human Nature, 112
Husserl, Edmund, 112, 182n2
hylomorphism, 50, 109–10

Ideal Game, 7, 98–108, 138, 161, 171
Ideas, 41–3, 136
identity of indiscernibles principle, 26–7, 29, 33, 35, 55, 62–4, 133, 135, 157
immanence, 79, 81, 93, 98, 115, 117
implication, 36, 70, 109, 154–61, 180
inclusive disjunction, 45–6
individuation, 50–6
inert matter, 73, 77, 115, 117–20, 189n56
infinity, 10–15, 42–3, 148, 172, 176
inflation, 169–70, 176
information theory, ix, 86–92, 123–4
intensity, 51, 57, 109–12
interruption, 77–8
invariance, 134, 171

James, William, 98

Kahn, Charles, 30
Kant, Immanuel, 80–1, 105–7
  Critique of Judgement, 83–4
  Critique of Pure Reason, 83–4
  and Leibniz (game analogy #1), 81–5
Kauffman, Stuart, 121–2, 153
Kerslake, Christian, 111

Klossowski, Pierre, 7
Kolmogorov, Andrei, 123
Koyré, Alexandre, 176

Lambert, Gregg, 68–70
Lampert, Jay, 112–14
Lautman, Albert, 39, 41–4, 138
Lawlor, Leonard, 4
laws, 6, 82, 162–3, 166–8, 172, 173, 176, 177, 179
  meta-laws, 168, 171
least resistance principle, 25, 31–3, 55, 184n2
Leavitt, Henrietta, 87–8
Leibniz, Gottfried Wilhelm, ix, 24–70, 128, 129, 133, 166–7
  'De incerti aestimatione', 30
  Discourse on Metaphysics, 25, 184n5, 191n13
  and Kant (game analogy #1), 81–5
  'On the Ultimate Origination of Things', 29–34, 55, 81, 86, 91, 97, 185n16
  principle of complete concept, 25–8, 29, 33, 44–9, 56, 62–4, 66
  principle of identity of indiscernibles, 26–7, 29, 33, 35, 55, 62–4, 133, 135, 157
  principle of least resistance, 25, 31–3, 55, 184n2
  principle of sufficient reason, 8, 24–34, 37–8, 44–9, 50–1, 55, 62, 66, 128–35, 163, 172, 177–8
Levinas, Emmanuel, 191n11
Life, ix, 7, 114–15, 116–18, 191n7
limitation principle, 47, 127–30, 147, 161, 198n28
limits, 38, 44, 60–8, 79, 118–19, 124, 127–30, 135–50, 163–4
Lineweaver, Charles, 18, 145, 166, 168–71, 205n71
Lloyd, Seth, 124

locality, 114, 142–3, 149–51, 154–5;
  see also non-locality
loop quantum gravity, 14, 21, 150–4
LS see Deleuze, Gilles: *The Logic of Sense*
Lucretius, ix
  clinamen, x–xi, 2, 95–7, 102–3, 129
  The Nature of Things (De rerum natura), 94–104

Mach, Ernst, 166–7
Massumi, Brian, 51–2
mathematics, 38–44, 57–8, 63, 71–2
Maupertuis, Pierre Louis, 184n2
maximal fall, 95–7
mechanism, 73–81, 111, 115, 117–18
Mee, Nicholas, 57
Meillassoux, Quentin, 15, 177–8
monads, 45–7, 49, 54
More, Thomas, *Utopia*, 193n42
Musser, George, 157, 202n39

natural kinds, 137, 146, 154, 163–6, 170–1, 172, 176, 177
necessity, 24, 26–8, 98
negation, 72–3, 79–80, 127–30, 161, 173
negative energy, 158–9
negative prehension, 47–8
Neoplatonism, 156
Nernst, Walther, 60–1, 66
networks, 86, 90–3, 105, 150–4, 176, 202n39
Neumann, John von, 22
Newton, Isaac, 67, 73, 74, 162
Newtonian Paradigm, 17, 82
Nietzsche, Friedrich Wilhelm, 5–8, 13–14, 22, 172
  eternal return, 8–9, 11–14, 22, 28, 36, 55, 57, 62, 66
  The Gay Science, 8
  Thus Spoke Zarathustra, 9, 11
Noether, Emmy, 59, 134, 171–2

noise, 87, 88, 90, 91, 192n28
non-locality, 114, 128, 135–55, 176
North, Jill, 200n15
NP see Deleuze, Gilles: *Nietzsche and Philosophy*
numbers, 36, 56–7

openness, 5, 19, 67, 138, 154, 163, 176–7
order, 68–70, 71–108, 177, 178–9
  as complexity, 109–30, 166–8
  generative, 70, 124–6, 130
  mechanistic, 73–81, 111, 115, 117–18
  vital, 75–81, 111, 117–18
  without law, 68–70
  see also disorder

Penrose, Roger, 10, 120, 135, 162, 199n13
physical systems, 50–6
physics, 15–23, 56–60, 67, 105, 119, 122, 128, 133–5, 136, 138, 144–6, 155, 172
  classical, 7, 10–11, 13–14, 35, 56, 59, 94, 139
  see also specific fields of
Platonism, 41–2, 82, 102, 186n39, 191n12
Poincaré, Henri, 3, 12, 13, 16, 171–2
Popper, Karl, 176, 206n1
PR see Whitehead, Alfred North: *Process and Reality*
prehension, 47–8, 127, 128
Price, Huw, 179–80
Prigogine, Ilya, 1, 50, 183n29, 206n1
probability, 101–2, 123, 194n47
  stochastic, 101–2, 104
problematic mode, 39–43, 57
Process Philosophy, 132
Protevi, John, 2, 3, 4

quantum field theory, 159–60
  vacuum energy, 49, 106, 144–5, 147, 158, 160, 169–70

quantum foam, 106, 144
quantum mechanics, ix, 2, 5, 19–22, 57–9, 61, 119–20, 122–3, 128, 139–42, 148–50, 156
　loop quantum gravity, 14, 21, 150–4

reciprocal determination, 34, 52, 82, 85–6, 90–8, 104–5, 153–5, 157, 162, 163
Rees, Martin, 64–6, 67, 107
relativity *see* general relativity
Renaissance, 156
retardation, 77–8, 92–7, 109, 111–18, 145, 147–9, 153–4; *see also* delay
Rölli, Marc, 180–1
Rosen, Joe, 132–3

Sauvagnargues, Anne, 52
Schrödinger, Erwin, 20
self-organisation, 50, 124
Selme, Léon, 63
series, 2–4, 34–5, 54–6, 101–3, 116, 163
Serres, Michel, ix, 71, 78, 82, 129
　The Birth of Physics (BP), x, 92, 94–8, 185n16, 185n22
　La communication, 85–6, 90–4
　and Shannon (game analogy #2), 85–6, 94–8
Shannon, Claude
　'A Mathematical Theory of Communication' (game analogy #2.1), 86–94
　and Serres (game analogy #2), 85–6, 94–8
Simondon, Gilbert, 7, 49–56, 57, 129
simultaneity, 3, 113–14, 190n6
singularity, 3–4, 52–4, 57
Smith, Daniel, 24, 27, 41
Smolin, Lee, 18–19, 78, 119, 131, 133–5, 153, 154, 162, 166, 199n6, 203n43

Solomonoff, Ray, 123
spatium, 143, 148, 149, 152, 158
Spencer, Herbert, 98
Spinoza, Baruch, 47, 128
Standard Model, 58, 145, 150
Stengers, Isabelle, 1, 15–16, 50, 128–9, 200n21
stochastic probability, 101–2, 104
string theory, 21, 106
sufficient reason, 8, 24–34, 37–8, 44–9, 50–1, 55, 62, 66, 128–35, 163, 172, 177–8
superior sufficient reason, 8, 22, 24, 28, 36, 38, 45, 51, 56
Susskind, Leonard, 151
symmetry, 7, 29–30, 33, 56–68, 131–2, 163, 171, 172, 199n6
　supersymmetry, 146, 148
　see also dissymmetry

thalweg, 95–6, 154, 169
thermodynamics, ix, 10–13, 32, 50, 52, 55–6, 101, 172–3, 184n2, 199n13
　first law, 32–3, 134, 172
　second law, 10, 13, 18–20, 22, 24, 32–3, 67–8, 121–2, 134, 135, 153, 168, 170, 171, 173, 175
　third law, 60–1, 66–7, 189n61
　see also energy
time, 73, 74–5, 93, 95, 100–5, 115–16, 167–8, 189n58
　Aion, 100–2, 161, 180, 188n46
　arrow of time, 115–16, 121, 149, 173, 179–80
　relational, 63–8
　as retardation, 73, 78–9, 113–14, 116
　see also delay; duration
topological theory, 145
transcendentalism, 80–1, 83–5, 103, 108, 180–1
Tryon, Edward, 144, 201n27

Unger, Roberto, 166–8, 171

vacuum energy, 49, 106, 144–5, 147, 158, 160, 169–70
vitalism, 75–81, 111, 117–18

wave-function, 57, 119–20, 137, 140, 200n15
Weaver, Warren, 86–7, 89, 90, 91
Weinberg, Steven, 58, 78
Welchman, Alastair, 83–4, 85
Westphal, Wilhelm, 84
Weyl, Hermann, 58, 131, 176
Whitehead, Alfred North, ix, 4, 15, 29, 46–8, 55, 119, 127, 135, 145, 147, 149–50, 152, 157, 161, 163, 171, 177, 200n21, 202n28
  Modes of Thought, 137, 200n17
  principle of limitation, 47, 127–30, 147, 161, 198n28
  Process and Reality (PR), 48–9, 80, 128–9, 139, 165–6, 186n39, 205n65
  Science and the Modern World, 128, 135–6, 138–9, 165
Wiener, Norbert, 90
Williams, James, 93
Woit, Peter, 58
WP *see* Deleuze, Gilles, and Félix Guattari: *What is Philosophy?*

Young's wave/particle duality, 119–20

Zarathustra, 6, 9, 11
Zee, A., 131–2
Zourabichvili, François, 45, 46

EU representative:
Easy Access System Europe
Mustamäe tee 50, 10621 Tallinn, Estonia
Gpsr.requests@easproject.com